WOMEN EMPOWERMENT AND FAMILY MANAGEMENT IN TRIBAL REGION

By the Same Author

Ecology and Quality of Life in Urban Slums : An Empirical Study

Economics of Social Sector and Environment

About the Authors

Udai Prakash Sinha (*b.* 1956) is Professor of Economics, T.M. Bhagalpur University, Bhagalpur. He has authored many books including Planned Development of Resources in a Developing Region (1985), Socio-Economic Dimensions of Integrated Development in India (1991) and IRDP for Weaker Sections (1996). He is editing 'Journal of Economic Issues' since 2000 published by Planning Forum, and Anga Economic Society, University Department of Economics, T.M. Bhagalpur University, Bhagalpur. He has also completed two UGC Major Research Projects and contributed more than 50 research papers to reputed national and international journals of Economics and other social-sciences. 28 Research Scholars have already been awarded Ph.D. degree under his able guidance. Micro-level planning and the regional economics are the areas of his interest and research.

Rekha Sinha (*b.* 1958) is currently Professor of Psychology, T.M. Bhagalpur University, Bhagalpur. She has contributed more than 20 research papers to the reputed national and international journals of Psychology and other social-sciences. She has completed two UGC Major Research Projects and has also authored one book, entitled: *Organised and Disorganised Personality : A Comparative Study.* Organizational, Industrial & Environmental Psychology are the areas of her interest in research.

WOMEN EMPOWERMENT AND FAMILY MANAGEMENT IN TRIBAL REGION

Udai Prakash Sinha
Professor of Economics
T.M. Bhagalpur University, Bhagalpur
and
Rekha Sinha
Professor of Psychology
T.M. Bhagalpur University, Bhagalpur

Concept Publishing Company, New Delhi-110 059

Cataloging in Publication Data—DK
Courtesy: D.K. Agencies (P) Ltd. <docinfo@dkagencies.com>

Sinha, U. P. (Udai Prakash), 1956-
Women empowerment and family management in tribal region / Udai Prakash Sinha and Rekha Sinha.
p. cm.
Study conducted at Santhal Parganas Division of Jharkhand State, India.
Includes bibliographical references (p.)
Includes index.
ISBN 13: 9788180694721
ISBN 10: 8180694720

1. Home economics—India—Santhal Parganas Division. 2. Rural women—Family relationships—India—Santhal Parganas Division. 3. Santal (South Asian people)—Family relationships—India—Santhal Parganas Division. 4. Sex role—India—Santhal Parganas Division. 5. Women in development—India—Santhal Parganas Division. I. Sinha, Rekha, 1958-, joint author. II. Title.

DDC 640.954 127 22

ISBN-13: 978-81-8069-472-1
ISBN-10: 81-8069-472-0

First Published 2007

Published and Printed by
Ashok Kumar Mittal
Concept Publishing Company
A/15-16, Commercial Block, Mohan Garden
New Delhi (INDIA)

Phones : 25351460, 25351794
Fax : 091-11-25357103
Email : publishing@conceptpub.com

Foreword

At the advent of new millennium, when one takes stock of where exactly Indian women stand in terms of empowerment and socio-economic emancipation, one is forced to notice that not much has changed in real terms, since notion of femininity were reshaped and reconstructed under colonial rule. Empowerment of women presupports a drastic dynamic and democratic change in the perception of and expectation from women in our society. To help women attain economic independence is the first priority of such changes.

Empowerment is a process and is, therefore, not something that can be given to people. The process of empowerment is both individual and collective, since it is through involvement in groups that people most often start developing their awareness and the ability to organize and take action to bring about the desired change.

Women's empowerment include both a personal strengthening and enhancement of life chances, and collective participation in efforts to achieve, equality of opportunity and equality between different genders ethnics, social classes and groups. It enhances human potential at individual and social levels of expressions. Empowerment is an essential starting point and a continuing process for realizing the ideals of human liberation and freedom for all.

Thus, when we talk of women's development and women's status, it is important for us to recognize that interventions at all levels, namely social, cultural, political and economic are required and are possible only if changes take place in the existing system and social structures, which are not at all favourable to women today.

Women account for more than half of the world's illiterate population and achieving literacy could be one of the first steps to empowering women to participate more equally in society and free themselves from economic exploitation and oppression. The empowerment of women and economic opportunity is a highly important end in itself. In addition, this also enhances their decision making capacity in vital areas, especially in the areas of reproduction. Education is one of the most important means of empowering women and giving them knowledge, skills and self-confidence necessary for their becoming full partners in the development process.

The absence of women at the politically powerful and socially visible leadership positions have also been responsible for the increasing devaluation and at the consequent atrocities against women. What is desired is to get more and more women to the political positions so as to enable them to collectively influence and direct the laws, policies and programmes in their favour.

The empowerment of women demand empathy, rapport building, participatory action, efficient management of resources in such a manner that contribute to equity, social justice and freedom while avoiding social and family conflicts and disruptions. This implies strong community participation of work.

It is, therefore, necessary to attract the women's issue from many fronts—seminars, conferences, researches, books and other writings, educational-cum-awareness programmes; and finally, ground-level help. The erosion of social value, the crumbling down of joint family system, and the rapidly changing socio-cultural matrix have had degenerating effect on the entire atmosphere. The need of the hour is to explore the problem thoroughly and thrash out the positive as well as negative effects of the present day conditions. There is no denying the fact that the woman today is not what she was a century or two ago. Thing have changed, though with the changes new problems have cropped up. It is high time to discuss the issue to pave our way for the future. The contribution by Dr. Udai Prakash Sinha and Dr. (Mrs.) Rekha Sinha is an important step in this direction. I hope that this would stimulate debate and discussion on this fundamental issue.

The contents of this book are expected to serve as a base material for teaching, learning, research and extension on women's issues and development. It is envisaged that the educated 'change-agents' would benefit from the findings in the book and reach the uneducated audience in the communities where awareness has to be spread on gender equality and women's role in the development and proper management of the family.

Prema Jha
Vice-Chancellor
T.M. Bhagalpur University
Bhagalpur

Preface

Women all over the world plays a very crucial role in the development and management of their families. From early ages of history the gender role differential exists in the management of household affairs. Women, according to the previous norms of our society are meant for looking their children and also to serve their best the needs of other members of the family.

Women constitute, roughly, half of the total population. The society however, does not always permit equal status to women with men. It is alleged that to most society including our own, women are exploited by men in various ways. Since the beginning of agricultural economy the status of women started dwindling in human societies all over because prior to the agricultural economy. Women used to work with men for subsistence which was based on food gathering and hunting. There was possibly a division of labour but the women were equally significant with men in economic persuits, with the advent of agriculture there was a surplus of production over consumption which permitted there was surplus of production over consumption which permitted people to enjoy leisure and to develop their culture, including religion, fine arts and philosophy. Food became more easily available and required less labour. Moreover, with the evaluation of agriculture people left their no made habits and became settled agriculturists. Gradually, men started working in field and women were entrusted with the responsibility of home management.

There is a wide spread belief both among men and women that the women have a natural instinct for the management of home. The anthropologist of earlier generation, like Brofault, suggested that the origin of the institution known as family was due to the in born tendencies of women. The presence of maternal instinct among the women made them include to seek security for their children which the men could provide them. Thus they preferred to live with her male companion and look after the children as well as household. The nucleus of the family was thus formed.

The role of women in home management differs from one society to the other. It not only depends on the tradition and norms of the society but also on the type of family *e.g.* Joint individual and extend, locational background of the family *viz.* rural and urban etc. The modern civilization has brought in a men new phenomenon of mechanisation in different spheres of life and family is no exception to this. In the urban household, particularly those which are economically well off, the various appliances, better known as gadgets, have not short the physical labour of women in home management and ensured them greater opportunities or possibilities to work outside the home. In super societies the picture is different. In villages which are dominated by agricultural economy, the women other than performing various types of domestic works like cooking, washing, cleaning and serving food to the members of the family are required to work in the field. This is more correct about the women belonging to the lower income strata. Women in rural areas start their domestic chores since early morning beginning with cleaning of cowshed, give them food, preparing meal for the family members as well as the labours employed by the family, supervising the works of the labourers, weighing the fertilizers etc. women are also supposed to make arrangement for the fuel required in the household to bring firewood after walking a long distance. They draw water from wells, clean the rooms with broom sticks and also clean the utensils.

Women belonging to the poor families perform various works related to agriculture, like boiling the paddy, drying the same, taking out the weeds from the paddy, crushing wheat, pulses and other corns to maintain a kitchen garden and applying fertilizer to the garden after making the soil ready for sowing vegetables.

In none of the societies of the world, however, women are paid for the domestic works, which they perform in their families, though they bear the responsibilities starting from reproduction to the upbringing of children. Inspite of hard labour women are denied appreciation as well as material return by the government, society and family. Unlike the works in industry or agriculture, in some cases, the women are not given any remuneration for their labour related to home management. The works performed by them are not considered productive because of the non-payment of remuneration. In case the women are freed from the sphere of domestic activities their labour becomes productive of women making in the machine meant for crushing the cereals and making fodder for the animal, working as creche attendants, working in hotels, restaurants, factory canteen, old age centers, tutors as well as in various business organization. From there it becomes clear that the works performed by the women are not unproductive. It is rather as well thought out conspiracy which acts as a barrier to the development of women and prevent their labour being treated as productive.

The present Research Project is an indepth study of the role of tribal women in family management and development of society and nation as well. In other words it probes into the gender role differentiation in a society which completely lack mechanisation and primarily guided by the traditional norm. I can further be claimed as an attempt to assess the role of women in tribal households. Various studies by social anthropologists in the past regarding the position of women in tribal societies have taken different aspects of the life of tribal women into consideration but very few of them attempted to pin point the role of the women in tribal societies in home management. They also failed, in most cases to discuss the status of women and the assessment made by the society as a whole of the roles performed by them *i.e.* whether productive made by the society, as a whole of the roles performed by them *i.e.* whether productive or unproductive.

The Santhals are the largest among all other tribes they living in Jharkhand state and it will not be exaggeration to say that compared to other tribes they are most prosperous. But still they are characterized with a simple life, economically poor and culturally traditional. Predominantly they are agricultural people and because of the climate or topographical condition forced to toil every hard to eke out their living out of the unfavourable natural condition. But men and women take part in economic and other social as well as cultural activities. The women according to their culture are free to work out side their homes. Moreover, this is also a necessity in their case. But like all other societies, but literate and literate (pre), their exists gender role of differentiation in their culture. The women are entrusted with the responsibility of home management.

The present research monograph provide an understanding to the scholars of different disciplines *viz.* Economics, Social Anthropology, Psychology and Sociology about the role of tribal women in home management and development of society and nation as well the changes, if any, have taken place as a result of the diffusion of non-tribal culture. Normally, any person from non-tribal area visiting Santhal villages are attract to their neat and clean style of living and also their artistic elements contained in it, particularly the households. It gives rise to a question in the minds of the visitors as to how the Santhal women arrange their households so nicely inspite of the poor economic condition. The present research may provide an answer to this question.

Udai Prakash Sinha

and

Bhagalpur **Rekha Sinha**

Acknowledgements

The conduct of field research investigation is a joint endeavour and in such cases the success depends upon wholehearted co-operation of everyone involved in the preparation of the present research report. It is the devotion to the work as well as proper suggestion, guidance and financial help that determine the outcome of such works.

First and foremost, we are extremely grateful to Dr. (Mrs.) Prema Jha, Vice-Chancellor, T.M.B.U., Bhagalpur who wrote the foreword of the book.

We owe deep sense of gratitude to Prof. U.P. Singh, Former Vice-Chancellor, S.K.M. University, Dumka for thought provoking suggestions on the subject emeritus Professor of Mathematics for his moral boost in the preparation of this work and also to Prof. T.N. Sinha, D.Sc.

We express gratitude to the authors and researchers whose writings and findings have benefited us in conducting the research and presenting this report. Important among them are Prof. M.G. Chitkara, Prof. A.K. Sen, Prof. Uday Pareekh, Prof. Amar Kumar Singh, Prof. Vir Bala Aggarwal, Prof. V.M. Rao, J. Bhagyalakshmi, Amrita Guha, Sujata Madhok, A.K. Jain and many others

We extend our very sincere thanks to Prof. P.K. Bhargava, Retd. Professor and Dean, Faculty of Social Sciences, B.H.U., Varanasi. The authors acknowledge the sincere thanks to all the colleagues and faculty members of the University Deptt. of Economics and Psychology, T.M.B.U., Bhagalpur for their help, comments and suggestions.

The authors are also grateful to Dr. (Mrs.) U.R. Singh, Prof. and Head of Deptt. Psychology & Dean, Faculty of Social Sciences, T.M.B.U., Bhagalpur and Dr. R.R.L. Das, Prof. & Head, University Deptt. of Economics, T.M.B.U, Bhagalpur. We acknowledge the sincere co-operation received from Dr. Naresh Jha and Dr. Ajit Kumar Sinha, Professors of Economics, T.M.B.U., Bhagalpur.

The present research would not have come to light without the invisible help, co-operation and encouragement received from Dr. V.N. Singh, Retd. Professor, University Deptt. of Psychology, T.M.B.U., Bhagalpur, and Dr. R.B. Mandal, Professor, University Deptt. of Geography, T.M.B.U., Bhagalpur. We express our gratitude to them.

We extend our warmest thanks to the librarian and staff of National Library, Kolkata, NJRD, Hyderabad, Centre for Advanced Research Institute, Shimla, Pune Central Library, Ratan Tata Library of Delhi School of Economics and Xavier Institute of Social Sciences, Ranchi.

We are very much thankful to Dr. Sanjeev Kumar Singh, research scholar, University Department of Economics, T.M.B.U., Bhagalpur in collecting and analyzing the data.

We must express thanks to our respondents for their ungrudging co-operation in answering our questions, which is definitely a tedious work.

We are also thankful to Dr. Ajay Kumar Singh, Office Assistant, University Deptt. of Psychology and Sri Namo Narayan Jha, Office Assistant, Accounts Section T.M.B.U., Bhagalpur for immense help in several ways.

Thanks are also due to Sri Raj Madhvan for cartographic work and Md. Reyaz who has painstakingly computer typed the manuscript in a short time.

Udai Prakash Sinha

and

Rekha Sinha

Contents

Foreword by ***Dr. (Mrs.) Prema Jha***	v
Preface	vii
Acknowledgements	xi
List of Tables	xv
List of Figures	xix
1. Introduction	1
2. Globalisation and Role of Women in Family Management	17
3. An Overview of the Past Literature	35
4. Methodological Framework	52
5. Women and Management of Household Economy	91
6. Women and Decision-making Management	123
7. Women and Leisure Time Management	150
8. Women, Energy and Food Management	174
9. Women Welfare and Social Development	197
10. Women and Communication Need	203
11. National Commission for Women : An Appraisal	209
12. Promoting Child Development and Governmental Programmes: An Assessment	214
13. Summary and Conclusion	237
Appendix-1	251
Appendix-2	258
Appendix-3	262
Appendix-4	264
Appendix-5	269
Bibliography	287
Index	300

List of Tables

1.1	Population of India	3
1.2	Life Expectancy at Birth in India	4
1.3	International Comparison of Life Expectancy at Birth	4
1.4	Literacy Rates in India	5
1.5	Statewise Female Literacy Rates in India	6
1.6	International Comparison of Illiteracy	6
1.7	Percentage Distribution of Female Workers	7
1.8	Literacy Levels of Female Workforce in India (1987-88)	8
1.9	Female Workforce Participation Rate in India	8
1.10	Distribution of Female Workers by Category of Employment	9
4.1	Comparative studies on the network of educational infrastructural facilities in different sub-divisions	61
4.2	Studies on the extent of children enrolled on different schools in different sub-division	63
4.3	Number of students in schools and high schools in different sub-divisions	63
4.4	Sub-division-wise number of Doctors and Para-medical Staff (1989)	67
4.5	Number of households and population density in different sub-divisions	70
4.6	Age and Education	72
4.7	Education and Earning	73
4.8	Education and Nature of Job	77
4.9	Nature of Job and Monthly Income	77
4.10	Age and Marital Status	78
4.11	Age and Husband's Education	78
4.12	Marital Status and Number of Children	79
4.13	Age and Question No. 9	79
4.14	Education and Question No. 10	80
4.15	Education and Religion	80
4.16	Education and Question No. 12	81

4.17	Education and Question No. 13	81
4.18	Clan Membership Question No. 14	82
4.19	Occupation and Monthly Income (Question No. 15)	82
4.20	Occupation and Question No. 16	83
4.21	Age and Question No. 17	83
4.22	Income and Number of Earning Members (Question No. 18)	84
4.23	Income and Number of Dependent Members (Question No. 19)	84
4.24	Source of Income and Question No. 20	85
4.25	Age and Question No. 21	89
5.1	Age and Question No. 22	107
5.2	Age and Question No. 23	108
5.3	Education and Question No. 24	108
5.4	Education and Question No. 25	109
5.5	Education and Question No. 26	110
5.6	Family Income and Question No. 27	111
5.7	Literacy and Question No. 28	112
5.8	Literacy and Question No. 29	113
5.9	Occupation and Question No. 30	114
5.10	Occupation and Question No. 31	114
5.11	Religion and Keeping Poultry	115
5.12	Age and Weaving (Question No. 33)	115
5.13	Age and Basket Making	116
5.14	Age and Question No. 35	116
5.15	Literacy and Question No. 36	117
5.16	Literacy and Question No. 37	118
5.17	Literacy and Question No. 38	118
5.18	Literacy and Question No. 39	118
5.19	Age and Question No. 40	119
5.20	Literacy and Question No. 41	119
6.1	Age and Question No. 42	134
6.2	Age and Question No. 43	135
6.3	Age and Question No. 44	135
6.4	Education and Question No. 45	136
6.5	Education and Question No. 46	137
6.6	Education and Question No. 47	138
6.7	Occupation and Question No. 48	139
6.8	Occupation and Question No. 49	139

6.9 Education and Question No. 50 140
6.10 Education and Question No. 51 141
6.11 Age and Question No. 52 142
6.12 Age and Question No. 53 142
6.13 Education and Question No. 54 143
6.14 Education and Question No. 55 143
6.15 Occupation and Question No. 56 144
6.16 Occupation and Question No. 57 144
6.17 Occupation and Question No. 58 145
6.18 Occupation and Question No. 59 145
6.19 Education and Question No. 60 146
6.20 Education and Question No. 61 146
6.21 Age and Question No. 62 147
6.22 Age and Question No. 62 147
7.1 Occupation and Question No. 64 161
7.2 Occupation and Question No. 65 162
7.3 Education and Question No. 66 162
7.4 Education and Question No. 67 163
7.5 Age and Question No. 68 164
7.6 Income and Question No. 69 164
7.7 Education and Question No. 70 164
7.8 Age and Question No. 71 165
7.9 Education and Question No. 72 165
7.10 Source of Income of Family and Question No. 73 166
7.11 Source of Income of Family and Question No. 74 166
7.12 Education and Question No. 75 167
7.13 Education and Question No. 76 168
7.14 Agc and Question No. 77 168
7.15 Age and Question No. 78 169
7.16 Age and Question No. 79 169
7.17 Age and Question No. 80 170
7.18 Age and Question No. 81 170
7.19 Age and Question No. 82 171
7.20 Education and Question No. 83 171
7.21 Occupation and Question No. 84 171
7.22 Age and Question No. 85 172
8.1 Income and Question No. 86 184
8.2 Income and Question No. 87 184
8.3 Income and Question No. 88 185

8.4	Income and Question No. 89	185
8.5	Occupation and Question No. 90	186
8.6	Occupation and Question No. 91	186
8.7	Education and Question No. 92	187
8.8	Education and Question No. 93	187
8.9	Income and Question No. 94	188
8.10	Main Source of Income and Question No. 95	188
8.11	Main Source of Income and Question No. 96	189
8.12	Education and Question No. 97	189
8.13	Source of Family Income and Question No. 98	190
8.14	Source of Family Income and Question No. 99	190
8.15	Source of Income and Question No. 100	191
8.16	Source of Income and Question No. 101	191
8.17	Occupation and Question No. 102	192
8.18	Education and Question No. 103	192
8.19	Source of Family Income and Question No. 104	193
8.20	Source of Income and Question No. 105	193
8.21	Age and Question No. 106	193
8.22	Education and Question No. 107	194
8.23	Education and Question No. 107	194
9.1	Number of Girls Enrolled in Schools and Colleges	197
9.2	Representation of Women in Lok Sabha	199
9.3	Women Empowerment and Social Development	201

List of Figures

1.1	Women Development and Child Care in Santhal Pargana	12
1.2	Women's Reproductive Health Conditions	12
2.1	Stage and Changing Scenario of the Tribal Women in Santhal Pargana	30
4.1	Location Map of Santhal Pargana	59
4.2	Educational Institutions in Santhal Pargana	62
4.3	Formal Girls Education Enrolment (ST) Santhal Pargana	64
4.4	Formal Girls Education Enrolment Santhal Pargana	65
4.5	Formal Girls Education Enrolment Santhal Pargana	66
4.6	Districtwise Population Santhal Pargana	68
4.7	Male and Female Population (0–6 age group) Santhal Pargana	69
4.8	Villages Surveyed in Tribal Blocks in Santhal Pargana (Situationwise)	71
4.9	Trends of Literacy and Education in Relation to Village Situation (SP)	73
4.10	Rural and Urban Literacy (%) Santhal Pargana	74
4.11	Districtwise Literacy (%)	75
4.12	Literacy and Education Status in Paharia Tribal Belt (Santhal Pargana)	76
4.13	Women's Average Annual Income of District Dumka	85
4.14	Women's Average Annual Income of District Godda	86
4.15	Women's Average Annual Income of District Deoghar	87
4.16	Women's Average Annual Income of District Sahibganj	88
5.1	A Framework	120
6.1	Action Steps in Organizing, Controlling and Evaluating	125
12.1	ICDS Projects Administrative Chart	215
12.2	Organisational set-up of ICDS Dumka (Jharkhand)	221

Appendix of Figures

1. Scheduled Tribe Population (Male and Female) 269
2. Rural Population 270
3. Urban Population 271
4. Population of S.T. (Rural and Urban) 272
5. Analysis (Age and Sex) of Paharia Population Structure 273
6. Male and Female Workers 274
7. Rural Workers (%) 275
8. Urban Workers (Male and Female) 276
9. Agricultural Workers (Rural and Urban) 277
10. Rural, Urban and General Workers 278
11. Construction Workers 279
12. Trade and Commerce Workers 280
13. Marginal Workers 281
14. Mining and Quarrying (Rural and Urban) 282
15. Cultivators Workers (Rural and Urban) 283
16. Other Workers (Services) 284
17. Transport, Storage and Communication Workers 285
18. Location Map of Godda District 286

1

Introduction

In spite of their differential access to resources and opportunities, women play a vital role in the social and economic transformation of a country. The contribution of women to economic development is a complex and multi-dimensional phenomenon. The UN Report, prepared at the time of the International Development Decade of Women, pointed out that women constituted half of the world work hours, but received only a tenth of the world's income and owned less than a hundredth of the world property. There is a need for evolution integrated policies and coordinated programmes to bring about substantial improvement in the quality of life of women, taking into account the complex reality of women's lives, their multiple tasks, responsibilities and the diverse yet inter-connected aspects of women's lives. In this context, an attempt is made in the present dissertation to examine the emerging trends in the role of women as equal partners in the process of socio-psycho and economic development and family management.

Earlier Schools of Thought

The classical and the neo-classical economic thoughts have not contributed much to the understanding of the contribution of women to the economy, as household activities were not included in the valuation of the national income of the country. The Marxian concept of exploitation is based on extraction of surplus value at the point of production and hence could not explain much of women's problems. On the other hand, Roemer's Theory dealt with exploitation even in the absence of employment relations. The Institutional School maintains that the role of women is confined to certain sectors of the economy and under restriction as imposed by the market. The radical approach focused on material and political benefits derived by the capitalists from the family. All these theoretical explanations have not been able to assess properly the women's contribution to the economy. Vehlen's efforts to evolve a theory of economic behaviour differentiating the role of women as against that of men, made a starting point of theoretical comprehension of women's behaviour in the labour market.

Until recently, the contribution of women to the Indian economy through self-employment and home-based work has not received much attention. The three major reports on women brought into focus the role-played by women as invisible inputs in the development process. The rapid changes in recent social conditions have drawn women in large number into the economic arena, transforming them into visible economic agents. The sizeable increase in the participation of female labour force in the Indian economy is attributed as much to economic necessity as to the emancipation of women.

Socio-psycho and Economic Development of Women

Human development involves widening the choices of the people. The three essential choices of the people are:

1. to lead a long and healthy life;
2. to acquire knowledge; and
3. to have access to resources needed for a decent standard of living.

The Human Development Report of 1998 suggested that having the highest per capita income alone is not an index of human development. According to the report:

1. nutritious food;
2. education;
3. availability of protected water; and
4. improved health and sanitation facilities are the real indicators of human development.

In the case of India, the Report has drawn attention to the progress achieved in terms of:

1. increase in average life expectancy,
2. increase in real income, and
3. increase in literacy rate of women and the progress in their role in the political and economic spheres.

Looked in this way, the long-term trends indicate a gradual improvement in the development of women. All over the world, women are living longer and are better educated that ever before.

Women's Development in India

Women constitute about 48 per cent of the total population of India. The vast majority of the women live in rural areas (Table 1.1). Life expectancy of women at birth increased from 40.55 years in 1961 to 61.7 years during 1991–96 (Table 1.2). Yet, international comparison indicate that female life expectancy in India is lagging behind that of countries like Sri Lanka, Mexico, Malaysia, Thailand, Brazil, Libya, Indonesia, Egypt and Kenya. Life expectancy of women is as high as 73.80 years in Sri Lanka compared to 60.7 years in India during 1990–95 (Table 1.3).

Table 1.1: Population of India

(in millions)

Year	*Total Population*	*Female Population*	*Rural Female Population*
1971	547.95	264.01 (48.18)	213.64 (80.92)
1981	665.28	321.36 (48.30)	247.55 (77.03)
1991	838.58	403.37 (48.10)	301.53 (74.75)
2001	1027.00	495.00 (48.19)	742.00 (72.25)

Source: Based on CMIE, India's Social Sectors, February 2002, p. 52

Table 1.2: Life Expectancy at Birth in India

Year	*Male*	*Female*
1961	41.89	40.55
1971	46.40	44.70
1980	54.10	54.70
1981	50.90	50.90
1981–86	55.60	56.40
1986–91	58.10	59.10
1991–96	60.60	61.70
1996–2001	62.80	64.20

Source: CMIE, India's Social Sectors, February 2004, p. 52

Significant gains are made in the spread of literacy among women. Female literacy in India increased from a mere 8.9 per cent in 1951 to 39.3 per cent in 1991 (Table 1.4). Kerala has the highest female literacy rate of 86.17 per cent, followed by 52.32 per cent in Maharashtra, 51.33 per cent in Tamil Nadu and 50.41 per cent in Punjab. However, except in the state of Kerala, increase in female literacy is influence more by the higher levels of the urban female literacy area. For example, the female literacy rate ranged from 11.59 per cent in the rural areas to 50.24 per cent in the urban areas, as in the case of Rajasthan. Further, there are also wide inter-state variations in the female literacy rates in India. The female literacy rate ranged from 20.44 per cent in Rajasthan to 86.17 per cent in Kerala. A number of important states like Orissa, Andhra Pradesh, Madhya Pradesh, Bihar and Rajasthan are trailing behind the average all India female literacy rate of 39.29 per cent (Table 1.5). International comparisons point to the glaringly high level of female illiteracy in India of about 61 per cent and Sri Lanka's female illiteracy rate of only 13 per cent (Table 1.6). Thus female illiteracy continues to plague the Indian economy adversely affecting the standard of living as well as the status of women in India. This is reflected in the nature and pattern of employment of women, as examined below:

Table 1.3: International Comparison of Life Expectancy at Birth

S.No	*Country*	*Female Life Expectancy*
1	Japan	81.60
2	France	80.80
3	Canada	80.70
4	Australia	80.10
5	USA	79.30
6	Germany	79.00
7	UK	78.70
8	Argentina	74.80
9	USSR	74.70
10	Sri Lanka	73.80
11	Maxico	73.60
12	Malaysia	73.00
13	Thailand	71.90
14	Brazil	69.10
15	Libya	65.00
16	Indonesia	64.50
17	Egypt	62.80
18	Myanmar	59.30
19	Pakistan	59.00
20	India	60.70
21	Nepal	53.00
22	Bangladesh	52.60
23	Afghanistan	44.03

Source: Based on CMIE, India's Social Sectors, Feb. 2004, Table 173, p. 170.

Table 1.4: Literacy Rates in India

(*Percentage*)

Year	*Male*	*Female*	*Total*
1951	27.2	08.9	18.3
1961	40.4	15.3	28.3
1971	46.0	22.0	34.5
1981	56.5	29.9	43.7
1991	64.1	39.3	52.2
2001	75.8	52.1	65.4

Source: CMIE, India's Social Sectors, February 2004, p.173.

Table 1.5: Statewise Female Literacy Rates in India

S. No	*State*	*Total*	*Rural*	*Urban*
1	Kerala	86.17	85.12	89.06
2	Maharashtra	52.32	40.96	55.52
3	Tamil Nadu	51.33	41.84	69.61
4	Punjab	50.41	43.85	66.12
5	Gujarat	48.64	38.65	67.70
6	West Bengal	46.56	38.12	68.25
7	Karnataka	44.34	34.76	65.74
8	Assam	43.03	39.19	73.32
9	Haryana	40.47	32.51	61.18
10	Orissa	34.68	30.79	61.18
11	A.P.	32.72	23.92	56.41
12	M.P.	28.85	19.73	58.92
13	U.P.	25.31	19.02	50.38
14	Bihar	22.89	17.95	55.94
15	Jharkand	20.01	16.40	42.68
16	Rajasthan	20.44	11.59	50.24
	All India	**39.29**	**30.62**	**64.05**

Source: Based on CMIE, India's Social Sectors, February 2004, p. 173

Table 1.6: International Comparison of Illiteracy

Country	*Female Illiteracy*	*Male Illiteracy*
Nepal	86	59
Pakistan	70	50
Bangladesh	74	51
India	61	35
Sri Lanka	13	07
World	38	21

Source: World Development Report, 1998

Employment of Women in India

Employment provides income and thereby leads to economic independence and decision-making power of women. Household production is a major user of time and labour of women which contributes significantly to the well-being of the household.

Employment of women in organized and unorganized sectors has drawn large number of women out of the family and the household who make their contribution to the economy visible. The majority of women in the third world countries are playing a predominant role in agriculture and allied activities. More than 65 per cent of women in these countries are engaged in agriculture and only 16–17 per cent in industry or services, while far-reaching structural changes have taken place in the developed countries with the shift of female labour force away from agricultural and industrial occupations to the services sector. In India, also there is a growing presence of women in the services sector especially in transport, communications and financial services. But these areas are open only to educated women.

Thus, it is in the unorganized sector, mostly in the rural areas, that the overwhelming proportions of women are finding employment. Table 1.7 indicates that 85.20 per cent of women in the rural areas and 20 per cent of the women in the urban areas are taking part in the primary sector activities. However, 82 per cent of the female workers in the rural areas and 52 per cent of the female workers in the urban areas are illiterate (Table 1.8).

Table 1.7: Percentage Distribution of Female Workers

Year	*Primary*	*Secondary*	*Tertiary*
Rural Areas			
1972–73	89.86	5.72	4.42
1977–78	88.36	6.62	2.07
1983	88.05	7.29	5.15
1987–88	85.10	9.81	5.21
1993–94	85.20	8.60	12.10
Urban Areas			
1972–73	33.47	28.40	38.14
1977–78	32.39	31.92	35.69
1983	29.40	31.25	39.35
1987–88	30.20	31.00	38.80
1993–94	20.00	28.80	51.00

Table 1.8: Literacy Levels of Female Workforce in India (1987–88)

Literacy Level	*Rural Areas*	*Urban Areas*
Illiterate	82.3	51.8
Literate Upto		
Primary	12.0	19.0
Middle	3.2	7.3
Secondary	2.1	12.3
Graduate and Above	0.4	9.6
Total	100.0	100.0

Source: CMIE, India's Social Sectors, February 2004, p. 222.

Further, female workforce participation rate in showing a decline from 27.93 per cent to 22.26 per cent in 1991. This decline is taking place in the rural as well as in the urban areas (Table 1.9).

Table 1.9: Female Workforce Participation Rate in India

Year	*Female Workers as a Percentage of Population*		
	Total	*Rural*	*Urban*
1961	27.93	31.42	11.16
1971	14.22	15.92	07.18
1981	19.67	23.06	08.31
1991	22.26	26.86	09.24
2001	27.41	31.85	08.82

Source: Based on CMIE, India's Social Sectors, February.

Women in the rural areas are mostly in self-employment, with only 3.8 per cent of the rural women being able to find regular salaries employment, whereas a greater number of urban workmen are enjoying the benefits of regular salaried employment (Table 1.10). Employment of women has grown at the rate of only 1.36 per cent per annum in the rural areas during the period 1977–78 to 1993–94.

The vast multitude of women in the unorganised sector are characterised by:

1. low earnings;
2. seasonal and insecure unemployment;
3. woefully inadequate and non-existent supportive services;

4. lack of access to credit facilities;
5. weak collective bargaining power; and
6. very few opportunities for personal growth.

Table 1.10: Distribution of Female Workers by Category of Employment

(*Percentage*)

Year	*Rural*	*Urban*	*Total*
Self-Employment			
1977–78	56.3	42.2	54.8
1983	54.1	37.3	52.0
1987–88	55.1	38.6	53.1
1990–91	58.6	49.0	57.2
2000–01	65.4	56.0	61.4
Casual Wage Employment			
1977–78	40.0	27.0	38.6
1983	42.2	30.9	40.7
1987–88	40.2	26.7	38.6
1990–91	37.6	25.1	35.8
2000–01	44.4	32.4	38.0
Regular Salaried Employment			
1977–78	3.7	30.8	6.6
1983–84	3.7	31.8	7.3
1987–88	4.7	34.7	8.3
1990–91	3.8	25.9	7.0
2000–01	5.2	31.4	6.5

Source: Based on CMIE, India's Social Sectors, Feb. 2004, Table 239, p. 226.

Policies and programmes to improve the conditions of women's lives are being implemented by governments in various countries. The most common interventions are those intended to increase women's income, to provide women with the means to control their own fertility and to increase levels of human capital investments in females so that the next generation of women will be better equipped to contribute to the well-being of their families and the nation.

Under successive Five Year Plans of the country, several measures have been initiated in India to provide employment and training to women. Development and children constitutes an integral component of the country's human resource development programme. The strategy for women's development consists of empowerment of women through:

1. employment;
2. economic independence;
3. education and nutrition facilities;
4. health and nutrition facilities;
5. welfare services;
6. legal support and safeguards.

The Integrated Rural Development Programme (IRDP) forms the core of Government's strategy for removal of rural poverty through employment generation. Other anti-poverty programmes include TRYSEM, JRY, NRY, PMRY and PMI UPEP which aim at:

1. employment;
2. creation of productive assets;
3. imparting technical and entrepreneurial skills; and
4. raising the income level of the very poor.

Gender focus is given to several of these schemes. For example, under IRDP, 40 per cent of the beneficiaries have to be women. Similarly, 30 per cent of employment generation under JRY is meant for women.

The DWCRA scheme which was started in 1983 is now in operation in 450 districts of the country with UNICEF assistance. During 1994–95, over 19,000 groups, with a 3.19 lac women contingent, were formed. Further, since its inception in 1987, the Support to Training and Employment Programme for Women (STEP) benefited more than 2.50 lac women. The programme seeks to train women for employment in the traditional sectors of agriculture, animal husbandry, dairy, handlooms and handicrafts. The Rashtriya Mahila Kosh (RMK) was set up in 1993 to meet the credit needs of poor women particularly in the unorganised sector.

Thus, women are being given importance in special programmes of poverty alleviation and employment generation as well as in several other social and family welfare programmes. But, most of the these programmes suffer from adhocism leading to only marginal benefits. The coverage is vastly inadequate and the programmes are not proportionate to the needs and numbers of women. The contribution of women and their work are grossly undervalued. The implementation machinery mostly lacks knowledge regarding the really poor amongst women and is sometimes insensitive to the basic needs of women in poverty.

Early Childhood Care and Education (ECCE)

Under this programme Integrated Child Development Service (ICDS) has been launched in 1996. This is currently the biggest programme of early childhood development with 2.90 lac Anganwadis serving nearly 140 lac children and about 27 lac mothers: 91.5 per cent ICDS projects are located in rural and tribal areas and 8.5 per cent in urban slums. Besides the ICDS, by the end of 1991–92 there were 12,470 creches with a coverage of about 3 lac children below 5 years, 4,395 ECE centers in 9 Educationally Backward (EB) states and the Balwadi Nutrition Programme serving nearly 2.30 lac children in the age-group of 3–5 years.

Over the recent years, a number of initiatives have been taken to make the programmes more focused. The measures under ICDS, include emphasis on practical training of Anganwadi Workers, and extension work by Anganwadi training centers, which are required to adopt 10 Anganwadis each for developing them as model Anganwadis. To build up resource capabilities in the field, action is afoot to develop CDPO's office into resource center. Instructional materials for Anganwadi Training Centres are also under preparation. Effort are also being made to distribute education-cum play materials to Anganwadis to improve their pre-school education component. Initiative has also been taken to improve the scheme of creches by reviewing norms for voluntary and community participation. A scheme has been worked out by the Department of Women and Child Development for converging the services under DWCRA, ICDS, pre-school education and related schemes of the Departments of Health, Family Welfare and Rural Development.

Targets and Phasing

The aim of ECCE is that every child should be assured access to the fulfillment of all basic needs. As such efforts will be made towards universalisation of ICDS of A.D. 2000. By the end of the Eighth Plan, 3.75 lac Anganwadi centers would be established and by A.D. 2000 seven lac Anganwadi centers. Anganwadis will be gradually converted into Anganwadis-cum-creches. By the end of Eighth Plan, 25 per cent of Anganwadis will be converted into Anganwadis-cum-creches. Qualitative improvement of ongoing ECCE programmes would receive high attention. New cost-effective designs of ECCE will also be encouraged and supported.

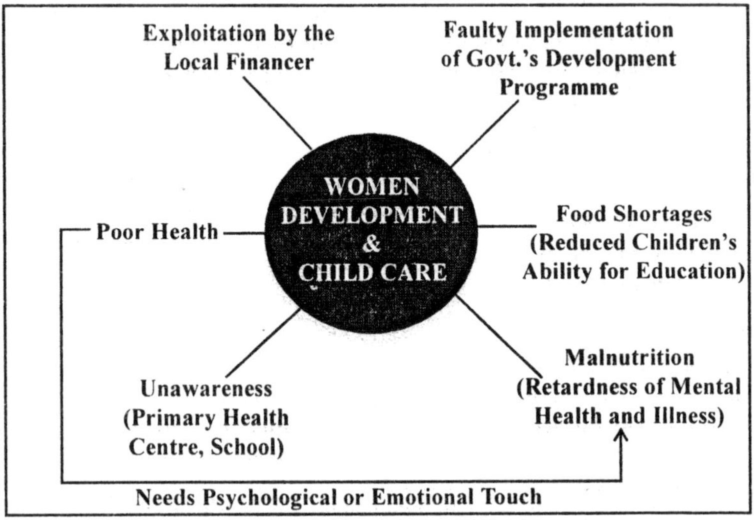

Fig. 1.1: Women Development and Child Care in Santhal Pargana

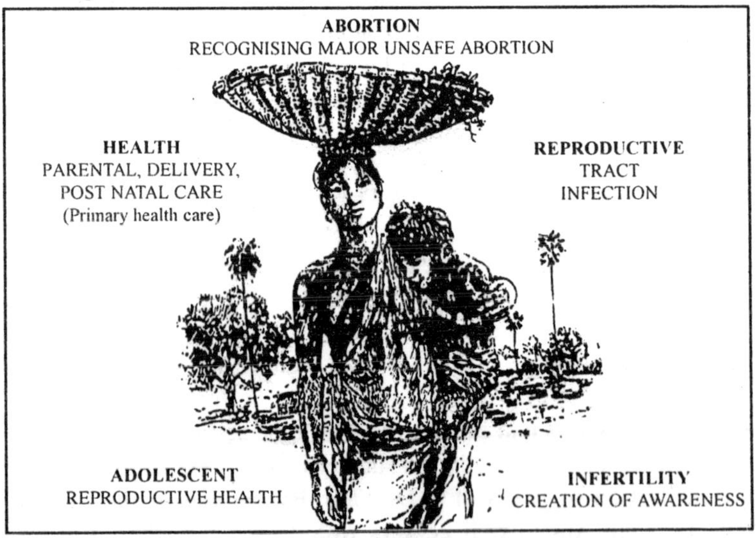

Fig. 1.2: Women's Reproductive Health Conditions

Strategy of Implementation

The ECCE involves the total development of child, *i.e.* physical, motor, cognitive, language, emotional, social and moral. The age span under consideration in ECCE is from conception to about 6 years. Even a modest development process during this period includes care of mother during pregnancy (ante-natal health check-up, support, control of anaemia, immunization for prevention of tetanus following delivery, etc., hygienic and skilled birth attendance, nutritional care of mother during lactation, correct infant feeding practices, immunization of infant from communicable diseases, mother's education in the child care, early childhood stimulation and health nutritional support throughout. Thus, ECCE is a complex integral function.

Women's Contribution to the Family Budget

Activities in the home are almost exclusively the responsibility of women, although: children may occasionally assist. These tasks return every day and absorb hours of time.

Throughout developing countries, women contribute substantially to the family budget through income-generating activities—food processing, trading of agricultural products and the production of handicrafts.

It is clear that women fulfill a great number of essential tasks, yet they and their labour are often unrewarded. "Although women represent half of the world's population and one-third of the official labour force, they receive only one per cent of the world income and own less than one per cent of the world's property".

Land particularly healthy soil, is the foundation on which life depends. If the land is healthy, then agriculture and pasturage will yields food in plenty. If it is not, the ecosystem will show signs of strain and food production will become more difficult. Because women are at the centre of world food production producing more than 80 per cent of the food in some countries—any analysis of land resources must include an appreciation of their central role.

The present world food situation is one of the great modern paradoxes: about 500 million people—the largest number ever—are seriously malnourished while world food production has reached the highest levels in history.

Many of those dispossessed of land by the increasing conception of ownership are women and their children. Women have title to only one per cent of the world's land. Yet they produce more than half of the world's food -and in countries of food scarcity the percentage is even higher.

As food providers, women play a central role in the nutritional intake of the family. But this is similarly affected by the development of large-scale monocultures, producing crops for export at the expanse of subsistence foods. The complementary structure of rural diet—beans and corns of lentils and rice, for example—has been undermined not only by these shifts but also by intensive marketing of commercially processed products such as Coca Cola and bread. Agriculture change linked to glistening images. Of progress alters nutritional intake and makes women's task of feeding the family that much more difficult. Health suffers and malnutrition increases.

Finally, large-scale agricultural expansion places impossible demands on women, who may have access to land but rarely to the capital or credit to invest in machinery, hybrid seeds or chemicals. The inputs required by Green Revolution agriculture are usually beyond their economic reach.

Most developing countries have a long history of colonial rule which imposed laws and social structures particularly harmful to women. Among these are inheritance laws, legislation on land ownership and transfer, and social restriction on women which seriously their activities and aspiration.

These same developments, especially since the Second World War, have fostered the growth of industrial centres which draw men away from rural communities, removing their labour from subsistence farming. The increasing migration of men to the cities, to mines, to export, agriculture, or to work abroad has caused the number of female-headed households to rise dramatically. This often means that the entire responsibility for feeding, clothing and housing children rests on the women's shoulders.

When rural women do participate in the wage labour economy, they face discrimination and lower rates.

Even development professionals usually ignore where women. Remain in subsistence agriculture their central position. Thus training and agricultural extension programmes often fail to reach women. In some Hindu are Christian cultures, too, customs preclude an open learning atmosphere between women and a male non-family member. But this is not sole problem. The teaching of non-family member. But this is not the sole problem. The teaching of non-middle-class women is not even considered of educational activity any where in the developing world. Yet illiterate women, out of reach of extension workers, are specially vulnerable to the injudicious use of dangerous chemicals, spraying of fields and local storage of unsafe chemicals are special hazards for these women, whose children also suffer if their mothers are poisoned during pregnancy.

Conclusion

Development of women is crucial for the social and economic transformation of a country in view of their complex and multi-dimensional roles. Women have been marginal players in the rapidly changing economic scenario. They have to be brought into the mainstream of the development process as equal partners by giving due recognition to the place, role, aspirations and achievements, which have undergone phenomenal changes in recent decades. Concerted efforts and greater thrust are needed to improve the quality of life of women in general and of poor women in particular. The implementation machinery of various women development programmes has to be strengthened through better targeting and constant monitoring so as to create a greater sense of well-being and status for the new generation in the next millennium.

REFERENCES

Cloud, K. (1994), "Women, Households and Development: A Policy Perspective", in Romy Borooah *et al.* (edu.) *Capturing Complexity*, Sage Publications, New Delhi, p. 81.

GOI (1974), Towards Equality, Report of the Committee on the Status of Women in India, Delhi.

Hirway, I. (2001), "Economic Reforms and Gender Issues in India", *The Indian Journal of Labour Economics*, Vol. 39, No. 3 July–September, p. 582.

Humphires, J. (1977), "Class Struggle and the Persistence of the Working Class Family", *Cambridge Journal of Economics*, Vol. 1.

ICSSR, Critical Issues on the Status of Women, Suggested Priorities for Action, New Delhi.

Mahajan. V.S. (ed) (1989). *Women's Contribution to India's Economic and Social Development* (quoted form). Deep and Deep Publications, New Delhi.

Marx. K. Kapital: *A Critique of Political Economy*, Vol. I.

Mitra, A. (1979), *The Status of Women: Literacy and Employment*, New Delhi.

Murthy, C.S. (1997), "Human Development in a Dynamic Setting: The Indian Case" (Mimeo).

Oppenheimer, V. (1990), *The Female Labour Force in the United States*, University of California, Berkeley.

Ramaswamy, U. 1992, "Women and Development", in A.N. Sharma and Seema Singh (eds.), *Women and Work: Changing Scenario in India*, B.R. Publication and Class, Havard, Cambridge, Mass.

Roemer, J. (1982), *General Theory of Exploitation and Class*, Harvard Cambridge, Mass.

Shanmugasundaram, Y. (1993), *Women Employment in India*, Allied Publishers, Madras.

Uma Devi, S. (1989), "Role of Women in Economic Development", in V.S. Mahajan (ed.), *Women's Contribution to India's Social and Economic Development*, New Delhi.

Veblen, T. (1934), *The Theory of the Leisure Class*, New York.

2

Globalization and Role of Women in Family Management

Globalisation is a fact of life. But we have underestimated its fragility. The spread of markets far outpaces the ability of societies and their political systems to adjust to them, let alone to guide the course they take. History teaches us that such an imbalance between the economic, social and political realms can never be sustained for very long.

Nobel laureate Amartya Sen said on October 13, 1998 that globalisation could be a major force for prosperity only if it was backed by adequate national policies in a conducive social and economic environment. He stressed that he was not against globalisation and said countries threatened by it were those where human development was very low. "There are major gains to be made in globalisation. So I am pro-globalisation", he said but, he added if a country has globalisation at the highest possible speed and pays no attention to lack of social opportunity, illiteracy and lack of health care, it was creating problems for itself.

In that case, the blame lies not with globalisation but with concomitant policies with which it was being married. Globalisation needs to be put in a broader context of social and economic policies. He suggested a "social safety net", as in the industrial countries of Western Europe, to take care of the people when things go wrong for one reason or another. India and Pakistan has opened up their economies suddenly, resulting in a "Lot of people" from these countries not being able to compete in the global world. India and Pakistan had neglected education, health care and land reforms in a truly regrettable way. "*The problems arise when people in the countries enjoying protective environment are suddenly pushed into a highly-competitive situation. And when they opened economies suddenly, there were a lot of people who were not in a position to compete in a global world".*

The first *mantra* of *Ishopanisad* says God envelops the world. He is the instrument, controlling whatever moves in this world of constant motion. It is better, therefore, to enjoy all pleasures of the world through renunciation, rather than derive pleasure from coveting what rightfully belongings to someone else.

The industrialized countries learned that lesson in their bitter and costly encounter with the Great Depression. In order to restore social harmony and political stability adopted social safety nets and other measures designed to limit economic volatility and compensate the victims of market failures. That consensus made possible successive moves towards liberalization, which brought about the long post-war period of expansion. Our challenge today is to devise a similar compact on the global scale, to underpin the new global economy.

The Role of Women in the Changing World's Economy

World is changing at galloping rate to meet various demands under changing circumstances. As population is rising at a very fast rate, we need to produce food for everyone besides other basic needs. Since we cannot increase our geographical area, we have to produce more with various scientific inputs to give us more with modern industries to supply various other industrial products. In this process besides meeting basic needs, we also try to improve our quality of life.

But the developmental process we practiced so far has caused enough of pollution. Therefore, while improving quality of life of privileged few, this process of development has in turn has ensured depletion of quality of life of bulk of home sapiens besides ensuring death of the planet itself, depletion resources at faster rate ensuring a barren earth for our descendants.

Therefore, to ensure a balanced growth we must plan for sustainable development which remained a slogan so far since the western world continued to grow fast at the expense of our global environment.

Sustainable development is the successful management of resources inclusive of human resource, for various development processes to satisfy changing human needs while maintaining or enhancing quality of the environment and conserving natural resources.

It is the developmental process, which is ecologically sound, economically viable, and adaptable, may result in sustainable development. That means we must have a developmental process that shall honour dignity of all, safety for all and adaptable by all with equal rights both for men and women in the entire system.

In order to achieve such development, women, particularly those living in the rural areas play a major role in managing natural resources—soil, water, forest and energy. Their tasks in agriculture and animal husbandry as well as in the household make them the daily managers of the living environment. They have a profound knowledge of the plants, animals and ecological processes around them.

Women also participate in the commercial sectors of society and the raw materials they use in rural enterprises are vulnerable to environmental degradation and contamination. As farmers and traders, then, women experience environmental problems as directly undermining the basis of their daily lives.

The principal victims of environmental degradation are the most underprivileged people, and the majority of these are women. Their problems and those of environment are very much interrelated. Both are marginalized by existing development policies. And because of the complex cycles of poverty, inappropriate development and environmental degradation, poor people have been forced into ways of living which induce further destruction. Third World women often have no choice but to exploit natural resources in order to survive, even though they may have the knowledge to promote sustainability.

Indian women, rural women have traditionally been the invisible workforce, the unacknowledged backbone of the family economy. Men go out to work, enter into chosen as spokespersons when it comes to dealing with government or development agencies. But when we look more closely at the types of work that women do, we can distinguish three main areas, all crucial to keeping the family and indeed three main areas, all crucial to keeping the family and indeed the rural generation, survival tasks are those essential for daily life, and it is for these the women are largely responsible. They grow the food, crops, provide water gather fuel and perform most of the other work, which sustains the family.

A certain division of labour is evident in the agricultural sector. Women are generally responsible. They grow the food crop, provide water, gather fuel and perform most of the other work, which sustains the family.

A certain division of labour is evident in the agricultural sector. Women are generally responsible for sowing, weeding, crop maintenance and harvesting as long as these tasks have not been mechanized. Men on the other hand, look after field preparation. Subsistence agriculture—the growing of food crops—is almost exclusively a women's task. But women's participation is increasing in cash-cropping as well. Care of small animals is often their responsibility. The supply of water vital for the survival and health of the family and for farming is exclusively the concern of women and children.

For their energy supplies, the rural areas depend mainly on biomass such as fuel wood, crop residues and manure. Fuel collection, where it is not commercialized, is mainly a task for women, with children's help. Depending on the ecological characteristics of the area in which they live.

Home-makers and Child-rearers

As home-makers and child-rearers, women are directly affected by the place in which they live. The prospects for their children are slender poor people in parts of many cities can expect to see one in four of their children die of malnutrition before they are five. Just as the lack of sanitation in the home affects women most strongly, so the destruction of water resources and fuel wood around settlements hits them, hardest. The environment, both inside and outside the home, has everywhere a great significance for women—a fact which is reinforced by cultural patterns.

Although, education and training opportunities for women neither automatically improve their position in society nor guarantee their equal participation in development, inequality in education is a vital constraint on women's progress in both rural and urban areas. Generally, women who are educated and trained improve their status within the family, the community and the nation. Evidence shows that educating girls may be one of the best investments a country can make.

> *"Educate a boy and you educate one person.*
> *Educate a girl and you educate a nation."*

Women are the first environmental educators. It is through contact with their mothers that young children first learn to see and understand what is happening around them, and begin to feel how they themselves are related to it.[1] The home, the groundwork is in place to demonstrate "connections". Children brought up learning "to connect" with their environment are more likely to "acquire in a formative age of imagination, a picture of themselves as citizens of a shared and indivisible planetary home".

Training is a dynamic and adaptable tool of interaction and a powerful means of bringing women into the development process. Social training can revive and strengthen traditional skills and build upon their enormous fund of indigenous knowledge so transforming it into the capacity for action. Training can also help to eliminate women's isolation and build confidence.

Women are vital, for in many areas of the world, they are the main environmental managers. They are traditionally responsible for a great deal of conservation activity—they protect soils, trees and water sources, they carefully select the seed-corn damage and their pioneer ways of reclaiming and severely degraded by bad management.

Women as Agents of Change

Women are the key agents of change. Yet women are the ones who could make a major contribution to environmental rehabilitation. First they have the knowledge and the skills of natural resource management that can be built upon. They know, for example, much better than imported "experts" which trees make the best fuel wood, which dry fast and burn well, which retain moisture in the soil and which ones give the best foliage for fodder or fertilizer.

Secondly, women have a remarkable ability to work together. The evidence from many women's groups is that women can share their skills and resource to take effective action. Some of the most successful examples, of sustainable development build upon women's initiatives—in the Chipko movement of northern India, in the Kenyan Green Belts and in the Boldia Sanitation project in Pakistan. Many women are experienced in cooperative working, something that male-dominated governments and multi-national companies have yet to learn.

Thirdly, in caring for children women have a powerful influence over changing attitudes to the environment. They can turn the short-term expediency of remedial action into a lasting habit of environmental protection.

Finally, perhaps most important of all, it is likely that restoring women's capacity to care for the environment will be associated with improvements in their independence and their status: there is a major convergence of interest between environmentally sound of sustainable development. And the development of women.

Basic problem of women is same. They are certainly considered second class citizens all over the world although with the passage of time and increase in awareness the brute treatment that was subjected to them is gradually being eliminated.

To improve the total situation violence or revenge is not the solution. It cannot be a solution for any of the problem, however, serious may be. What we lack is our capacity to analyse, situation shall certainly change. Thinking process infact is the other name of spiritualism. If we shall become tools for exploitation and surrender to meaningless dogma. This will lead to torture ultimately leading to oppression of women. One can imagine how analysis and thinking power of Raja Rammohun Roy could change the situation of women creating a new order of humanity. If one man can think and change the total situation, we can create heaven if every one of us think and analysis instead of surrendering to meaningless rituals, that leads to many social evils.

Women do have their constructive roles in various activities which we normally ignore to various chain reactions. Not only in our home-front, traditionally women and various roles in agriculture, sericulture, spinning, weaving, dyeing and printing. But male dominated society normally neglects women. While with chain of changing dimension superstitions and dogmas are gradually vanishing atrocities on women is also being reduced in one perspective. In most of the cases women are not being subjected to torture as part of ritual except in some countries. But modernization and mechanization also brings fresh wave of atrocities. As we opt mechanization and automation role of women in various economic activities is reduced making them unwanted in our society. Thus they are reduced to a commodity for sex and machines for producing children.

Gender Issues

Women's lives in India and the World over are
Circumscribed by what can be termed as the 'five Ps'—
Patriarch;
Productive resources access inadequacy;
Povery;
Promotion advancement insufficiency; and
Powerlessness.

At the core of this circle of denial of and discrimination in their rightful entitlements of life, education and training for a scientific technological world, health and social security, lies the gross violation of the human rights of women embodied in invisible structural and outward forms of violence perpetrated by the triple concentric circles of the family, community and society at large, now being compounded by the state under pressure of policy prescriptions of Structural Adjustment Policies.

The authors maintain that the "gender relationship of dominance and subordination is a political relationship which derives material sustenance from conditions and structures of production and its legitimacy from a tradition/culture which upholds subordination of women".

Female members of a poor household are often worse off than male members because of gender based difference in the distribution of food and other entitlements within the family. The Jakarta Document for the Advancement of Women in Asia and the Pacific (June 1994) brings this fact of absolute poverty in South Asia, as the foremost point of critical concern. What has been noted in that the SAP, in spite of increasing the employment for women has concentrated them in low-status, low paying job, thus, increasing their poverty. The disproportionate resource flow from the North to the South and the factor of reverse net outflow has "aggravated the poverty and dependency situation of women".

The strategy to eliminate poverty is to open every avenue for economic achievement. Occur in markets, for the rural poor, the strategy ought to be massive statal investments in a transport infrastructure connecting villages to town and city markets.

Housing the *jhuggi* market. It is the lowest component of the overall real estate market. Quite obviously then, if the shackles imposed from above on his important market were to be removed, the *jhuggi* market would each a higher level. Without urban land ceilings the real estate market would reach a higher level. Without urban land ceilings, the real estate market would take off. Fast road and rail connections would bring in vast reaches of vacant countryside into play.

Cities would decongest, small towns would develop land for housing would become cheap and plentiful. The key to integrating the *jhuggi* market into the overall expansion of the real estate industry lies in making its activities legal. For that, the removal of rent control is a must. Without rent control, there is the distinct possibility of a private market developing in the supply of low cost rental housing with sewer connections and priced electricity. With rent control, the urban poor have no hope. They will forever remain the constituency of slumlords, adding to the criminalisation of policies.

In banks are awash with funds, expansion of housing finance can fund a real estate boom. This will ultimately deliver poor people a house—on mortgage or on rent that is fit for human habitation. The state is intervening in his process today—hence jhuggis.

Hindu economics emphasizes plentiful supplies and moderation in consumption. It lays down the principle that the prices should be based on cost of production. And Buddhist economics emphasizes restriction on demand.

A book has been published with a title: "*Buddhist Economics*" it is edited by Guy Mint. R.C. Majumdar in his book, "*Corporate Life in Ancient India*", describes all sorts of corporate activities in ancient India—corporate activities in the economic, social, political and religious life, but leads us fundamentally to wonder as to what this "corporate life" really means.

Membership of the Buddhistic Samha was not determined by descent and no body could have any birth-right to it. As such an entry into it could not merely be a matter of the attainment of maturity. It is adoption. And an extraordinary, elaborate, democratic sanction is naturally a precondition for this in the tribal society. "Among the Iroquois", says Morgan, "the ceremony of adoption was performed at a public council of the tribe, which turned it practically into a religious rite".

Role of Santhal Women in Family Management

Management process essentially consists of three steps—planning, controlling and evaluating the outcome. Planning is vital to the success of management process. It is a necessary action for guiding action in meeting the demands of the family. It is essentially mapping out the courses of action to reach the goal. The need to develop a plan in derived from a felt need to resolve a problem or achieve something. During planning, standards are set which refers to the quantitative and qualitative measures of establishing standards depending on resources availability and other demands placed upon resources. The type of food served in family is determined by the money available, the requirement of the people and the facilities and people available for preparation. Planning is essentially the formation of a plan of action based on analysis of available opportunities and options, focusing on objectives determined in this stage.

We can apply the process of management to practically all activities in the home, whether they are economic activities, performance tasks or childcare and control activities. Some tasks are shared among parents and children. In Indian situations more household tasks are still considered to be women's prerogative. The responsibility of getting every thing done within the resource limits, necessitates the need for effective and productive management process.

The major managerial responsibilities in a family consists of: (*a*) Identifying values and selecting goal; (*b*) Create healthy environment in home and community; (*c*) Nurture, growth and development of the young; (*d*) plan work for long range financial security; (*e*) Maintaining a pleasant and comfortable home; (*f*) providing suitable food and clothing for the family; (*g*) purchase consumer's goods and services; (*h*) Maintaining health of all the family members; (*i*) perform task of maintaining the home, using time and energy wisely; (*j*) Guiding the educational and social development of the individuals in the family group and (*k*) participate intelligently in community, legislatives and social action affairs.

Examinations of all these marginal responsibilities shows inter-relationships. Some are the direct outcome of the others and some responsibilities like providing nutritious meal would be helpful in maintaining the health of all family members. Likewise, financial management permeates through all aspects of management. Another area of emphasis is time and energy management. In order to accomplish the days work without undue strain and tension, home makers, must constantly think in terms of time and effort in connection with each managerial responsibility and its related tasks.

From time immemorial women have filled diverse roles in their home activities; as wives, in their personal lives with their husbands, as mother, in their responsibilities for the development of their children; and as home makers, in charge of the operation of their houses. In early years the woman was the director of home production and her role in an agricultural economy was of permanent importance.

Clearly women are biologically different from men. Though there is disagreement about the exact nature and consequences of this differences, some sociologists, anthropologists and psychologists argue that it is sufficient to explain the basic sexual division of labour in all societies.

Anthropologists Lionel Tiger and Robin Fox argue that social scientists who assume that human being behave simply in terms of the culture of their society are ignoring what they call the human "Biogrammar". The biogrammer is a genetically based programme which predisposes mankind to behave in certain ways. These predisposition are not the same as instincts since they can be considerably modified by culture but they remain basic influence on human behaviour. In part, they are inherited from mans primate ancestors, in part they have developed during man's existence in hunting and gathering bands. Since 99.9 per cent of man's existence has been spent as a hunt and gatherer. Tiger and fox argue that it is reasonable to assume that to some degree, he is genetically adapted to this of life. Although the biogrammers of men and women are similar in many respects, there are important differences between them.

Tiger and fox argue compared to women, men are more aggressive and dominant. These characteristics are genetically based in particular they result from differences between male and female hormones. These differences are due partly to genetic inheritance from man's primate ancestries, partly to a genetic adoption to a hunting way of life. Males hunt, which is an aggressive activity. They are responsible for alliance or wars with the other bands. Thus man monopolies positions of power. Since tiger and fox see dominance as a "sex-linked characteristics" it comes as no surprise that politics is the province of men from the male elders in Austrian Aborigine hunting and gathering bands to the House of Commons and House of Lords in present day Britain.

By comparison women are programmed by their biogrammars to reproduce and care for children. Tiger and fox argue that the basic family unity consists of mother and child. In their words, "Nature matter how this basic unit is supported and protected. It can be by the addition of single male, as the case of the nuclear family, or by the impersonal services of a welfare state.

The close emotional bond between mother and child is a genetically based predisposition for both parties and it is particularly important for the welfare of the child. Tiger and fox maintain that "The mother is totally essential to the well being of the child". Unless this close emotional bond obtains the child will be unable to establish successful relationship in later life.

Though an anthropologists like tiger and fox, George Peter Murdock operates from very different assumptions. He sees biological difference between men and women as the basis of the sexual division of labour in society. However, he does not suggest that men and women are directed by genetically based predisposition or characteristics to adopt their particular roles, instead, he simply suggests that biological difference such as the grater physical strength of men and the fact that women bear children, lead to gender roles or out of sheer practically. Given the biological difference between men and women, a sexual division of labour is the most efficient way of organizing society.

In a cross cultural survey of 224 societies ranging from hunting and gathering bands to modern nation states. Murdock examines the activities assigned to men and women. He find tasks such as hunting, lumbering and mining to be predominantly male roles, cooking, gathering wild vegetables products, water carrying and making and repairing clothes to be largely female roles. He states that "Man with his superior physical strength can better undertake the more stenuous tasks, such as lumbering, minings, quarrying, land clearance and house building. Not handicapped, as is women by the physiological burdens of pregnancy and nursing, he can range further a field to hunt, to fish to herd and to trade. Women is at no disadvantage, however, in lighter tasks which can be performed in or near the home, *e.g.* the gathering of vegetable products, to the fetching of water, the preparation of food and the manufacture of clothing and utensils. Thus because of her biological function of child bearing and nursing, women is tied to the home base, because of her physique she is limited to less strenuous tasks. Murdock finds that the sexual division of labour is present in all of the societies in his sample and concludes, "The advantages inherent in a division of labour by sex presumably account for his universality.

Though women in Santhal society enjoys equal right with the men in various spheres of life, they are not given equal right in religious activities. The religion of the Santhals is essentially a man's religion. Women are not allowed to be present at sacrifices except when they are offered in the house to the ancestors and family gods, and then only if there are no men to help the sacrificer. When a sacrifice taken place in the holy groves they many not eat the flesh of the offspring. The men burning what they do not eat. This prohibition does not apply in the case of animals sacrificed to Marang Buru or the head of any animal, the latter is cooked with rice and eaten by the men. On the other hand, when the sacrifice is offered in the holy groves, only the village priest can eat the head. No women is permitted to climb the consecrated trees in the holy groves and no women belonging to the another household, in most cases not even a daughter of the house if she is or has been married is allowed to enter the "bhitar", a small closed inside the house partitioned off by a low well, where the family Gods and ancestors are supposed to reside, and where the offerings are made to them and to Marang Buru. If any one breaks either of these rites, sacrifices must be offered to appease the offend bongas "who otherwise will revenge themselves by sending sickness and death on their worshipers".

The Santhal from one of the major tribal groups in India. This community has its own traditional history of migration and settlement. They are very much sensitive towards their language and culture. As a result they try to retain it in a original from even in the complexities of modernization. It is queer thing to investigate anything like status in the Santhal community. Because such idea is virtually absent in the society, characteristic feature of Santhal community is that no body seeks one's status in the society but keeps an eye on any anti-social activity amimed against social solidarity. Her man and woman share the social lives on equal footings. Though educationally backward, Santhals exhibit a remarkable advanced attitude towards individual in the society. It is an age old convention for men and women to have equal status in the society. This can be understood from the popular Santhal saying "eramurme hernsaria, stom koys bharam sahaways *i.e.* if you understand women (here wife) you will be able to keep the balance between nature and power in your march of life. Another Santhali saying "legati re ne dare ho marang dare" means left hand in equally powerful as the right one. The term *legati* stands for women in Santhal society.

In Santhal traditional narration women is found since the beginning of human creation. They believe that present generations of the community is pongra (offspring) of "pilchuharam and pilchubudhi". They were first men and women in Santhal community. They had the five sons and six daughters who married when young pilchuharam and pilchubudhi brought up their sons and daughters. So the children never knew that they were brothers and sisters, pilchuharam taught his sons how to use bow and arrow and for what purposes. On the other hand pilchu budhi taught her daughters how to look after their shelter.

One day while hunting sons of pilchuharam moved away from their locality and entered into the area of daughters of pilchubudhi. When they first met they become very much surprised and wanted to know each other.

Thus sons and daughters of pilchuharam and pilchubudhi know each others as different group members. It encouraged them to see

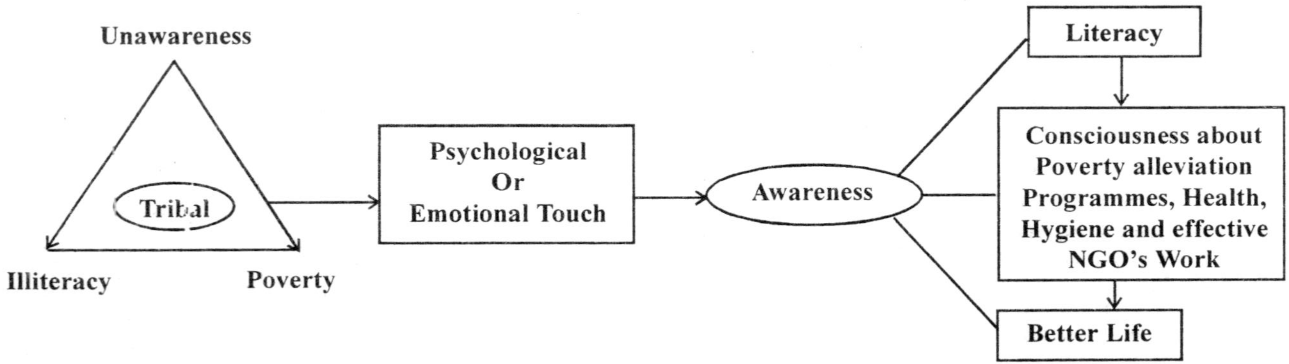

Fig. 2.1: Stage and Changing Scenario of the Tribal Women in Santhal Pargana

each other to meet each other and ultimately they married and thus the Santhal population increased.

In Santhal society the whole village organizations is called "Morekoturnika" five and six respectively stands for five sons (moreko) and six daughters (Turm-ko) of pilchuharam and pilchubudhi. They were the first group in Santhal community. They themselves and their descendents move from place to place in search of livelihood. The places where "Lepocteral or Lepectorrel, petorbare, sananbeda, Cirunge, Erestne, Khoj-kheman, khodemetkom and Sari-Sari Jomadisom (particularly known as Singdisom or Eaenes disom champs). In this journey for settlement and livelihood woman took part in equal footing with men endured great pains and sufferings. So they were not subordinates, but they were participants enjoying equal authority. The evidence of participation in this journey is found in baha song:

> *"On elder sister, listen more-ko searched rute-baha and metkobaha. And turuiko collected rute-baha and matkeombaha."*

Virtually Santhals first settled at Chae-champa areas. At that time this community called themselves. The name Santhal has been given to them in a latter period by non-tribal population. Any Chae-champa they first met with the sources for minimum requirements of livelihood. In Santhali such is called Ja-ha-re are thirto *i.e.* a place where food need may be sown.

There, they established Jaher-sra (mother Goddess) and other duties as Morang bare-More-ka Turuiko and Dharam. In Santhali a women (particularly married one or mother) is called "era" possibly the term "era" has been derived from Jaher-era.

The formal head of village organization is called kajhi and sometimes nayko. This term has been derived from nay and key or keys. Nay means goodness or welfare and key or keya means work benevolent service. So a nayke serve for the welfare of the villagers. How, this term stands for a priests in Santhal village. Similarly when a woman assists nayke she is called naykers. A naykera or manjhi can help the manjhi or mayke during puja and other social activities. In spring seasons flowers, namely, shoree-rebus ta and basis latifolio begins bloom. Santhals utter certain religious chant recapitulating the ancient history of searching:

Morekorenajing Sarjom baha
Turuikoren ejing matkum baha.

Ajing is very important term used to give respect to women. This term originated by Lite, Lita, Dhorom and Jaher-era where brothers and sisters. Jaher-era was the eldest, Lita and Dhorom were younger to her. They called Jaher-era ajing. Lita was the messenger God in Santhal pentheon. He moved from place to place to collect news and supply them to his elder sister. Keenly he observed the activities of Santhals and their attachment towards surroundings and time-to-time informed Heherera.

Lita brought up twin brother and sister pilchuharam and pilchubudhi. He only knew who was elder between the two. He would never express this thing publicly. But the term ajing indicates that pilchubudhi was elder. So, Lita tactfully put this term in use as a convention to show respect to Santhal women.

It has been mentioned that nayke-era also occupies a place of honour in village worship. Particularly during baha puja she is considered the divine incarnation of Jaher-era. So villagers conventionally convey to her all good news first as a mark of great respect and love.

From the occasional presence of seasonal bird, namely "wood-packer" and animal like gotrot Santhals come to know that earth is revolving in the cycle of seasons. This massage is communicated to Nayke-era and this alerts her to get ready for celebrating beha festival.

Man and women enter the social life through marriage. Marriage negotiations in Santhal community is organized by ryabar (mediator) and initiative is taken by groom's family. In Santhal society dowry system is absent but gonong (bride-price) is given to the parent of bride. Though, the amount of gonong is little, but it is a mark of honour shown to the bride. Many opined that gonong and two cows means some economic compensation to the bride's parents. However, the exact reason behind a practice is not known.

Conjugal life of the Santhal is based on co-operation, mutual sharing and good understanding. When the husband goes to field, the wife never site idle at home but attends him. Husband and wife love each other. They mutually share joys and sorrow. Even women join or participate with their husband during hunting. The evidence is collected from this baha song.

Particularly, for household affairs women shoulder all responsibilities. They prepare household budget and keep the daily account. Besides, they go to market and purchase necessary materials either for consumptions or other purposes. In this respect male members solely depend on females. But in this changing situation Santhals have been influenced by Hindus. Many families have adopted Hindu mode of living. This may have some impact on the rights and privileges of the Santhal women. But exact nature of its influence is not known.

Force application of over million on a virgin's head was an evil practice in Santhal society and it derogated the position of grown up girls. One day this form of force marriage was getting social recognition. This practice not get a place of honour in rituals. In some rear occasions it has been that though the women take part in preparing the puja materials in the house or at Jaher, yet she is not given any shape of boholete (main puja pressed) prepared from the heads of sacrificed animal.

A woman in Santhal society has many rights and privilege to move for divorce from the husband, if he is allegedly involved in extra-marital relations or for any other mal-adjustment in their conjugal life. The decrease is given to the wife and she is permitted to remarry elsewhere. This demonstrated that Santhal women are not wholly downtrodden.

As any other advanced society of the world, Santhal is a free society. After certain age young boys and girls do have social freedom to mix and participate in all spheres of social activities and social gatherings. In fact social functions become more lively and gay through equal and active participation of youths.

Every head of household cares for his wife's opinion in family matters. Traditionally Santhal women are equal to their men both in rights and privileges. They are equally respected and have equal responsibilities for contributions to make in the Santhal society.

REFERENCES

Amartya Sen, Individual Freedom: "Basis for a Social Commitment", *The Times of India,* October 16, 1998, p. 12.

Dr. Ashu Pasricha, Department of Gandhian Studies, Punjab University, Chandigarh, "The Women in Changing World".

Balasaheb Dev Ras, *RSS—A Force for Social Change* (1981), pp. 11–22.

Mr. Justice S. Mohan, "Social Justice in India", A.I.R., 1995, *Journal Section,* p. 98.

M.G. Chitkara and Harbans Garg (Retd.) Director, Art, Culture and Language, Himachal Pradesh, Shimla.

Mukhopadhyay, Maitrayee, *Silver Shackles: Women and Development in India,* Oxford: Oxfam.

Swarup, Hem Lata, "Ethnicity, Gender and Class" in *Ethnicity, Class and Gender,* (2005).

Swarup Hem Lata and Pam Rajput (ed.), *Women and Globalisation* (1994), p. 102.

3

An Overview of the Past Literature

As discussed in the earlier chapter, ever since the advent of Independence in 1947, the country has witnessed enormous rise in education of women and their emancipation from tradition bound ethos. Like educated, uneducated women throughout the world, the Indian women's attitude towards the stereotyped sex roles has also undergone a change. Kapur (1974) has discussed in great length the changing status and attitudes of working educated women in India. They carry strong concern for status and social equality. But there are good deal of inter and intra social variations in the status and attitude of women. Even the educated women differ sharply in their concern for status. Why it so happens? What socio-psychological variables determine or influence the individual differences among the educated women in this regard? The present research addresses itself to provide an answer to this question. Among the variables which have been studied here as correlates of women's concern of status are certain socio-personal background factors, personality dimensions and value orientations. This chapter presents review of the relevant literature on the concept, dimensions and significance of the selected variables for the present research.

Socio-economic Factors

While education about which discussion has been made in great length in the previous chapter is the prime personal determinant of women's concern for status. The other relevant factors in this regard appear to be age, socio-economic status, parental attitude and control, family discipline and child rearing practices etc. Halas (1974) has shown the influence of childhood socialization experience on sex-role stereotypes of adult women. Prager (1986) studied

86 undergraduate students and found that their overall identity status showed a significant association with the age and college experience of the subjects.

Women of different age groups differ in their needs and values. Erdwins *et al.* (1982) have shown that the university girls student differ significantly in needs measured by the EPPS from the full time home-makers (aged 40—50 yrs), particularly the former expressing more dependence and affiliation needs. Reinke (1985) collected data from 124 women of varied ages of 30—60 years and reported significant changes in the attitudes and psycho-social makeup of women of different age groups. Major mental transitions take place in women around 30, 40 and 60 years of age. Lebe (1986) has discussed the female ago ideal conflicts which frequently emerge in women during their 20's, 30's, and 40's as they have to make decisions regarding motherhood and career. Junge and Laya (1986) have found that women in their forties have problems of ageism as well as sexism. They are the generation of both tradition and liveration and have to cope with integration of conflicting demands and expectations. Bell (1975) on the basis interview conducted on 439 women living in Melbourne Metropolitan Area (Australia) has concluded that age and education are crucial variables in understanding of the changing social roles for women. Stinnet *et al.* (1983) reporting data collected from Romanion samples have shown that urban subjects and those with higher education were of the married women in the age group of 31–45 years are androgynous in their attitude than those in age group of 20–30 years. Younger women in India have, therefore less concern for status and equality than the matured aged women. But so far education is concerned, college students, whether male or female, have relatively more liberal attitude towards the sex roles (Phillips and Johnson, 1985; Lyson and Brown, 1982; Crealock, 1978).

A number of studies have indicated influence in family situations and background on ideals of equality between the sexes (Stinnet *et al.*, 1983). Symonds (1986) has shown that a family background in which the girls receive inferior treatment as compared to the boys creates chronic depression in the female child which influences her throughout her life. Mother-daughter emotional bond is equally important. This is manifested on imprint of mother on the daughter's cultural and social blues (Bouchart-Godard, 1978). It has been noticed that daughters of working women have more keenness for jobs and employment. Koening and Juni (1981) found in their study that girls from father, dominated families exhibited greater anti-women attitudes than the girls from mother dominant families. In families having dominant in conversation (Mayes-Sharon, 1979). Similarly, arthorltarian parents have more dogmatic and tradition loving children (Thomas, 1975; Sharma, 1982) and they are expected to believe more in sex differentiated roles. Khoo *et al.* (1984) have however, shown that mothers occupation has more influence on son's that daughter's attitudes towards married women's employment and the motherhood role in Australia.

Stinnet *et al.* (1983) after collecting data from a large number of 20—49 years only married Romanian women have reported that urban subjects and those with higher education are more egalitarian in their attitude. They hold that women should receive equal education and equal pay for the same work, because they are as intelligent and capable to take important decisions as men. They no longer subscribe to the traditional family ideology, but still believe that males should be head of families and women's place should be in the home. Gupta *et al.* (1982) have also confirmed the positive effect of education on women's attitude towards social equality, although they could not find socio-economic status as a significant factor in this regard. A few studies have shown girls receiving special training or education courses have more egalitarian sex role attitudes (Bennett and Grasser, 1981; Harris, 1983; Khoo *et al.*, 1984).

Apart from age and education, employment and marriage are two most important determinants of sex roles, values and attitudes. Kapur (1974) has dealt in great lengthy the problems and changing status and attitudes of working educated women in urban area. According to Desai (1957) educated women consider self-respect and development in offices, professions and business provides them opportunity to realize these goals. It provides them personal status, independent social standing, self-confidence and a changed outlook. They hold that mission of their life does not end with becoming good wives and wise mothers. If we analyse the reasons, which impel an educated woman to join job outside her home, we find that it is not just earning money. There are a number of socio-psychological factors as well, due to which wives and mothers do jobs outside (Hafstrom *et al.*, 1978), no doubt, those women, who are economically hard pressed, get engaged in paid jobs and serve as bread earners for the family. But a large number of them come from middle and upper middle class families who take jobs to supplement family income, improve their social status and worth, gain independence and seek engagement and self-fulfilment (Kapur, 1970; Oppengeimer, 1977; Frenkel *et al.*, 1982). Welch (1979) has reported from her study that the working wives (especially professionals) are more 'androgynous' than the house wives. They score high on masculinity. McCall (1977) has called a working lady as "work wife" who, according to him, is more concerned for personal identity and is quick to identify with new role model demanding individuality. Krohg (1985) has shown that among the employed women there is a significant positive correlation between sex role orientation and number of hours worked by them each week. Nodelson and Eisenberg (1977) have shown that female personhood is enriched by professional commitment. As a result, the woman with a career become a more stimulating marital relationship. The successful female executives have positive attitudes toward themselves, their families, and their work environment (Keown and Keown 1982). It is a question of developing suitable strategy to cope with problems. Lang (1978) has suggested strategies for a woman to cope with non-traditional occupations. She should be conscious of her identity, values and attitude, and be prepared for loneliness, office politics and opposition.

Due to change in interest and hobbies, the working wives differ from the non-working wives in their family purchases and major items of expenditures as well (Strober and Weinberg, 1977). Explaining this Lazer and Smallwood (1977) report that working women spend heavy amounts on expensive household appliances, on their looking youthful and impressive, and on convenient and fast foods. They are more education oriented and interested in self-improvement, travel and leisure. According to Huser and Grant (1978) husbands and wives of dual career families are more inner directed and feeble in applying personal values that husbands and wives of traditional career families. Fuchsle (1983) has found that employed women in Germany have equalitarian sex role preferences. All these lead to suggest that working educated women have greater concern for status than the non-working women or housewives.

Marriage is an important event in a girl's life. It bestows especial roles and responsibilities on her. In Indian culture where inspite of breaking of joint family system, the family does not mean only husband, wife and minor children. The girl, after marriage has to adjust with a large number of inlaws, *i.e.* father, mother and other relatives of the husband. She has to observe *purdah* and a lot of complicated roles. In such a circumstances if she joins some vocational occupation she is put to great strain. Literature shows that dual roles of a housewife and a job-person are full of stress for the married women in all societies of the world howsoever advanced and progressive it may be. The demands of home and job are sometimes incompatible and they cause conflicts and problems of adjustment for the working women (Nye, 1959): Usher and Fels, 1985: Sanders *et al.,* 1984). Walker and Friendman (1977) have studied the professional women's attitude towards the dual role of women by developing their own test. Fine-Davis (1979) interviewed 240 Irish married women of 18—65 years age and found that the employed and the non-employed married women differed significantly on several characteristics including attitudes toward the role and status of women, religiosity, expected family size and use of contraceptives etc. Studies have shown that housewives and professional women (occupying high job status) demonstrate least role conflict (Nevill and Damico, 1978). Davis (1981) using the USA census data covering 29 years period starting from 1950 has shown that the strain on account of the household affairs and outside working responsibilities result in more married women committing suicide. Staines *et al.* (1978) have found that the working wives employed in positions having status, feel dissatisfied with their employed husbands and think of divorce significantly more often than housewives, but still they do not score lower on ratings of marital satisfaction or marital adjustment. On the basis of case studies St. John Passons (1978) has shown that in dual career families the kinship ties are loosened and social life decreased and the couples experience severe overload problems. Nadalson (1981) reports that many women living "single" life point out that marriage increases stress for women and so they prefer remaining "single" status. But Travis (1976) studying university students found that the "single" subject tended to see marriage and children as the most important life experience for a women and they planned to alter their career plans significantly to accommodate children.

However, not all findings are unanimous on married women doing jobs outside. There are findings which indicate no significant difference in adjustment of married working woman and whole time housewives (Locke and Mackeprang, 1949; Smith, 1981: Lovell-Troy, 1983). On the other, several studies have shown that the full time employed married woman have better mental health and marital adjustment (Powell, 1977: Hemekeeht and Mocke, 1981). Newberry *et al.* (1979) have reported that working women derived considerably more satisfaction from their outside jobs that either they or the housewives did from their work in the home. On the basis of survey of 400 West German housewives, Hofstalter (1979) has found that 85 per cent of the working women and 46 per cent of the underemployed women were in favour of women holding jobs. This conforms the result obtained by Trinsley and France (1978) that it is not the employment but the type of occupation, which causes dissatisfaction, strain and problems to the working ladies. In an earlier study Jephcott *et al.* (1962) has also found that "married women's employment, far from threatening good relations, helped to improve them".

These conflicting findings indicate that material adjustment and family happiness of married women are not necessarily adversely affected by their employment, rather they are influenced by a number of other factor (Havdesty and Betz, 1980). Kapur (1970) on the basis of data obtained from urban educated employed women found that 55 per cent of them were found to be well adjusted in their married life and had combined their role of worker with that of wife and mother successfully. She isolated the following factors as conducive to marital harmony—(a) consistent premarital SES of spouses; (b) compatible and congenial personality traits of spouses; (c) harmonious sexual relationship. Bhattacharya (1980) has shown that organizational commitment and satisfaction with job, feeling of guild, and behaviour towards children of the working women are important factor in this regard. Similarly according to Bhattacharjee and Bhatt (1983), whether employed or not, women's adjustment is a function of her personality traits expectations and perceptions combined with those of her spouse and family members.

Wojciechowski (1982) has discussed the role confusion and self-image problems that the working mothers experience which demand a supportive network at home. This has been supported by other studies which indicate that the conflicts and strain of the married working women are well-managed with the cooperation of family members and more particularly by the supportive and accommodative husbands who take interest in their work and problems (Gray, 1983; Houseknecht, 1981). Miyahira (1975) has found that husband's attitudes towards his wife's employment constitute one of the most important factors affecting a women's work status. Bentell *et al.* (1983) have reported that such women experience more role conflict whose husbands hold relatively traditional sex role attitudes. Fenchel (1979) has emphasized the need of both husband and wife for affectionate caring from one another which make the marital life happy. Holahan and Gilbert (1979) have found that with support of husbands, the working women suffered less role strain that the non-working group of women. Such women use effective coping strategies like greater use of reward with children, making presentations to family members and keeping helping hands etc. (Singh and Sharma, 1975). Similarly a large number of research findings indicate that if the woman's employment serves her aspirations and the needs of the family and adds to her worth and status, she does not perceive the role strain and feels satisfied and adjusted in her life (Yogev, 1982; Frankel *et al.* 1982; Bingham and Turner, 1981; Huth, 1978; Molm, 1978). It is for this reason that the female school teachers do not perceive more role conflict than their male counterparts (Prasad and Bhushan 1984).

Whether working or non-working women have to perform the household duties which include kitchen work, child care and home arrangement/decorations etc. almost exclusively. There are required to conform to the traditional sex roles more than the unmarried women. As such, the unmarried women carry greater concern for identity and status and hold stronger belief in social equality for women (Shah and Varshney, 1982). Similarly the women in status jobs and professions carry strong concern and anxiety for equal status (Moulton, 1977).

Another factor which deserve a special mention here is the job conditions for the working women. A girl or woman just can not do any and every work outside her home because of socio-cultural conditions and fear of sex assault on her for being a female. Perception of woman as a source of pleasure and weaker sex continues almost throughout the world. This has resulted in large number of sex crimes, which has shown a growing trend in recent years (Krishna, 1982). In a developed country like America, one out of every 10 women is victim of sexual assault. In India during the year 1979, as many as 4,300 were the cases of rape crimes as admitted by the Government (Bureau of Police Research and Development, 1983). If the number is considered in the background of the research findings that because of social humiliation and psychological constrains hardly one third of the rape cases are recorded (Shorter, 1977; Singh 1981; Chaudhary, 1984; Wilson, 1978), the picture appears to be horrible. Pandey (1986) has very rightly remarked that so many women in a free democratic India are raped every year is, indeed a sad commentary on our society which claims to be progressing in terms of education, and socio-economic growth. The fact is that a considerable number of students and working educated or uneducated women have to experience sexual harassment in getting the due of their work (Benson, 1977; Farely, 1978; Mackinnon, 1979). The physical, psychological and social consequences of rape have such magnitude (for details see Pandey, 1986) that women of all age groups in the West perceptually suffer from the fear of being raped (Garofalo, 1979; Mc Dermott, 1979; Yin, 1980). Growing lawlessness indiscipline and violence in public life and poor imitation of Western fads (in order to be called mods') have created situations in which the women feel more and more unprotected and unsecured everyday. In every town or city of India escorting large number of girls and ladies to and from their educational institutions or work places by the male members of the family is a common sight. It presents a social paradox that on the one hand, we are imparting education and training to the girls to grow independent and stand on their own feet, and on the other they are being victimized and punished in the society for their independent growth. The moves to unstill security and confidence in women are being frustrated by the anti-social trends. Such situations develop conscious inferiority in some. But in many educated women it manifests in stronger concern or status and gives rise to protest and reaction to fight the evil designs on their legitimate independence and growth of personality.

Psychological Factors

The psychological make up of the present educated women is much different than what is was few decades back. This has contributed to their refusal to accept the stereotyped sex roles and treating themselves as inferior or subservient upon men. Their cognition, attitudes, needs and personality serve as important predisposing conditions to create strong concern for status among them.

In every culture sex-role identity has been conceptualized in terms of 'masculinity' and 'femininity'. Although societies differ in the specific tasks they assign to the two sexes, all societies allocate various role on the basis of sex. Boy and girls are expected to acquire sex specific self-concepts and personality attributes to be masculine or feminine as defined by that particular culture (Barry, Bacon and Child, 1957). So far as the Indian society is concerned although our stereotypes about sex-roles have crumbled a bit, but have not disappeared yet. Little boys are supposed to grow up to be masculine, dominant and aggressive men. In contrast, little girls are expected to develop into feminine, submissive and obedient women.

Cross cultural findings however, show that masculinity and femininity represent complementary traints and behaviour. Theorists have offered different models and domains of traits for two sexes. According to Parsons Bales (1955) masculinity is associated with 'instrumental' orientation, a cognitive focus on getting the job done or problems solved, where as feminity is associated with 'expressive' orientation, *i.e.* an effective concern for the welfare of others. Similarly, Bakan (1966) has suggested that masculinity is associated with an 'agentic' orientation, *i.e.* a concern for one-self as an individual, and feminity is associated with a 'communal' orientation, *i.e.*, a concern of interpersonal relationship and group. Erickson (1964) presented the distinction in terms of 'inner' (female) and 'outer' (male) pshychological characteristics.

Recently however, there has been a rising dissatisfaction with this orthodox sex labelled psychological characteristics or sex-role stereotyping. As discussed in the earlier chapter, the stereotyped sex-roles have undergone change in every society. If there is anything which characterises modern Indian society, it is the rapidly changing idea about the roles of men and women. The differences between men and women and the roles these differences seemed to dictate sometimes back were wide and clear. Now these differences have narrowed. A girl can not play football or any other game played by men but these things were unthinkable even a few years ago.

In consonance with the social movement like the "Women Lib" efforts have been made to develop a conception of mental health which is free from culturally imposed definition of masculinity and faminity (Bem, 1977). Androgyny was used as the term to denote integration of masculinity and faminity within a single individual. Androgynous individuals develop and integrate personality traits, which are called both masculine and feminine. Women doing work outside the home and displaying leadership and self esteem examples of their acquisition of traditional male characteristics. Such women do not rate themselves as inferior to men and have a high concern for status.

As regards the personality characteristics of such androgynous women, findings are not many. However, the available findings suggest meaningful dimension. Small *et al.* (1984) have found in their study that androgynous persons have the lowest level of dysphoria, anxiety and hostility. A series of studies by Bem and her associates (1977, 1976) show that androgynous individuals are behaviourally and emotionally more adaptable and better adjusted than uni-sex typed individuals. Studies have shown strong relationship of androgyning with self esteem (Spence *et al.*, 1975), self actualization (Halgund, 1978), modernity (Sahoo and Dash, 1983) and flexibility (Sahoo *et al.*, 1985). In a recent study conducted on 200 married middle class urban women of Ahmadabad, Nalini Sastry (1990) has found that the androgynous women of both young (20—30 years) and matured (31—45 years) age groups have the least anxiety as compared to the uni-sex or undifferentiated sex women. Besides, the women of younger age group are lower in androgyny and masculine sex role orientation and higher in anxiety and undifferentiated sex-role orientation than the women of matured age group of 31—45 years. The results are broadly in conformity with earlier findings that androgynous individuals show better personal and social adjustment than the persons of undifferentiated and feminine orientations (Harris and Schwab, 1979), and that they are low in neuroticism (Jordon *et al.*, 1976).

The personality characteristics of women with liberal and equalitarian attitude is very similar to that of the androgynous women.

Erickson (1977) while making his study on girl students found a close relationship between ego maturity and equalitarian attitude of the girls. Loo and Logan (1982) administered an Attitude Towards Women Scale and Eysenck Personality Questionnaire. The result indicated a significant positive relationship between liberal attitude toward women and emotional stability, but the attitude scores were independent of the Lie-scores. Hanson (1978) reported a negative correlation between attitude towards women's liberation and dogmatism. He found that the "feminist" were less dogmatic than the "antifeminists" and that the results did not support the hypothesis that dogmatism was related to extremity rather than to the content of the attitude.

Ghaffaradili Doty and Carlson (1979) have reported that women high in liberal attitude to act in more liberated way in cooperation of their friend and leader of Women's Liberation Movement. In another study on women, the labelled women liberationists were found to differ from the pseudo women liberationists in their beliefs about sex role socialization practice, perception about social priorities and perception of the properties of various kinds of male-female relations (Teleponos, 1977) Stein and Weston (1982) found that women who were profeminist in their attitudes toward women's role in contemporary society scored significantly higher on measure of identity achievement then women whose attitudes were more traditional. Biaggio *et al.* (1985) reported from their study that "anti liberation", women expressed greater personal in child rearing than "pro-liberation" women. The groups have also been found to differ in certain personality dimensions measured by 16 PF. Ferree (1983) showed that experienced, personal satisfaction and self-esteem were important motivating factors among the supporters of Women's Liberations Movement.

Shainess (1980) has concluded from her study that highly achieving and successful married women (in addition to playing their roles as wives and mothers) have a greater sense of independence and determination. Faver (1982) has also shown that the careerist women are generally high in their general achievement orientation and career values. This is further confirmed by the findings of Krogh (1985) which show that the mothers of young children, who have high achievement motivation, are more keen to have a job than subjects with low achievement motivation. Also it is reported that among the employed there is a significant positive correlation between sex-role orientation and number of hours worked each week.

Betz (1982) has analysed the needs of "career workers" and found them different than those of the "home markers". The results showed the "home makers" scored highest on security, safety, and social needs, while the professionals, managerial and clerical/sales workers scored highest on esteem needs. According to Stafford (1984) it is not the women's role, but the occupational congruencies which has positive relationship with women's self-esteem. Stane and Morrow (1981) have, however found racial differences in feminism and guilt. So the findings relating to the needs of women should be interpreted and generalized with caution.

Selected Personality Dimensions and Values Orientations

In the present study, apart from the background factors, efforts have been made to investigate the relationship of women's concerns for study with certain personality factors and value-orientations. Among the personality dimensions selected for the study are extraversion, neuroticism and ego-strength. The first two factors according to Eysenck, constitute the most comprehensive description of personality and so were selected for study as possible correlates of the women's concern for status and development.

Thus, an over view of the studies indicate that age employment, marital status, socio-economic status, parental education and residence (rural-urban) etc. are some of the significant personal and background factors in respect of women's concern for status, development and management. Similarly, the studies do suggest that feeling of protest against inferior status and roles among educated women have roots in their values and personality. Judging from the viewpoint of relevance, availability of suitable measures and manageability of the study.

REFERENCES

Bakan, D. (1966). *The Duality of Human Experience,* Chicago: Rand McNally.

Barry, H., Bacon, M.K. and Child, I.L. (1957). A cross cultural survey of some sex differences in socialization. *Journal of Abnormal and Social Psychology,* 55, 327–32.

Bell, Rber R. (1975). Significant roles among a sample of Australian women. *Australia and New Zealand Journal of Sociology*, 11(1), 2–11.

Bem, S.L. (1977). On the utility of alternative procedures for assessing psychological androgyny. *Journal of Consulting and Clinical Psychology*, 45, 196–205.

Bennett, Barbara W. and Grasser, George, S. (1981). Movement towards androgyny in college females through experimental education. *Journal of Psychology*, 107(2), 177–83.

Benson, Donna (1977). *Sexual Harassment: A Hidden Issue*. Published by Project on the Status of Women, Association of American College.

Betz, Ellen L. (1982). Need fulfillment in the career development of women. *Journal of Vocational Behaviour*, 20(1), 53–66.

Biaggio, Mary K., Mohan, Philip J. and Baldarn, Cynthia (1985). Relationships among attitudes towards children, women's liberation and personality characteristics. *Sex Roles*, 12(1–2), 47–62.

Bingham, William C, and Turner, Carol J. (1981). Modified questionnaire on the occupational status of women. *Educational and Psychological Measurement*, 41(3), 909–15.

Bouchart, Godard A. (1978). One kills the mother: Liberation of women and paternal space (Fren.) *Bulletin de Psychologie* 32(3–7), 383–87.

Chattarjee, Pratima and Bhatt, Kusum K., (1983). Family adjustment of married working and non-working women. *Indian Journal of Clinical Psychology*, 10(2), 497–501.

Choudhury, Neerja (1984). Cornered in the Dark. *The Statesman*, Delhi, Oct. 29.

Davis, Richard A. (1981). Female labour force participation, status integration and Suicide 1950–1969, *Suicide and Life Threatening Behaviour*, 11(2), 111–23.

Desai, Neera (1957). *Women in Modern India. Bombay:* Vohra and Co.

Erdwins, Card. J.: Tyer, Zita E. and Mellinger Jeanne C. (1982): Achievement and affliation needs of young adult and middle age women. *Journal of Genetic Psychology*, 141(2), 219–24.

Erickson, E. (1964). Inner and outer space: Reflections and Womenhood. *Daedalus*, 93, 582–606.

Farley, Lin (1978). *Sexual Shakedown*. New York: McGraw Hill, 20–21.

Faver, Catherine A. (1982). Achievement Orientation attainment values and women's employment. *Journal of Vocational Behaviour*, 20(1), 67–80.

Fenchel, Gerd (1979). Patternity and changing role of women. *Issue in Ego Psychology*, 2(1), 5–11.

Ferree, Myra M. (1983). The women's movement in the working class. *Sex Roles*, 9(4), 493–505.

Fine-Davis, Maragret (1979). Social psychological predictors of employment Status of married women in Ireland. *Journal of Married and the Family*, 41(1), 145–58.

Frankel, Judith; Monogul, Mary A. and Paaludi Michelle (1982). The employed mother: A new social norms? *International Journal of Women's Studies,* 5(3), 274–81.

Fuchsle, Traude (1983). Partnerschaft bei berufrataligen and nicht berufrtstigen jungeren und alteren Frauen, Intimage. Relationship of younger and older working and non-working women (Germ). *Parterberatung,* 20(2–3), 128–42.

Garofalo, James (1979), Victimisation and the Fear of Crime *Journal of Research in Crime and Delinquency,* 16, 80–97.

Gray Janet, D. (1983). The married professional women: An examination of her role conflicts and coping strategies. *Psychology of Women Quarterly.* 7(3), 235–43.

Gupta, Sarita; Shah, M.A.; Beg, M.A. (1982). Education and Socio-economic status as determinants of Indian women's attitudes towards equality of women. *Journal of Social Psychology,* 118(1), 139–40.

Hafstorm, Jeanne I and Dunshing, Marilyn M. (1978), Socio-economic and Social Psychological influences on reasons wives work. *Journal of Consumer Research,* 5(3), 169–75.

Halas, Celia M. (1974) Sex-role stereotypes. Perceived childhood socialization experiences and the attitudes and behaviour of adult women. *Journal of Psychology,* 88(2), 261–75.

Halgund, S.V. (1978). Relationship among adjustment variables and sex-role orientation in college women: A construct validation of psychological androgyny. *Dissertation Abstracts International,* 38, 3880-B.

Harris, T.L. and Sejwan, R. (1979). Women's liberation extremity and dogmatism. *International Behaviour Scientist,* 8(4), 57–58.

Holahan, Carolek and Gillbert, Lucia A. (1979). Inter-role conflict for working women: Career versus jobs. *Journal of Applied Psychology,* 64 (1), 86–90.

Houseknecht, Sharon K. and Macke, Anne S. (1981). Combining marriage and career: the marital adjustment of professional women. *Journal of Married and the Family* 43(3), 651–61.

Huser, Willa R. and Grant, Claude W. (1978). A study of husbands and wives from dual career and traditional career families. *Psychology of Women Quarterly,* 3, 78–89.

Huth, Carol M. (1978). Married women's work status; the influence of parents and husbands. *Journal of Vocational Behaviour,* 13(3), 272–88

Jephcott, P.; Seear, N. and Smith, J.H. (1962). Married women working; London: George Allen and Unwin Ltd.

Jordon, V., Fassberg; E.S. and Michael, V.T. (1976). Feminism, Androgyny and Anxiety. *Journal of Clinical and Consulting Psychology,* 44, 870–71.

Junge, Maxine and Maya, Vernetts (1985). Women in their forties: A group portrait and implications of phychotherapy. *Women and Therapy,* 4(3), 3–19.

Kapur, Promilla (1970). *Marriage and the working women in India.* New Delhi: Vikas Publication.

Kapur, Promilla (1974): Women's liberation in America, Span, 15 (I) 20–27.

Keown, Chares F., and Keown, Ada, L. (1982) Success factors for corporate women executives. *Group and Organisaion Studies*, 7(3), 445–46.

Khoo, Seiw-lan, Krishnamoorthy, Soorirajulu and Trlin, Andrew D. (1974). Attitudes towards roles, women's employment and anticipated family size among young unmarried adults. *Australian Journal of Sex, Marriage and Family*, 5(3), 147–57.

Koening, Esther J., and Juni, Samuel (1981). Attitudes toward police women. A study of inter-relationships and determinants. *Journal of Police Science and Administration*, 9(4), 463–74.

Krishna, K.P. (1982). Rape and its victim in India. *Journal of Social and Economic Studies*, 10(1 and 2), 89–100.

Krogh, Kathryn M. (1985) Women's motives to achieves and to nature in different life stages *Sex roles*, 12(1–2), 75–90.

Lang, Katherine, A. (1978) Suggestions for counseling women who want to enter a non-traditional occupation. *Journal of Employment Counseling.*

Lazer, William and Smallwood John, E. (1977). The changing demographics of women. *Journal of Marketing*, 41(3), 14–22.

Lebe Doryann, M (1986) Female ego ideal conflicts in adulthood. *American Journal of Psychoanalysis*, 46(1), 22–32.

Locke H.J. and Mackeprang, M (1979). Material adjustment and employed wife. *American Journal of Sociology*, 54(6), 329–30.

Loo, Robert and Logan, Pamela (1982). Personality correlates of the Attitude towards woman scale. *Personality and Industrial Differences*, 3(3), 329–30.

Lovell-Tory, Lawrence. A (1983). Anomia among employed wives and housewives: An exploratory analysis. *Journal of Marriage and the Family*. 45(2), 301–10.

Mackinnon, Catherine (1979). *Sexual Harassment of Working Women*. New Heaven: Yale University Press.

Mayes, Sharon. S. (1979). Women in positions of authority: A case study of changing sex roles. *Sighns*, 4(3), 556–68.

Mc Dermott, M.J. (1979). *Rape Victimization in 26 American Cities, Washington, D.C.*: U.C. Department of Justice.

McCall, Suzanne, H. (1977). Meet the wok wife: *Journal of Marketing*, 41(3), 55–56.

Miyahira, Sarah D. (1975). Marriage and the employment of women. In S.H. Osipow (Ed.) *Emerging women: Career analysis and outlooks. Columbus, Ott:* Charls E Merill XIII, 95.

Molm, Linda, D. (1978). Sex role attitudes and the employment of married women. The direction of casually *Sociological Quarterly*, 19(4), 522–33.

Moulton, Ruth (1977). Women with double lives. *Contemprorary Psychoanalysis*, 13(1), 64–84.

Nadelson, Carol C., and Notoman, Malkah, T. (1981). To marry or not to marry: A Choice. *American Journal of Psychiatry*, 138(10), 1352–56.

Nadelsons, Theodore and Eisendberg, Leon (1977). The Successful Professional Women " On being married to one. *American Journal of Psychiatry,* 134(10), 1071–76.

Nevill, Dorothy, D., and Damico, Sandra (1978). The influence of occupational status on role conflict in women *Journal of Employment Counseling,* 15(2), 55–61.

Newberry, Phyllis: Wiessman, Myrna. M. and Myres, Jerome K. (1979). Working wives and housewives: Do they differ in mental status and social adjustment? *American Journal of Orthopsychiatry,* 49(2), 282–91.

Nye, I.F. (1959). Employment status of mothers and adjustment of adolescent children. *Marriage and Family Living,* 21.

Pandey, Rajendra (1986) Rape crime and victims of rape in free India. *The Indian Journal of Social Work,* 47(2), 169–86.

Parsons, T. and Bales, R.F. (1955). *Family Socialization and Interaction Process* New York: Free Press.

Phillips, Susan D, and Johnston, Susan L. (1985). Attitudes towards work roles for women. *Journal of College Student Personnel,* 26(4), 334–38.

Powell, Barbara (1977), The empty nest employment and Psychiatric symptoms in college-educated women. Psychology of women Quarterly, 2(1), 35–43.

Prager, Karne, J. (1986): Identity development age and college experience in women. *Journal of Genetic Psychology,* 147(1), 31–36.

Prasad, Pramil, and Bhushan L.I. (1984). Perceived role conflict among school teachers. *Research in Psychology, ;* 3, 41–48.

Reinke, Barbara J. (1985): Psychosocial changes as a function of chronological age. *Human Development,* 28(5), 266–69.

Sahoo, F.M., and Dash, P. (1984). *Androgyny and Life Stress.* Unpublished Reprot, Utkal University, Bhubaneshwar.

Sahoo, F.M., Rout, Jayashree and Rout, A.K. (1985). Androgyny and psychological rigidity. *Psychological Studies,* 30–(2), 111–15.

Sastry, Nalini (1990). Anxiety, Sex role orientation and age. Married women in Urban India. *The Indian Journal of Social Work,* 51(4), 659–68.

Shah, M.A. and Varshney, K. Mukul (1982). A comprehensive study of the attitude of married and unmarried women towards religion, equality of women and birth control in relation to their adjustment. *Asian Journal of Psychology and Education,* 9(1), 15–20.

Shaines, Netalie (1980). The working wife and mother: A new women? *American Journal of Psychotherapy,* 34(3), 374–86.

Shorter, E. (1977). On writing the History of Rape. *Sings* 3, 2.

Singh, D.R. (1981). Current Trends and Forms of Crime Against Women. *The Indian Journal of Social Work,* 42(1), 33–40.

Singh, S.N., and Sharma, Neelima (1975). Child rearing practices of Working and non-working educated women. Manas, 22(2), 113–19.

Smith, Elsie J. (1981). The working mother: A critique of the research. *Journal of Vocational Behaviour,* 19(2), 191–211.

Spence, J.T., Helmreich, R. and Stapp, J. (1975). Ratings of peers on sex role attributes and their relation to self esteem and conceptions of masculinity and feminity. *Journal of Personality and Social Psychology,* 32, 29–39.

St. John-Parsons, Donald (1978). Continuous and dual career families: A case study. *Psychology of Women Quarterly,* 3(1), 30–42.

Stafford, Inge P. Setan Hall U. (1984). Relation of attitudes toward women's roles and occupational behaviour of women's self-esteem. *Journal of Counseling Psychology,* 31(3), 332–38.

Stane, Steve and Morrow, Lisa (2005). Race differences in feminism and guilt. *Journal of Economic Issues,* 61(1), 70–74.

Stein, Sandara L. and Weston, Louise C. (1982). College women's attitudes towards women and identity achievement. *Adolescence,* 17(68), 895–99.

Stinnet, Nick; Knaub, Patrica K., O'Nal, Sunny and Waltors James (1983). Perceptions of Panamonian women concerning the roles of women. *Journal of Comparative Family Studies,* 14(2), 273–83.

Strober Myra H., and Weinberg, Charles B. (1977). Working wives and major expenditures. *Journal of Consumer Research,* 4 (3), 141–47.

Symonds, Alexandra (1986). The dynamics of depression in functioning women: Sexism in the family. American Academic of Psycho-analysis seminar on Women's Emerging Identity. *Journal of Ameircan Academy of Pswycho-analysis,* 14(3), 395–406.

Teleporas, Elizabeth (1977). Motivational patterns in attitudes towards the Women's Liberation Movement. *Journal of Personality,* 45(4), 481–500.

Travis, Cheryl B. (1976). Women's liberation among two samples of young women. *Psychology of Women Quaterly,* 1(2), 189.

Usher, Sarah and Fels, Mort (1985). The challenge of feminism and career for the middle aged women. Special issue: Feminist Psychology: Single life and married life and women's sexuality. *International Journal of Women's Studies,* 8(1), 47–57.

Walker, Loraine and Friedman, S. Thomas (1977). Professional women's attitudes toward the dual role of women. *Psychology Report,* 41(1), 327–34.

Welch, Reenate (1979). Androgyny and derived identity in married women with varying degrees of non-traditional role involvement. *Psychology of Women Quarterly,* 3(3), 308–15.

Wojccichowski, Denise (1982). I am a working mother but who am I? *Journal of Employment Counseling,* 19(3) 106–12.

Yin, R.P. (1980). Fear of Crime Among the Elderly, Some Issues and Suggestions. *Social Problems,* 27: 492–504.

Yogev, Sara (1982). Are professional women over worked? Objective versus subjective perception of role leads. *Journal of Occupation and Psychology,* 55(3), 165–69.

4

Methodological Framework

Method is of permanent interest in any research. It is true of all the discipline. Without the application of appropriate methodology the outcome of any research falls short of it scientific nature. In other, word in the modern day academic world no body is ready to accept the findings of any research as reliable or scientific in nature if the research is not done in accordance with methodology appropriate for the nature of research. If it is otherwise the result will be treated as philosophy, guess, hunch or even nonsense. Of course the methodology differs according to the field of study. The methodology applied in physical sciences can not be suitable for social science and the same is also done true about the biological sciences. But on the whole unless the finding of the researcher is free from biás it can not be leveled as scientific in nature. The bias, starting from individual bias, can be of various nature. The methodology is the most reliable means of avoiding bias and make the study objective in nature.

An interdisciplinary research in social science is interesting and existing not simultaneously it is intriguing and difficult. Because social phenomenon which is complex and puzzling constitutes the subject of socio-logical research. Although intention, common sense and guess work have in important part of play in sociological research yet they can not produce any reliable evidence of their own. Reliable and factual evidence and analysis can be produced only by using a reliable methodology or in other works by the application of scientific method.

Any one who has a serious interest in comprehending and examining society, its various aspects, processes and segments must give some thought to the way in which social facts can be and are gathered. Thus we find a range of needs which require the application and use of research techniques, as that can provide the way to make the study scientific and logical. Social phenomenon are complex and intriguing. Therefore, to provide accurate account and reliable knowledge about them is very difficult. However, since few recent decades, sociologist and other social scientist have developed the science of research method with a view to make scientific equity and interpretation of the problems of social research.

The social scientist face numerous problems in studying their object world scientifically which the natural scientists are spread of. Because the basic concern of any social researcher is to investigate into the social phenomenon or social world which is complex and complicated and thus are inherently incapable of scientific enquiry. But this claim has been reputed and disapproved by the social scientists as they have succeeded in studying and treating the social phenomenon in a realistic and systematic manner with the help of scientific method. There is no short cut to truth. No way to gain the knowledge of the universe except through the gateway of scientific method. The unity of all sciences consists along us in its methods, not in its material alone.

The present study as stated earlier is also a research endeavour which attempts to provide the knowledge of gender-role differentiation in Santhal society particularly in the sphere of home management. This study is empirical in nature and therefore the tools and procedures needed for scientific social research have been followed and applied to collect the informations.

The unique and more distinctive features of the scientific is its ability and capacity to obtain definite and verifiable knowledge, discover casual relationship between diverse and scattered facts to predict future according to Encyclopaedia Britannica.

Scientific method is collective term denoting the various processed by the aid of which the sciences are built up. In a wide sense any method of investigation by which scientific or other empirical and systematic knowledge is called a scientific method namely, observation, experimentation, classification and explanation also exhibit their systematic nature. According to Lundberg, "Scientific method consists of systematic observation, classification and interpretation of data. The main difference between our day to day generalisation and conclusions and the scientific generalisation lies on the fact that the latter is derived by the application of scientific method which contains degree of formality, rigorousness, verifiability and general validity. This means that compared with common sense thinking the scientific thinking is more formal, strict, empirical and goal directed. The scientific method observes, classifies and interprete data according to rigorous test. The primary task of scientific method is the discovery of casual relations in the diverse facts under it and to generalise about these. It is to the credit of the scientific method that it can predict about the future. There are only six primary forms of scientific methods and all others are merely variations of the some forms.

The primary forms are the following:

(a) Induction: The movement of knowledge from particular fact to a general rule or principle is known as induction.

(b) Deduction: A movement of knowledge from a general rule to a particular case is called deduction.

(c) Historical: Historical methods is a backward movement in knowledge to trace out the entecedent cause or causes of a phenomens. Darwin's theory of evolution and Marx's law of Economic Deteria-nism are examples of this method.

(d) Comparative: Analysis and comparision of two contem-porary phenomena is known as comparative method.

(e) Structural: A study of what is a thing what are its outlines and significant feature is a structural study.

(f) Functional: In contrast to the structural method, functional method studies the processes and their causes *i.e.* how and why a thing physiology is a functional study.

The scientific knowledge involves not only the discovery of new facts but also tests the practical validity of ideas and theories. If the facts confirm our theory it is accepted as true and it attains the status a scientific role or law and facts refute the theory has either to be suitable modified or rejected together depending upon the nature and kind of reputation.

Techniques are thought of as comprising the specific procedure by which the sociologist together and orders his data, the main techniques of social science research are observation, study of historical documents, questionnaire, schedule, case study, social survey, sociometry and interview.

Various efforts are made in relation to scientific investigation which may to some extent differ from each other but we can consider it as a complete process and divide it into four stages: formulation of hypothesis, observation, data collection and its analysis and drawing conclusions. According to Lundburg, "A hypothesis is a tentative generalization, the validity of which remains to be tested. In most elementary stages the hypothesis may be by human gushes, imaginative dies which becomes the basis for action or investigation. According to Goode and Hatt, "It is a proposition which can be put to a test to determine its validity". A scientific hypothesis consists of two or more variables linked by some inter-relationship. A working hypothesis is necessary before the intelligent collection of data begins. The working hypothesis is a tentative generalization based on a cursory empirical examination of certain data.

The word "Research" during our contemporary period has become equally significant to the word "Science". Research signifies, "A searching for something or somebody, especially with care also, a continued careful enquiry of investigation into a subject in order to discover facts or principals". According to Mzarry Staphenson and D. Slesinger, "Research is the manipulation of things, concepts, or symbols for the purpose of generalization to the extent. Correct and verify knowledge". According to Rodmen and Mary, "Systamatised effect to gain new knowledge" we call research. F. Austin says, Research may or may not come to success, it may or may not add anything to what is already known. It is sufficient that its objectives by new knowledge of atleast a new mode or orientation of knowledge.

In social research the design is prepared on the basis of the nature of the problem or hypothesis, "Design" according to Ackoff, is the process of making decisions before the situation arises in which the decision is to be carried out.

Designs are of three types

(a) Explanatory or Formulative Design: Explanatory research is necessary to obtain the experience which will be helpful in formulating relevant hypothesis for more definite investigation.

(b) Descriptive and Diagnostic Design: These two are very closely related to each other.

(c) Experimental Design: The concept of experimental design in sociological research refers to "systematic study of human relation by making observation under controlled conditions". In the present study use has been made of the explanatory descriptive designs.

Finally, we will discuss the techniques used in the study which include sampling, schedule and interview. According to E.S. Bogardus, sampling is the selection of certain percentage of a group of items according to predetermined plan. Sampling method can be of various types but significant among them are: Random sampling, Purposive Sampling Method. Stratified sampling method, Multi-stage Sampling and Areas Sampling. In this study has been made of random sampling drawn by means of lottery method. And for removal of bias as well as testing the validity and reliability necessary precautions were taken. Schedule is prepared specially for collection of relevant data.

"An Interview" according to Hacooby and Macooby is a peculiar verbal interactional exchange in which one person, the interviewer, attempts to elicit information or expression of opinions or belief from another persons, "Interview" can be classified as:

According to function—diagnostic, treatment and research interview. According to formality: formal interview and informal interview. According to the number of persons participating: personal interview and group interview. According to roles assumed by interviewees and informants: non-directive interview, focused interview and repeated interview.

Hypothesis of the Study

The study is based on the hypothesis that in tribal society, particularly among the Santhals, the management is almost an exclusive domain of the women. Like non-tribal society the sex-role structure is differentiated in Santhal society leading to status, differential. The study is a social survey aiming at the exploration and description of role played by Santhal women in home management.

Tools of Data Collection

Data were collected with the help of structural schedule, personal interview, participant and non-participant observation and informal interview. In addition, secondary sources were also utilized.

Interview Methods

An interview schedule was used for conducting interview with the respondents. Some of the questions were open ended and some were closed. A copy of the schedule is appended.

Observation

Some relevant materials and data on the ceremonies and unique rituals of marriage, voting behaviour etc. were collected with the help of both participant and non-participant observations.

Informal Interview

Informal conversations with people and particularly the elderly educated persons in the villages were of great help in understanding the different aspects of inter-caste relations and caste and politics in the villages.

Secondary Data

Data and materials were also collected from secondary sources which included village handbooks, panchayat records, District Gazetter, Census reports, acadamic journals, news papers etc.

Analysis of Data

The data collected through various sources were tabulated and analysed on the basis of several variables like age, caste, income, education, occupation etc. These variables were used in consideration to their relevance in the analysis of the data.

Fieldwork

The data were collected by the principal investigator, co-investigator and project fellow between October 2003 to December 2005. The usual difficulties such as non-availability of the respondents, lack of co-operation in some cases, time constraits, etc. were encountered by researcher.

Majority of the respondents were interviewed at their residence while a few outside their residences. The interview lasted between one and two hours. However, in general the respondents were considerate, courteous and co-operative. As times the researcher had to make the meaning of some questions clear to the respondents in order to get correct answers.

Objective

The prime objective of the study as the title suggests was to study the role of Santhal women in Home management; the specific objects were to study the contribution of women in household economy, participation in decision-making, practice, leisure time activities of women and how did women manage energy and food problem in the household.

Universe

The universes of the study is comparised of 45 villages within all the districts of Santhal Parganas. Before it was elevated to the rank of a fulfledged District Deoghar, Dumka, Godda, Sahebganj, Pakur and Jamtara formed a part of the Santhal Parganas.

Area and Location

The Santhal Parganas covers an area of 14.2 thousand sq. kms lying between latitudes 23.45° N and 25.30° N and Longitudes 86.20° E and 88.00° E. It is bounded on the north by the river Ganga and the north Bihar district of Katihar; on the south by the district of Dhanbad and Burdwan on the west by the district of Giridih, Munger and Bhagalpur and on the east by the Ganga and the West Bengal district of Maldah, Mursidabad and Birbhum. Area and location of Santhal Parganas has been depicted in Fig 4.1.

Geology

The Santhal Parganas constitutes the farthest north-east extension of the Chotanagpur plateau which forms part of the peninsular hills and Plateaus of India. As in the adjacent plateau district of Dhanbad and

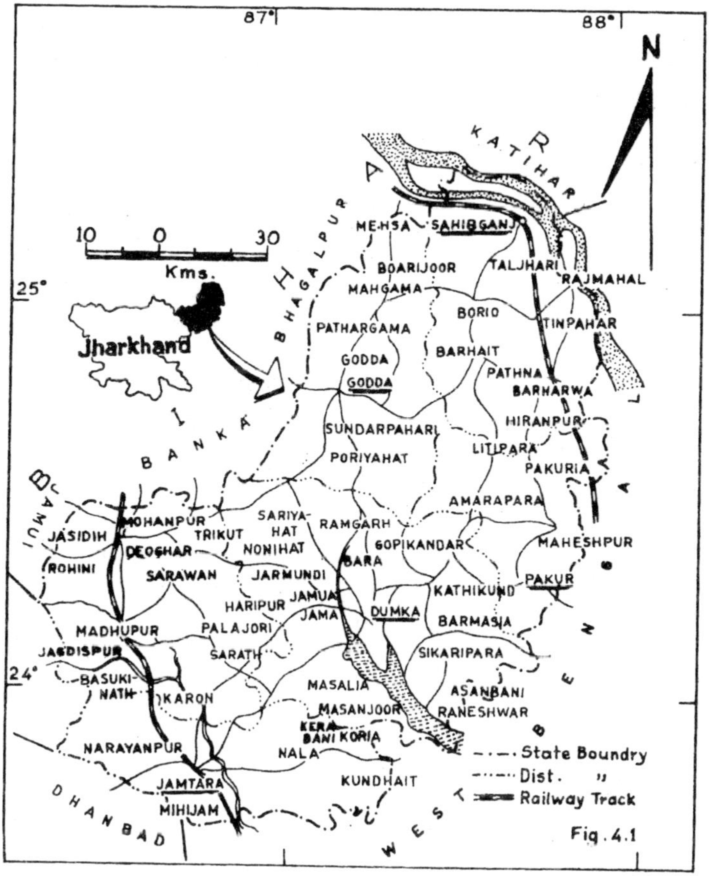

HILL TOP (T)		HILL SLOPE (S)		HILL FOOT (F)	PLAIN
1. Bara Kera	12. Pergoda	1. Agaia	12. Kortika	1. Khizuria	1. Chandana
2. Bara Berma	13. Surla	2. Anamu	13. Loha Tamba	2. Pokaria	2. Kusumghati
3. Beldiha	14. Talkunda	3. Bara Churi	14. Maridih	3. Tamili	3. Lelabhita
4. Bandgora	15. Tatardiha	4. Bara Amra	15. Maliguda		4. Muchura
5. Chhota Berma		5. Bararu	16. Telotok		5. Persia
6. Chhota Chapri		6. Bangru Tola			6. Ratanpur
7. Chhota Kera		7. Chhota Amra			7. Rajabhita
8. Chhota Soni		8. Chhota Boarijot		Total = 45	8. Raja Pokhar
9. Dolna		9. Chhota Churi			9. Talbaria
10. Dewdant		10. Dobri			10. Malbhita
11. Kasrigora		11. Gadgaria			11. Bador

Fig. 4.1: Location Map of Santhal Pargana (Jharkhand)

Giridih, a major portion of the Santhal Parganas is covered by granite of Archaean formation. The lower interprapean beeds contain well preserved plant fossils.

Topography and Natural Division

The western and southern parts of the division and rolling terrain interspersed with long ridges, or isolated hills. There is a narrow fringe of low-lying land between the Ganga and Rajmahal hills. The division thus consists of following natural division:

1. The central block mainly of the Rajmahal hills and the adjacent, Damin-j-koh-Damin. This region is about 160 kms. long and 20 to 40 kms. wide and has a total area of approximately 2140 sq. kms.
2. The western and south-western parts of the division with undulating terrain and isolated hills, covers the greater part.
3. The alluvial belt extending over an area of 900 sq. kms. between the Ganga and Rajmahal hill on the north-eastern periphery of the division.
4. Rainfall: The normal annual rainfall in the division of Santhal Pargana has been estimated by the Poona observatory as 1377 mm. Distributed as follows:
   (a) June–September (South-west monsoon)
   (b) October–December
   (c) January–February
   (d) March–May

Thus, about 90 per cent of the total precipitation falls over a period of only four consecutive months (June–September).

Infrastructural Facilities

A perusal of data presented in Table 4.1 reveals that out of six sub-division in the district Dumka is the largest (3776 sq. kms.) and Deoghar is the smallest (1807 sq. kms.) sub-division in respect of the area. Likewise number of inhabited villages is also maximum (2666) in Dumka and minimum (1067) in Deoghar sub-division. Dumka being superior to all sub-divisions in respect of area and inhabited villages accounts for maximum number of primary (921) and middle (143) schools while Jamtara though ranking second in respect of area and inhabited villages have the lowest number of primary (440) and middle (64) schools. Godda ranking third in respect of area and inhabited villages occupies the super most position is having high school as many as 38. Pakur sub-division has the lowest number of high schools. Dumka occupies the first place in respect of total number of educational institutions (1091) followed by Godda (900) while Jamtara sub-division has the lowest (519) total educational institutions.

Table 4.1: Comparative studies on the network of educational infrastructural facilities in different sub-divisions:

Sub-division	*Area in sq. kms*	*No. of inhabited villages*	*No. of primary schools*	*No. of middle schools*	*No. of high schools*	*Total*
Dumka	3776	2666	921	143	27	1091
Deoghar	1807	1067	706	121	24	851
Jamtara	2479	2320	440	64	15	519
Godda	2319	1572	729	133	38	900
Pakur	1817	1113	559	73	08	640
Rajmahal	2018	1289	555	88	22	665
Total	**14216**	**10027**	**3910**	**622**	**134**	**4666**

Sub-division Dumka accounts for the highest population (7.13 lac) followed by Godda (6.01 lac) and Deoghar (5.85 lac) while Jamtara has the lowest (3.78 lac) population. Dumka has the highest scholars (51,096) in primary schools. Taking into consideration the percentage of children out of total population of sub-division into consideration. Pakur is the best sub-division in primary school followed by Dumka 7.1 per cent and Deoghar 7.1 per cent while Rajmahal having only 6.2 per cent children enrolled in primary schools is the worst sub-division. The percentage of male child going to primary schools is 5.2, 5.1, 5.0, 4.96 and 4.6 in Deoghar, Jamtara, Dumka, Godda and Pakur, respectively. The present girls going to primary school is 1.9, 2.3, 2.1, 1.89 and 1.8 in Deoghar, Jamtara, Dumka, Godda and Pakur respectively. Godda accounts for highest percentage of students (3.8) enrolled in middle school followed by Deoghar (3.6) and Dumka (3.5) while Pakur has the lowest

District	*Primary*	*Middle*	*Sec.*	*Hr. Sec.*	*Degree*
Dumka	1462	206	58	10	8
Godda	875	166	44	2	4
Deoghar	775	165	40	4	7
Sahebganj	1147	208	53	9	3
S. Pargana	4260	745	195	25	22

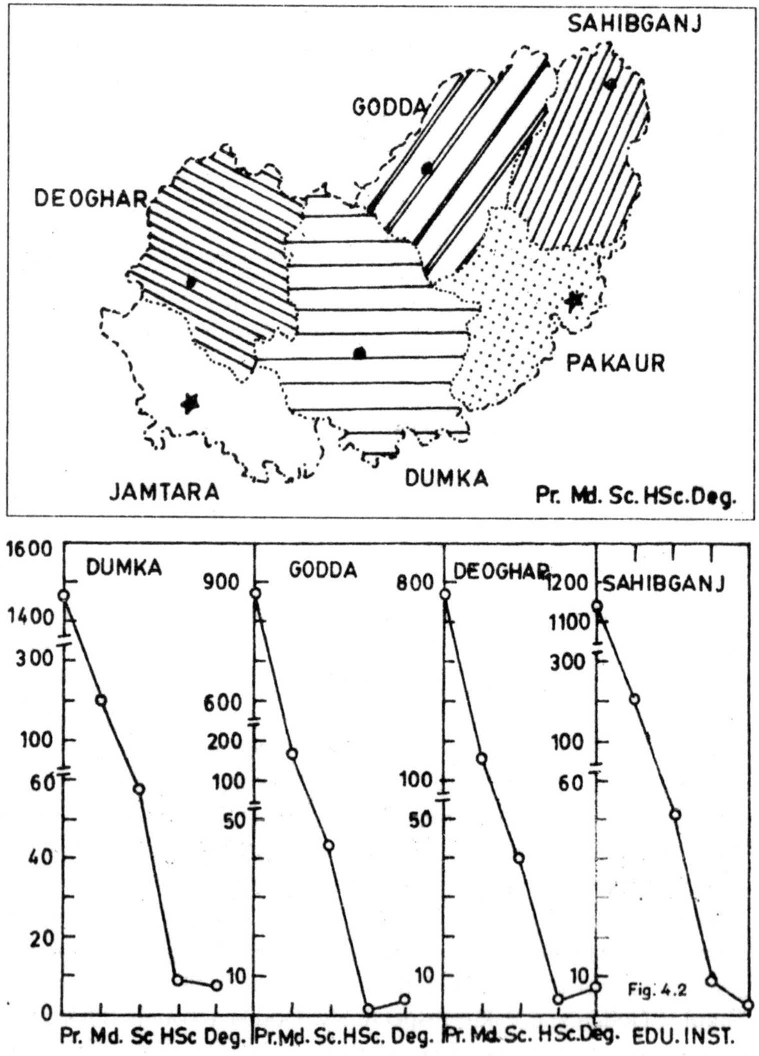

Fig. 4.2: Educational Institutions in Santhal Pargana

percentage (3.1) of students going to middle school in Godda, Deoghar, Dumka, Jamtara, Pakur and Rajmahal are 2.8, 2.7, 2.5, 2.3, 2.2 and 2.2 respectively.

Table 4.2: Studies on the extent of children enrolled on different schools in different sub-divisions

Name of the sub-division	*Total population (in lakh)*	*Number of Students in high school*			*Total number of school students*		
		Boys	*Girls*	*Total*	*Boys*	*Girls*	*Total*
Dumka	7.13	36237	14859	51096	18026	7077	25013
Deoghar	5.85	30368	11383	41751	15646	5801	21447
Jamtara	3.78	19415	7201	26616	8984	3404	12388
Godda	6.01	29851	11367	41218	17077	5778	22855
Pakur	4.03	18453	7408	25861	8899	3693	12592
Rajmahal	5.07	20858	10637	31495	11200	6394	17594
Total	**31.87**	**155182**	**62855**	**218037**	**79832**	**32147**	**111889**

Rajmahal accounts for highest percentage (1.2 per cent) of girls going to middle school followed by Dumka (1 per cent) and Godda (1 per cent) while remaining sub-division having only 0.9 per cent girl students in middle school have the lowest literacy among girls.

Table 4.3: Number of students in schools and high schools in different sub-divisions

Name of the sub-division	*Number of students in high school*			*Total number of school students*		
	Boys	*Girls*	*Total*	*Boys*	*Girls*	*Total*
Dumka	5693	1380	7073	59956	23316	83272
Deoghar	6828	1104	7932	52842	18288	71130
Jamtara	3550	377	3927	31949	10982	42931
Godda	6961	944	7905	53889	18089	71978
Pakur	1905	506	2411	29257	11607	40864
Rajmahal	4662	1774	6436	36726	18805	55525
Total	**29599**	**6085**	**35684**	**264161**	**101087**	**365700**

The above table depicted that Deoghar ranks first in respect of number of students in high school (7073) while Pakur has the lowest number (2411) of students in high schools followed by Jamtara (3927).

District	*Class 1—5 (%)*	*Class 6—8 (%)*	*Class 9—10 (%)*
1. Dumka	39.43	27.30	23.30
2. Godda	37.05	22.40	17.98
3. Deoghar	29.16	15.62	12.77
4. Sahebganj	36.40	28.38	20.45
5. Santhal Pargana	35.51	23.43	18.63

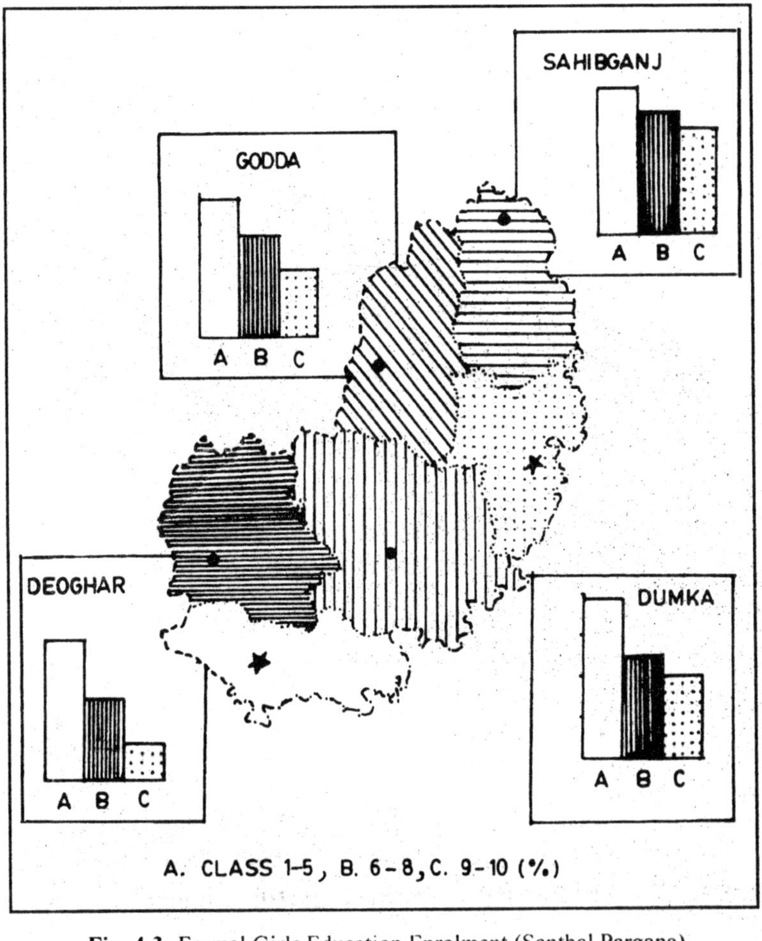

Fig. 4.3: Formal Girls Education Enrolment (Santhal Pargana)

	Class 1—5 (%)	*Class 6—8 (%)*	*Class 9—10 (%)*
1. Dumka	39.05	24.88	19.89
2. Godda	33.60	24.61	15.94
3. Deogarh	33.93	19.83	9.33
4. Sahibganj	36.05	29.86	26.18
5. Santhal Pargana	34.91	24.80	17.4

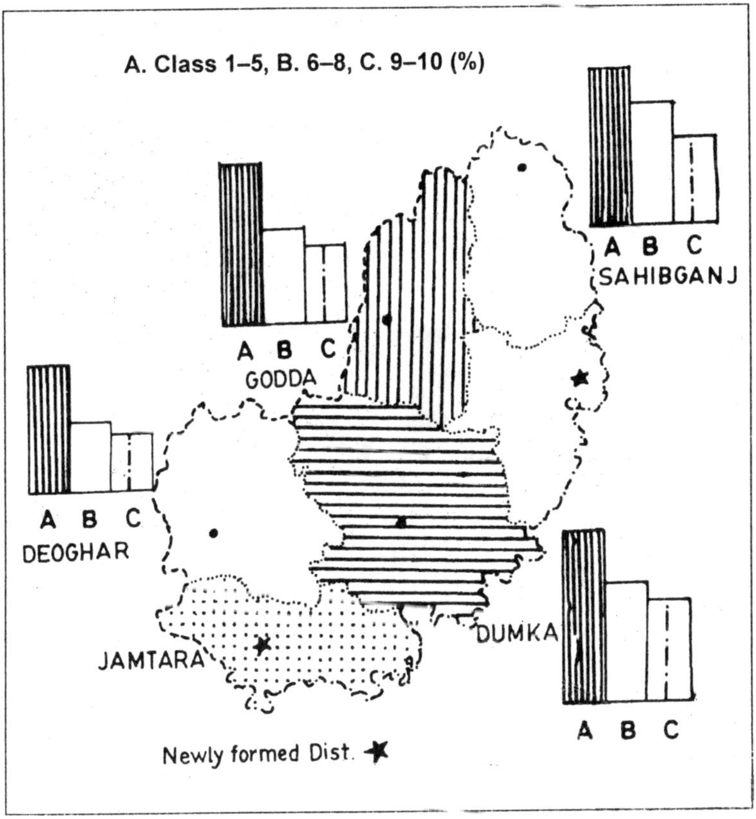

Fig. 4.4: Formal Girls Education Enrolment (Santhal Pargana)

	Class 1—5 (%)	*Class 6—8 (%)*	*Class 9—10 (%)*
1. Dumka	37.88	29.09	27.74
2. Godda	35.81	29.33	24.22
3. Deogarh	31.40	25.80	18.30
4. Sahibganj	36.84	36.01	28.98
5. Santhal Pargana	35.48	30.06	24.06

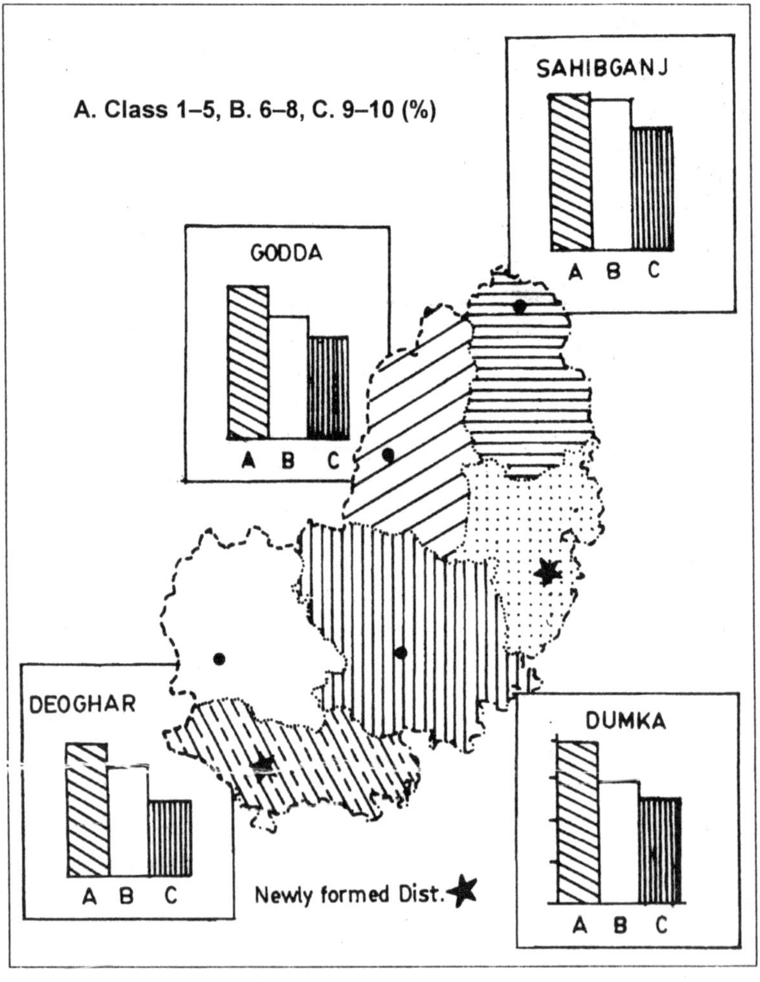

Fig. 4.5: Formal Girls Education Enrolment

According to per cent students going to high school these sub-divisions may ranked in the following descending order.

Deoghar (1.35) >Godda (1.31)>Rajmahal (1.27)>Jamtara (1.04)> Dumka (0.99)> Pakur (0.06). On the basis of the percentage of girls students in high school these sub-divisions may be arranged in respect of superiority in the following descending order:

Rajmahal (0.36)>Dumka (0.20)>Deoghar (0.19)>Godda (0.16)>Pakur (0.13) > Jamtara (0.10).

Medical Facilities

Below table reveals that Dumka avails the opportunity of being superior to others in having provision of 48 sanctioned posts of doctors and 268 posts of para-medical staffs. While Jamtara has been provided with the best least medical facilities with only 13 doctors and 94 para-medical staffs. Other sub-divisions have the medical facilities between these two extremes.

Table 4.4: Sub-divisionwise number of Doctors and Para-medical Staff (1989)

Number of Sub-division	*No. of Doctors*		*No. of Para-medical staff*	
	Posts sanctioned	*In position*	*Posts sanctioned*	*In position*
Dumka	48	30	256	240
Deoghar	30	24	182	165
Jamtara	13	8	94	86
Godda	25	18	174	165
Pakur	22	15	187	170
Sahibganj	23	18	174	158
Total	**161**	**113**	**1076**	**984**

Sex Ratio

The male-female ratio *i.e.* number of female per thousand male in Santhal Pargana work out to 959 (1991) as against 954 for Bihar as a whole. Although statistical data relating to distribution of population by marital status is not readily available, it is known that marriages are almost universal, and take place generally at a family early age and that girls are mostly married 14 to 18 years of age. The remarriage

	Population		*Male*		*Female*	
	Total	%	Total	%	Total	%
1. Dumka	1495709	6.85	765002	51.15	730707	48.85
2. Godda	861182	3.94	448072	52.03	413110	47.97
3. Deoghar	933113	4.27	488229	52.32	444884	47.68
4. Sahibganj	1301088	6.95	671731	51.63	629357	48.37
5. Santhal Pargana	4591092	21.02	2373034	51.69	2218058	48.31

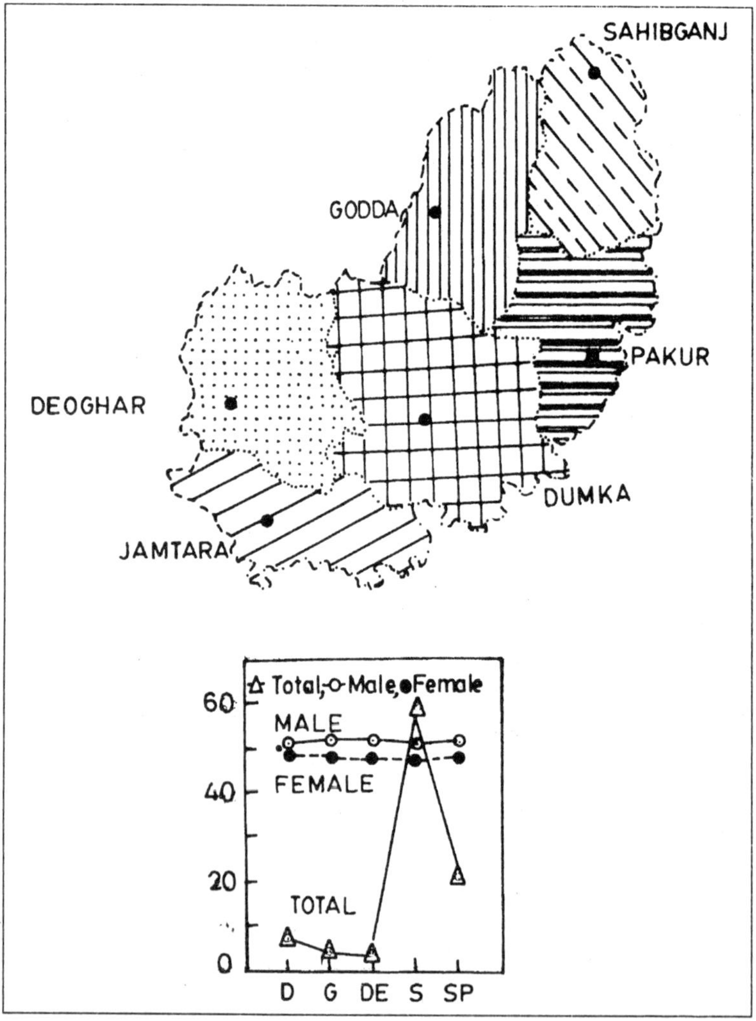

Fig. 4.6: Districtwise Population (Santhal Pargana)

	Population		*Male*		*Female*	
	Total	%	Total	%	Total	%
1. Dumka	298698	19.17	150528	50.39	148170	49.61
2. Godda	172502	20.03	86933	50.40	85569	49.60
3. Deoghar	201870	21.63	101607	50.33	100263	49.67
4. Sahibganj	274587	21.10	139140	50.67	135447	49.33
5. Santhal Pargana	947657	20.64	478208	50.48	469449	49.54

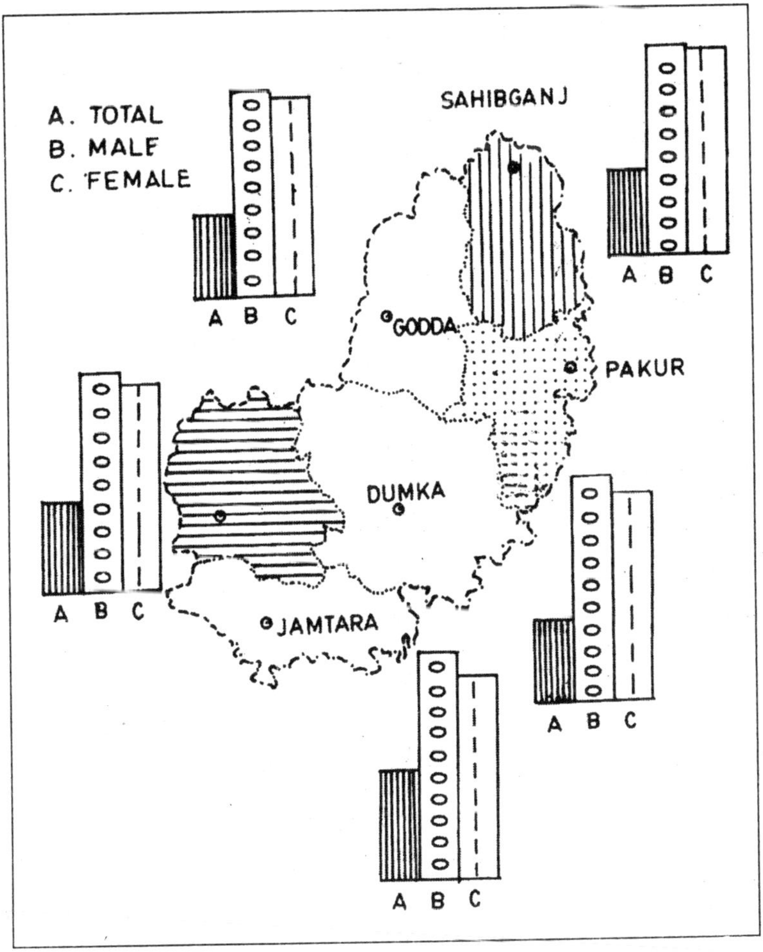

Fig. 4.7: Male and Female Population (0–6 age group) (Santhal Pargana)

of widows is also a common practice except the high caste Hindu who constitutes relatively a small section of the total population.

Structure of the population at the 1991 Census not less than 42.63 per cent of the total population belongs to age group 0—14 while 23.56 per cent is in age group 15—29. The percentage of population in the dependent age group *e.g.* 0—14 and 60 and the above works out to 47.53.

Table 4.5: Number of households and population density in different sub-divisions

Name of sub-division	*No. of house hold in thousands*	*Total population in lac*	*Density per sq. kms.*
Dumka	133	7.13	192
Jamtara	68	3.78	210
Deoghar	106	5.85	236
Godda	113	6.01	286
Rajmahal	94	5.07	317
Pakur	76	4.03	223
Total	**590**	**31.87**	**224**

Santhal Parganas is pre-dominantly a rural district. In 1991, only 5—9 per cent of the total population was urban and 94.1 per cent rural. The corresponding figure for the plateau region are 16 per cent (urban) and 84 per cent (rural), and for Bihar state as a whole, 10 per cent (urban) and 90 per cent (rural). The very low level of urban growth in this district is clearly indicate of the fact that the development of industry and commerce has been very much lagging behind in comparison with adjacent areas in the plateau region and Bihar state generally. As will appear from the table below, among sub-division, Deoghar has the largest urban population (0.68 lac) followed by Rajmahal (0.51 lac). Urban development has been lowest in Godda sub-division, the urban population being less than 10 thousand out of a total population of 4.97 lac.

Sampling

Respondents included in the study were selected on the basis of random sampling. The specific technique used was the lottery method.

At the first step forty five villages from a total number of seven blocks of the division *viz.* Deoghar, Sarath, Palajori, Karon, Sarawan, Mdhupur and Mohanpur were selected from a list of villages provided by the block offices having high concentration of trible population in their respective areas. The villages were selected by using the lottery method of random sampling. Thereafter, because of the small size of the villages the female heads or the female member of each of the tribal families were included in the sample. Total number of respondents thus came to 312 but during the study 22 of the total respondents could not be contacted and thus, the total number of sample included in the study came to 290.

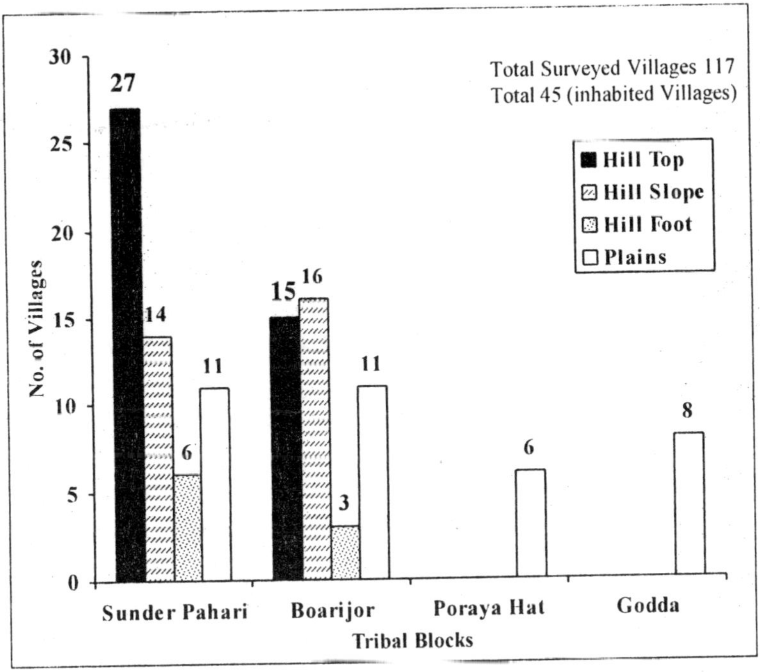

Fig. 4.8: Villages Surveyed in Tribal Blocks in Santhal Pargana (Situationwise)

Regarding the socio-economic characteristic of the respon-dents the analysis of the demarkated that out of the total number of respondent 8.27 per cent were below 35 years of age, 15.51 per cent between 35 to 40 years 20.68 per cent between 40 to 45 years, 23–10 per cent were between 45 to 50 years and 32.41 per cent of the total 290 respondents were above 50 years of age.

Data regarding literacy showed that 47.93 per cent were illiterate 30.68 per cent literate 14.48 per cent less than Matriculates and 6.89 per cent were Matriculate and above. The percentage of higher literacy was distinctly marked in the lower age. Groups, that was probably due to the increasing availability of the educational facilities in tribal areas since independence of the country.

Table 4.6: Age and Education

Education Age	*Illiterate*	*Literate*	*Less than matriculate*	*Matriculate and above*	*Total*
Below35 years	26.63	37.50	25.00	16.66	8.27
35 to 40 years	26.66	31.11	24.44	17.77	15.51
40 to 45 years	48.33	30.00	13.33	8.33	20.68
45 to 50 years	53.73	28.35	13.43	4.47	23.10
Above 50 years	60.63	30.85	8.31	—	32.41
Total	**47.93**	**30.68**	**14.48**	**6.89**	**290 (100.00)**

Source: Based on the SAWC Rating Questionnaire.

Out of the total respondents 67.93 per cent reported that there were earning members of their families. That included 70.50 per cent of the illiterate, 75.28 per cent of the literate, 57.14 per cent of those who were less than Matriculates and 40 per cent who were Matriculates and above, the significant feature which came out of analysis was that the women having low rate of literacy or no literacy were breed concerns of their families in higher number of cases than those who were comparatively there educated. That could be analysed on the ground that the women with higher education did not in most cases worked either as manual labourers or agricultural labourers or even petty traders in which most of the tribal women were engaged in 32.06 per cent of the respondents said that they were not earning members.

Table 4.7: Education and Earning

Response Education	*Yes*	*No*	*Total*
Illiterate	70.50	29.49	47.92
Literate	75.28	24.71	30.68
Less than matriculate	57.14	42.86	14.48
Matriculate and above	40.00	60.00	6.89
Total	**67.93**	**32.06**	**290 (100.00)**

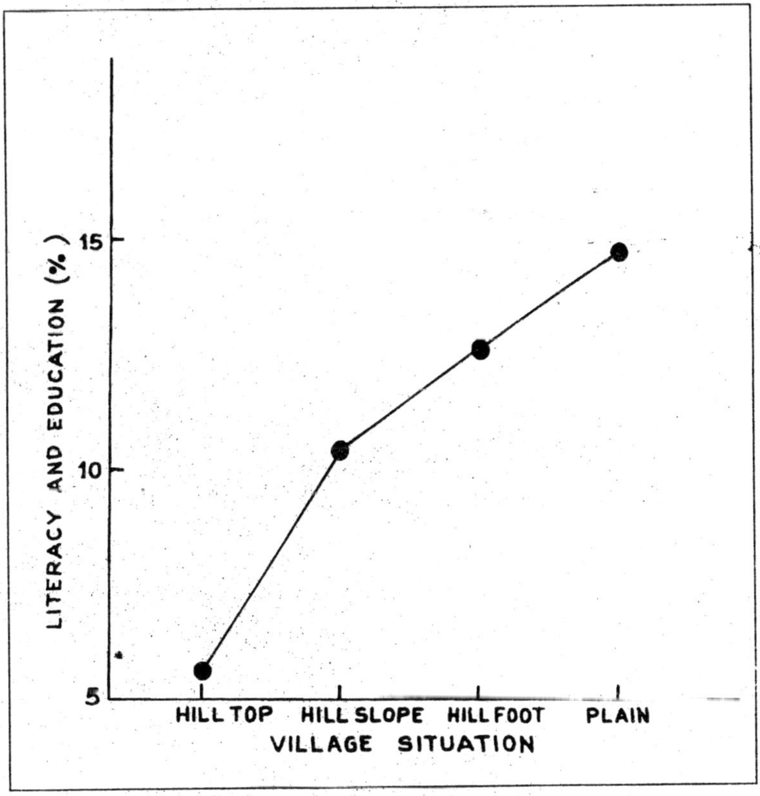

Fig. 4.9: Trends of Literacy and Education in Relation to Village Situation (Santhal Pargana)

District	*Rural %*	*Urban %*
Dumka	31.47	71.79
Godda	32.92	71.75
Deoghar	32.11	73.00
Sahebganj	23.68	67.98
S. Pargana	33.05	71.13

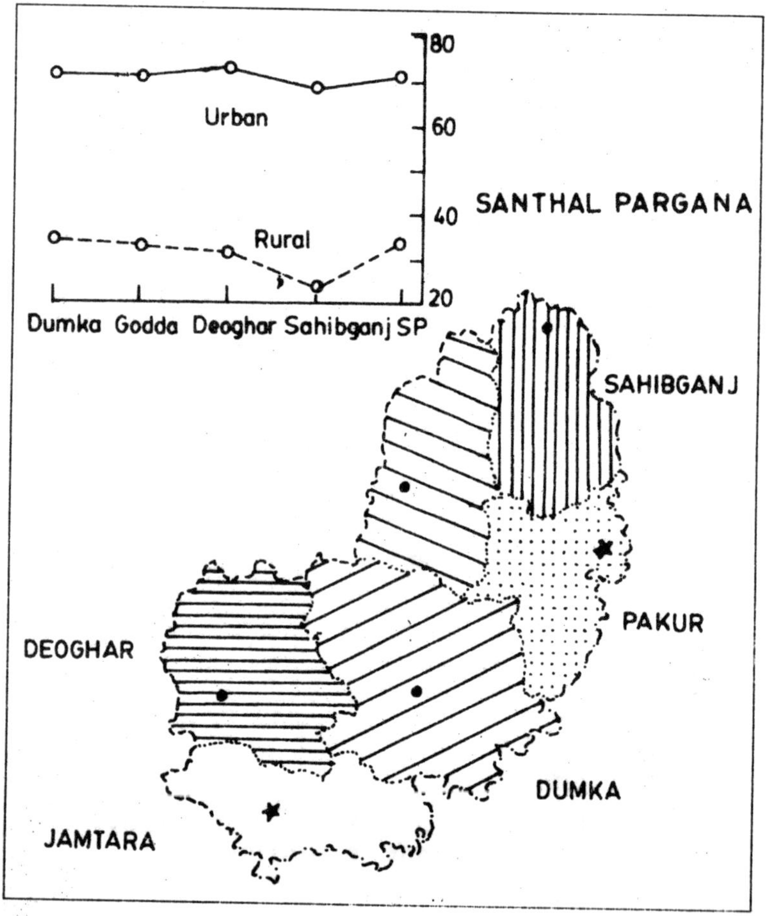

Fig. 4.10: Rural and Urban Literacy (%) (Santhal Pargana)

	Total %	*Male %*	*Female %*
1. Dumka	34.02	49.29	17.91
2. Godda	34.02	48.56	18.00
3. Deoghar	37.92	45.12	19.74
4. Sahibganj	27.03	36.97	16.32
5. Santhal Pargana	33.25	74.24	18.01

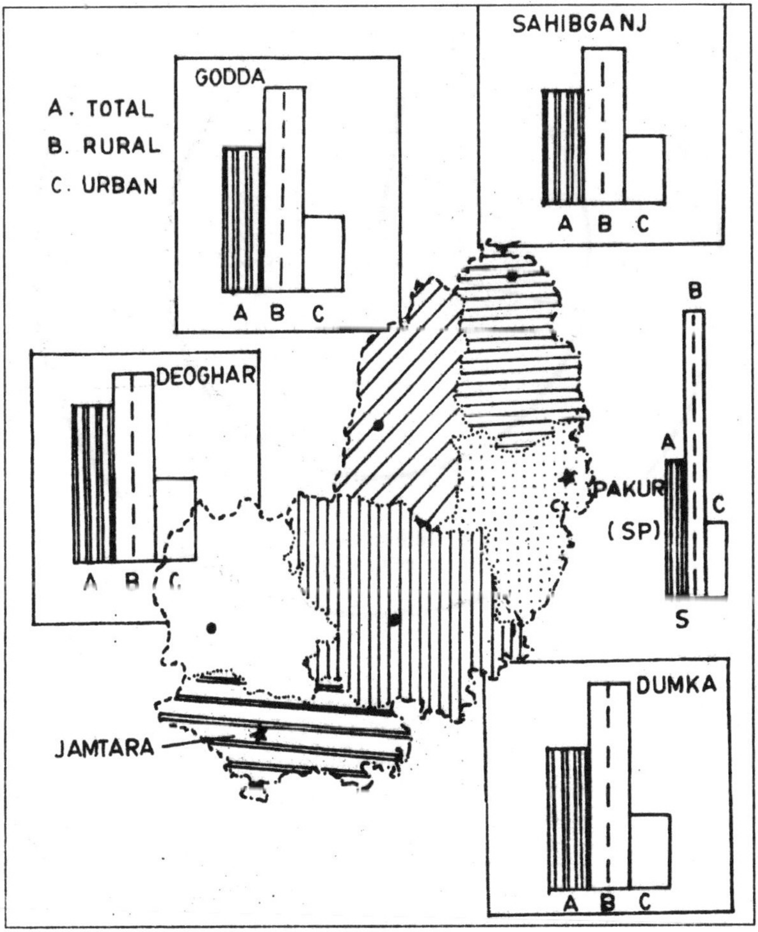

Fig. 4.11: Districtwise Literacy (%), Santhal Pargana

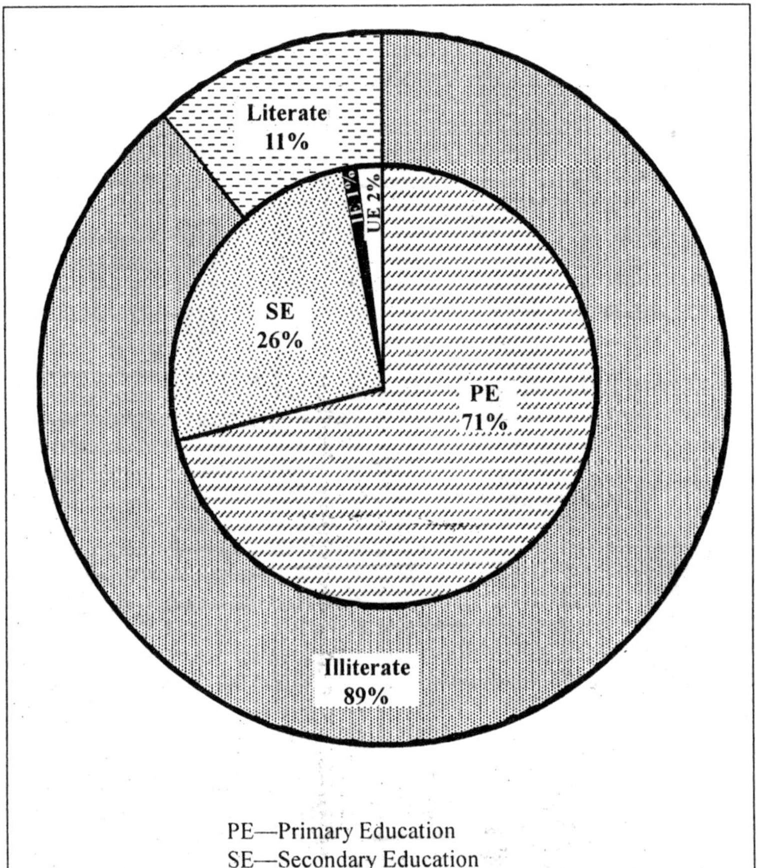

Fig. 4.12: Literacy and Education Status in Paharia Tribal Belt (Santhal Pargana)

The subsequent two questions were meant for those respondents who were earning members. In the first question they were asked to specific the nature of their job and in the second question they were asked about the amount they were earning per month. In reply to the first question 10.15 per cent reported that they were doing different types of official jobs. 75.00 per cent of those who were Matriculates and above were included in most cases marketing of commodities in the local markets or latias. In this group 58.33 per cent of less than matriculates 43.87 per cent of illiterates 40.29 per cent of the literates and 25.00 per cent of the Matriculation and above were included 46.19 per cent were working as manual laborers. In that group 56.12 per cent of the illiterate 47.76 per cent of the literates and 16.66 per cent of the less than Matriculates were included.

Table 4.8: Education and Nature of Job

Nature/Education	*Service*	*Business*	*Manual Labour*	*Total*
Illiterate	—	43.87	56.72	43.87
Literate	11.94	40.29	47.76	34.01
Less than Matriculate	25.00	58.33	16.66	12.18
Matriculate and above	75.00	25.00	—	4.04
Total	**10.015**	**43.65**	**46.19**	**290 (100.00)**

Regarding monthly income 43.14 per cent including 44.18 per cent of tracer and 51.69 per cent of manual labourers reported that they were earning less than 400 per month 41.62 per cent were earning between Rs. 400 to 800 per month, 9.13 per cent between 800 to 100 per month and 60.09 per cent were earning more than Rs.1000 per month. In that group only 60.00 per cent of service holders were included.

Table 4.9: Nature of Job and Monthly Income

Income	*Less than Rs. 400 per month*	*Rs. 400 to 800 per month*	*Rs. 800 to 1000 per month*	*More than Rs. 1000 per month*	*Total*
Service	—	—	40.00	60.00	10.15
Business	44.18	44.18	11.62	—	43.65
Manual Labour	51.64	48.35	—	—	46.19
Total	**43.14**	**41.62**	**9.13**	**6.09**	**290 (100.00)**

The data related to the marital status revealed that 71.03 per cent including 75.00, 75.11 per cent 80.00 per cent, 71.64 per cent and 63.82 per cent of the respondents in the respective age group of below 35 years, 35 to 40 years, 40 to 45 years, 45 to 50 years and above 50 years were married. 18.27 per cent which included 23.40 per cent of the respondents above 50 years, 20.00 per cent of the respondents in the age group of 35 to 40 years, 14.92 per cent of those who were between 45 to 50 years and 8.35 per cent of the respondents below among the Santhals in some cases women widows till their marriage do not take place, 10.68 per cent of the total respondents were deserted by their husband.

Table 4.10: Age and Marital Status

Marital Status/Age	*Married*	*Widow*	*Deserted*	*Total*
Below 35 years	75.00	8.33	16.66	8.27
35 to 40 years	71.11	15.55	13.33	15.51
40 to 45 years	80.00	20.00	—	20.68
45 to 50 years	71.64	14.92	13.43	23.10
Above 50 years	63.82	23.40	12.76	31.41
Total	**71.03**	**18.27**	**10.68**	**290 (100.00)**

Asked about the educational qualifications of their husbands 48.27 per cent of the respondents reported that they were married to persons who were illiterate, 46.66 per cent, 56.71 per cent and 61.70 per cent of the respondents in the age group of 40 to 45 years 45 to 50 years and above 50 years respectively were included in that group, 27.58 per cent of the total respondents reported that their husbands

Table 4.11: Age and Husband's Education

Husband's Education/Age	*Illiterate*	*Literate*	*Less than Matriculate*	*More than Matriculate*	*Total*
Below 35 Years	16.66	25.00	20.83	37.50	8.27
35 to 40 Years	26.66	33.33	22.22	17.17	15.51
40 to 45 Years	46.66	25.00	20.00	8.33	20.68
45 to 50 Years	61.70	29.78	8.51	—	32.41
Total	**48.27**	**27.58**	**14.28**	**9.31**	**290 (100.00)**

were literates, 14.82 per cent reported that their husbands were less than matriculates and 9.31 per cent which include 37.50 per cent of the respondents below 35 years of age, were married to persons who were matriculates and above.

Regarding number of children 11.03 per cent reported that they were not having any child. This included 25.80 per cent of the deserted women, 10.34 per cent were having only one child, 23.10 per cent were having two children, 33.44 per cent were having children and 22.06 per cent were having more than three children. The analysis, therefore, revealed that the average size of the family among the Santhal is not very big. This was to some extent also due to high rate of infant mortality agony toss people.

Table 4.12: Marital Status and Number of Children

Children/ Marital Status	*None*	*One*	*Two*	*Three*	*More*	*Total*
Married	8.73	10.67	24.27	30.09	26.21	71.03
Widow	11.32	15.09	32.07	22.64	18.86	18.27
Deserted	25.80	—	32.25	41.93	—	10.68
Total	**11.03**	**10.34**	**23.10**	**33.44**	**22.06**	**290 (100.00)**

In case of 18.27 per cent of the respondents the male holding the family was working outside the villages, 81.72 per cent reported that they were working in the village itself or in the adjoining villages. This shows that the Santhals do not appreciate the idea of moving out of their villages in search of job but poverty and lack of employment force. There to migrate to places outside there villages.

Table 4.13 : Age and Question No. 9

Response/Age	*Yes*	*No*	*Total*
Below 35 years	25.00	75.00	8.27
35 to 40 years	26.6	73.33	15.51
40 to 45 years	16.66	83.33	20.68
45 to 50 years	19.40	80.59	23.10
Above 50 years	12.76	87.23	32.41
Total	**18.27**	**81.72**	**290 (100.00)**

In the next question the respondents were asked to express their opinion about bearing the major burden of running the families on their society. The respondents were asked who according to them—male or female bear the major burden. In reply 47.24 per cent including 44.02 per cent, 60.00 per cent, 37.20 per cent and 40.70 per cent of the respondents who were illiterates, less than Matriculates, Matriculation and above respectively said that the male members were bearing the major burden, 43.44 per cent mentioned female member as bearing the major burden and 9.31 per cent were undecided.

Table 4.14: Education and Question No. 10

Response/Education	*Male*	*Female*	*Undecided*	*Total*
Illiterate	44.28	40.00	15.71	40.27
Literate	60.00	40.00	—	27.58
Less than Matriculate	37.20	51.16	11.62	14.82
Matriculation and above	40.76	59.25	—	9.31
Total	**47.24**	**43.44**	**9.31**	**290 (100.00)**

In the religion-wise break up of the respondents the analysis revealed that out of the total respondents, 32.41 per cent were Hindus, 32.10 per cent were Christians and 34.48 per cent were professing bongaism.

Table 4.15: Education and Religion

Religion/Education	*Hinduism*	*Christianity*	*Bongaism*	*Total*
Illiterate	31.42	20.00	48.57	48.27
Literate	28.75	43.75	27.50	27.58
Less than Matriculate	41.86	46.51	11.62	14.82
Matriculation and above	33.33	48.14	18.51	9.31
Total	**32.41**	**33.10**	**34.48**	**290 (100.00)**

Opinion of the respondents was also sought about the women being head of the family, 35.51 peı cent of the total respondents including 55.55 per cent of the Matriculates and above, were in favour of women being head of the family, 47.58 per cent including 60.00 per cent of the literates were opposed to that idea and

16.89 per cent were undecided. The analysis thus, pointed out the hold of family, they do not want to exert one superiority over males who were held superior to women according to the tradition. The cake of custom however appeared to be breaking in case of the educated women and the high percentage of Matriculates and above were in favour of women being head of the family.

Table 4.16: Education and Question No. 12

Response/Education	*Yes*	*No*	*Don't know*	*Total*
Illiterate	32.14	44.28	23.57	48.27
Literate	32.50	60.00	7.50	27.58
Less than Matriculate	39.53	37.20	23.25	14.82
Matriculation and above	55.55	44.44	—	9.31
Total	**35.51**	**47.58**	**16.89**	**290 (100.00)**

The relationship between the mother-in-law and daughter-in-law not very cordial irrespective of the culture. In the tribal society also it seems that the mother-in-law in most cases in a per-sons-non-grate. In this study the respondents were asked whether they would like interference of mother-in-law in their family affairs. In reply 50.00 per cent of the total respondents gave negative answers. There had been no considerable difference of opinion in the different educational categories. This indicated the presence of generation gap in the tribal society as found among the non-tribals. 35.17 per cent however, did not express any opposition to the interference of mother-in-laws in their family affairs, 14.82 per cent were undecided.

Table 4.17: Education and Question No. 13

Response/Education	*Yes*	*No*	*Don't know*	*Total*
Illiterate	41.42	48.57	10.00	48.27
Literate	25.00	56.25	18.75	27.58
Less than Matriculate	34.88	46.51	18.60	14.82
Matriculation and above	33.33	44.44	22.22	9.31
Total	**35.17**	**50.00**	**14.82**	**290 (100.00)**

The Santhals like other tribes of our country are divided into several classes. The Santhals are divided into 11 major classes. The respondents were asked about their clan membership. Analysis of the answers given by them revealed that 46.0 respondents out of total 290 were Hunsdahs, 49 Murmus, 21 Kishkus, 53 Hembrum, 58 Sorens, 29 Tudus, 23 Baskags, 7 Besras, 11 Powriyee and 8 Bedias. No one reported belonging to the clan. Known as Chandey. The clan membership is not only confined to the tribals professing Bongism. The Hindu as well as the Christian tribals were also aware of their ancestral clan.

Table 4.18: Clan Membership Question No. 14

Hansda	41	Baske	23
Murmu	49	Basra	7
Kisku	21	Powriya	11
Hembrom	53	Chandey	—
Soren	58	Bedia	8
Tudu	29		
Total			**290 (100.00)**

Asked about the monthly income of the family 37.93 per cent of the respondents reported that the total monthly income of their family was less than Rs. 2000 per month that included 59.54 per cent of the manual labourers, 41.37 per cent reported the monthly income of their families was between Rs. 1000 and Rs. 1500 per month and 20.68 per cent including 50.00 per cent of the service holders that their monthly income were more than Rs. 1500 per month.

Table 4.19: Occupation and Monthly Income (Question No. 15)

Response/Occupation	*Less than Rs. 1000 per month*	*Rs. 1000 to Rs. 1500 per month*	*More than Rs. 1500 per month*	*Total*
Service	30.00	30.00	50.00	6.89
Business	23.25	50.00	26.74	29.65
Manual Labour	59.34	35.16	4.49	31.37
Not earning	34.40	41.93	23.65	32.06
Total	**37.93**	**41.37**	**20.68**	**290 (100.00)**

The subsequent question was meant for the respondents who were earning members. Their total number was 197, out of 290 *i.e.*, 67.93 per cent of the total respondents. They were asked whether they thought that the women were discriminated against man while working outside. In reply 47.71 per cent of the total respondents including 45.00 per cent of the service holders, 46.51 per cent of the businessman (Petty traders) and 49.45 per cent gave affirmative replies, 39.08 per cent including 30.00 per cent, 37.20 per cent and 42.85 per cent in the respective occupational categories did not complain receive as service holders, 29.65 per cent mentioned business as the main source of income, 31.37 per cent reported manual labour as the main source of their family income.

Table 4.20: Occupation and Question No. 16

Response/Education	*Yes*	*No*	*Don't know*	*Total*
Service	45.00	30.00	25.00	6.89
Business	46.51	37.20	16.27	29.65
Manual Labour	49.45	42.85	7.69	31.37
Total	**47.71**	**39.80**	**13.19**	**290 (100.00)**

In the following question the respondents were asked about the earning members of their family. In reply 29.65 per cent said that there was only one earning member in their family, in case of 32.41 per cent the number were two, 25.86 per cent as reported having three earning members.

Table 4.21: Age and Question No. 17

Response/Age	*Service*	*Business*	*Manual*	*Agriculture*	*Total*
Below 35 years	25.00	25.00	29.16	20.83	8.27
35 to 40 years	17.27	33.33	22.22	26.66	15.51
40 to 45 years	5.00	46.06	26.66	21.66	20.68
45 to 50 years	4.47	37.31	23.88	34.32	23.10
Above 50 years	—	12.76	44.68	42.55	32.41
Total	**6.89**	**29.65**	**31.37**	**32.06**	**290 (100.00)**

Table 4.22: Income and Number of Earning Members (Question No. 18)

Number/Income	*One*	*Two*	*Three*	*More*	*Total*
Less than 1000 Per Month	36.36	33.63	30.00	—	37.93
Rs. 1000 to 1500 Per Month	26.66	29.6	23.00	19.16	41.37
More than 1500 Per Month	23.33	36.66	20.00	20.00	20.68
Total	**29.65**	**32.41**	**25.86**	**12.06**	**290 (100.00)**

Regarding number of dependents in their families 17.24 per cent of the respondents said having only one, 25.51 per cent reported having two, 40.00 said that they had three dependent members in their families and 17.24 per cent were having more than three dependent members in their families.

Table 4.23: Income and Number of Dependent Members (Question No. 19)

Number/Income	One	Two	Three	More	Total
Less than 1000 Per Month	19.18	23.63	41.81	16.36	37.93
Rs. 1000 to 1500 Per Month	13.33	26.66	39.99	20.00	41.37
More than 1500 Per Month	23.33	26.66	36.66	16.33	20.68
Total	**17.24**	**25.51**	**40.00**	**17.24**	**290 (100.00)**

In the next question the respondents were asked whether any of their married daughters was living with them? Normally the girls after their marriage join their husband. But there are certain exceptions. In some cases the son-in-law comes to live with their daughters were livings with them. But in case of 34.25 per cent of the respondents the married daughters were accommodated in their father's families.

Table 4.24: Source of Income and Question No. 20

Response/Occupation	*Yes*	*No*	*Total*
Service	20.00	80.00	6.89
Business	24.41	75.58	29.65
Manual Labour	29.67	70.32	31.37
Agriculture	23.65	76.34	32.06
Total	**34.25**	**74.48**	**290 (100.00)**

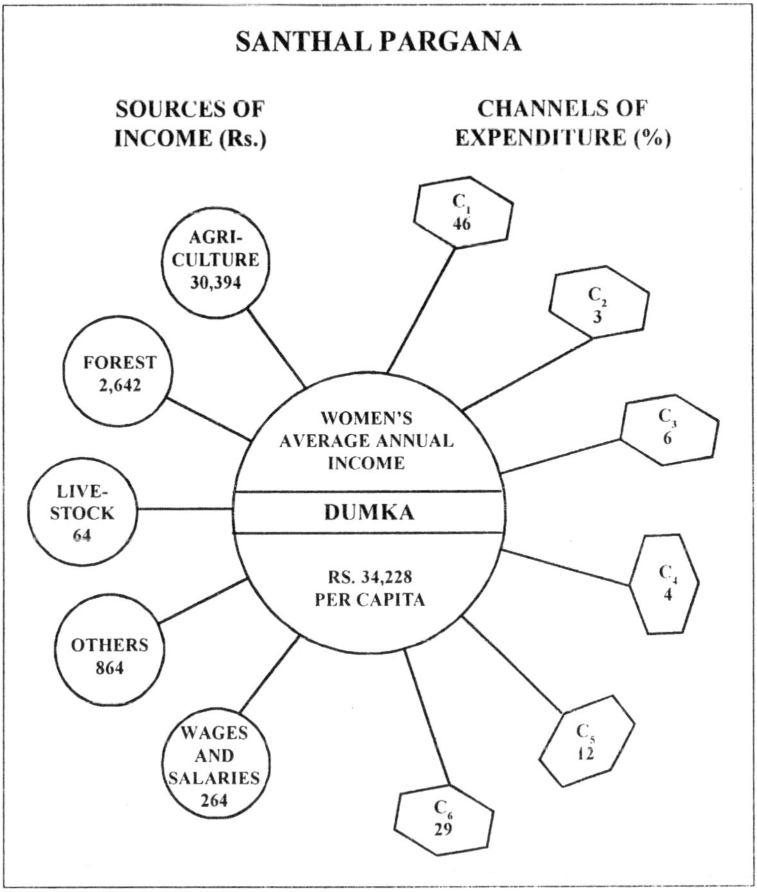

Fig. 4.13: Women's Average Annual Income of District Dumka

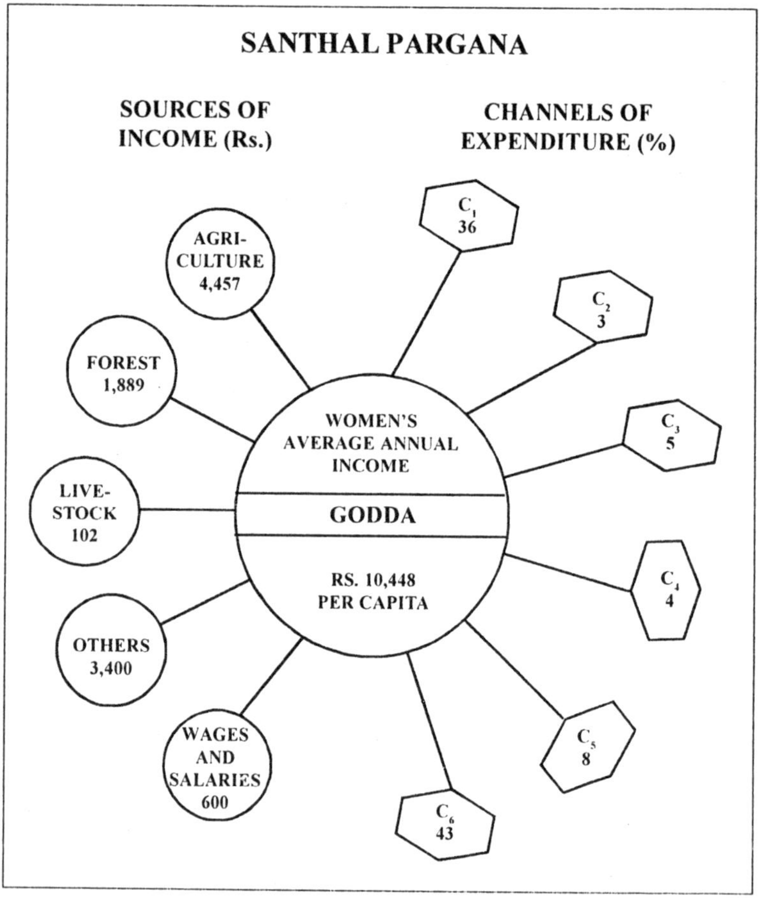

Fig. 4.14: Women's Average Annual Income of District Godda

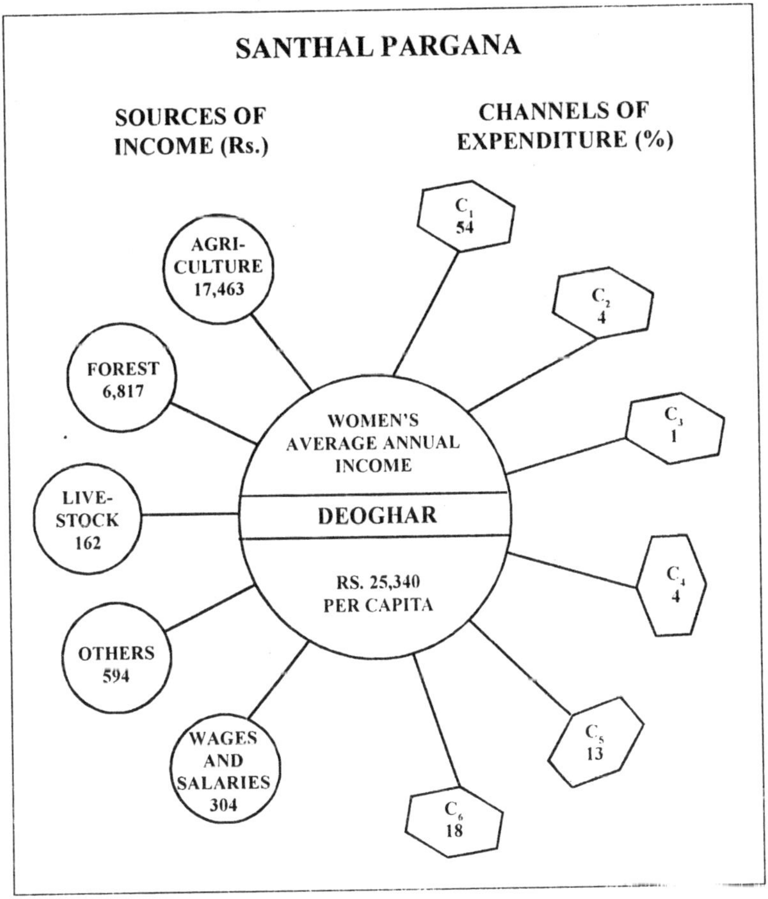

Fig. 4.15: Women's Average Annual Income of District Deoghar

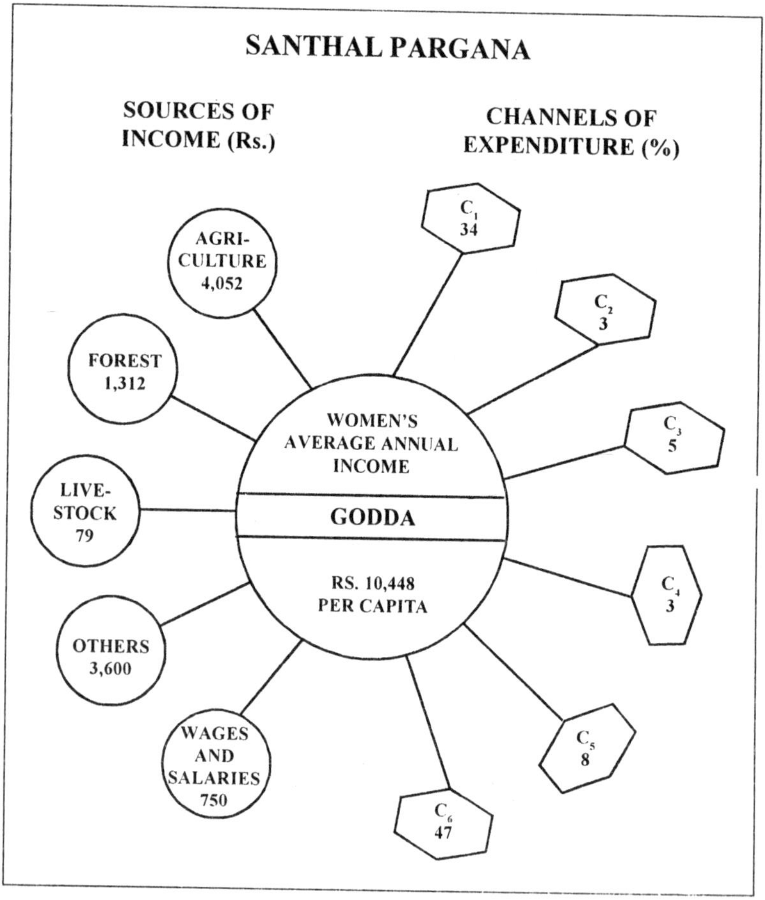

Fig. 4.16: Women's Average Annual Income of District Sahibganj

Lastly the respondents were asked whether they thought that the status of women in Santhal society had changed in recent years? This question was significant because of the fact that all respondents in this study were women. In reply 53.10 per cent of the total respondents 62.50 per cent in the age group of below 35 years, and 58.51 per cent in the age group of above 50 years said that there has been changes in the status of women in Santhal society during recent years. 34.62 per cent were opposed to this idea and 12.06 per cent were undecided.

Table 4.25: Age and Question No. 21

Response/Age	*Yes*	*No*	*Don't know*	*Total*
Below 35 years	62.50	37.50	—	8.27
35 to 40 years	48.88	35.55	15.55	15.51
40 to 45 years	43.33	38.32	18.33	20.68
45 to 50 years	53.73	34.32	11.94	23.10
Above 50 years	58.51	31.91	9.57	32.41
Total	**53.10**	**34.82**	**12.06**	**290 (100.00)**

Thus, the discussion tries to draw the linkage that a women's social status *i.e.*, her education, her participation in economic activity and in taking crucial decisions regarding marriage, family size, her health, status and contraceptive use are related to our efforts for population control in India in General and Santhal Parganas of Jharkhand state in particular on the basis of SAWC Rating Questionnaire.

REFERENCES

Bajpai, S.R.: *Samajik Anusandhan Tatha Sarbekshan*, Ketab Ghar, Kanpur, 1984, p. 9.

Bodding, P.O.: Taboo, Customs amongst the Santals, J.A.S.B., Part III, 1898.

Doshi, S.L.: *Praramvik Samajik Manav Vigyan*, Vikas Publishing House Pvt. Ltd, Kanpur, pp. 140–50.

Encyclopaedia of Social Science: Vol. XIII, Macmillan, London, 1924, p. 330.

Goode, W.J.: *Methods in Social Research*, Prentice Hall, New Jersy, 1975, p. 40.

Hambrum, P.C.: *Status of Women in Santal Society.*

Heralambos, M.: *Sociology, Themes and Perspectives*, Oxford University Press, Walton Street, Oxford, 2005, pp. 369–71.

Lundberg, G.A.: *Social Research,* Longman Green and Co., New York, 1942, pp. 118–19.

Mazumdar, M.: The Santhal: A Study in Culture Change, Govt. of India Press, Calcutta.

Mukherjee, R.N.: *Samajik Manavshastra Ke Rooprekha,* Vivek Prakashan, Jawahar Nagar, New Delhi, p. 201.

O'Malley, L.S.S.: *Bihar District Gazetteers, Santhal Parganas,* Logos Press, New Delhi, pp. 89–95.

Saxena, R.D.: *Tribal Economy in Central India,* Firma K.L. Mukhopodhyaya, Calcutta, 1964.

Smith, H.W.: *Strategies of Social Research,* Prentice Hall, New Jersy, 1975, p. 10.

Tomar, R.S.: *Social Research with Statistics,* Shriram Mehra and Co. Agra, 1959, p. 49.

5

Women and Management of Household Economy

Family income is that stream money, goods, services and satisfaction that come under the control of the family to be used by them to satisfy needs and desires and to discharge obligation. As streams of water may be caught behind a dam and sent on through dynamics or to generate power so may this stream of income be controlled and directed to creative and in a family's living by the process of management.

Chief among the family's concern is the use of its major non-human resource, money, because that is the income people know about. Much thought and effort are expended on its size its source and the circumstances around which it is derived. Money income in an exchange economy conditions the content of a family's living through the standard of food, clothing and housing it allows, the cultural opportunities it provides, and the experience, possessions and comforts it furnishes. However any consideration of the way money is spent must bring into focus the other resources which are used in conjunction with it and are often used alternatively with money namely, knowledge, energy and skills of family. The result of using all of these resources including money and in a flow of satisfaction which is called psychic income.

The concept of management may be defined as planning organizing, controlling and valuating the use of all types of income. Its purpose is simply to get the greatest satisfaction from the resources at hand. Included in such satisfaction are three to be especially remembered, the development of the various individuals in the family, the furthering of group happiness and the opportunity to contribute to civic well being.

The process of income management is the same for the family as for an individual. There is a difference, however in ultimate goals, the individual's goals are usually more or less personal, whereas those of the family involve both the individual of the group and as a whole.

To be thoroughly workable and satisfactory any plan of using income must be worked out by or at least for the person or group concerned. Any family that expects to accomplish it goals by having someone else direct the plan or by following some readymade plan is bound to meet with disappointment. Patterns of expenditure that 'fit' a family do not exist. Plans must be evolved by an appraisal of all income and by careful analysis of each phase of an essential need in order to bring the two together and to arrive at a satisfactory plan.

The force and speed of social and economic changes in present day economy leave no place for rigid patterns or models of expenditures. No to families, even though they have identical incomes, will have identical needs and desires. An ideal budget for a family of four, a model budget for a professional women, and other such readymade plan have been the cause of the misdirected effort. They have been looked upon an easy solution to financial problems whereas nothing can substitute for thinking making decisions about what is important and planning for the use of money by the individual family.

The information reported by studies on standards of living and levels of consumption is invaluable in social planning and in providing basic information about consumption habits. Such data do not provide a method by which an individual or family can learn to manage income. The fact that certain individual do as a group send their money in a certain average way does not mean that each individual in the group has such a spending pattern, nor is there any reason to assume that any particular degree of wisdom attaches to the pattern. For the individual family, working day by day and year by year to meet its own particular situations or problems, the informations in such studies can be revealing but only suggestive at best.

Studies have run through several years are more helpful in showing how families have made adjustments to change in income or other situations. These studies seldom deal with plans that have been evolved through weighing values and making critical decisions. They are rather record of the results of spending in a certain way through a period of years, they show the affect of changed needs of families upon the way money is spent and also the changes in the cost of living through the years.

In our modern society "fringe benefits" have grown increasingly important to a family in financing its living, sometimes making up as much as 20 per cent of the total income. Hospital, insurance, unemployment insurance, pensions and such items paid by the employer or by both employer and employee sharing-spare current income to be used for other family needs. Literally these benefits become a part of a family's income and where they are received they should be considered in total planning for financing the family.

The amount of money income above the minimum for subsistence is not the entire for family accomplishment. Families with ample money often accomplish much less in terms of development of individuals and civic contributions than others with considerable income. Mismanagement of family funds may be due to a failure to realise or understand of the place that management takes in modern life. Ingenuity, foresight, intelligence, and the stamina to carry through well conceived plans for financing pay a high divided in reaching goals.

Before we venture into the study how to manage money, we should examine the kinds of income that are at a family's disposal.

There are three types of income that families work with making up their realized income which will be discussed. All should be understood to appreciate the total content of family living. They are: Money, Income, Real income and Psychic income.

We are familiar with money income which is the purchasing power in dollars and cents that goes into the family treasury in a given period of time, weekly, monthly and so forth. It may occur to the family in the form of wages, salary, sick benefits, dividends and interest, profits, net rent, gifts, pensions and social securities or royalties. Money income is converted into goods and services required for daily living and often a part is diverted into savings for delayed use or for investment.

For the salaried group with regular employment, money income is usually predictable. Recognition of human resources which determine and condition the amount of real income may not be so easily recognized. For those who have irregular money incomes or those with a large part of their income in the form of real income and little money, planning is not only more difficult but also necessary.

Real income (non-money) is the flow of goods and services used or available for any given period of time. Real income is derived from the use made of money income, together with that added without the use of money but as a result of the efforts of family or household members, it includes the services derived from owned property and possessions used by family members. Specially it includes such things as food furnished by a garden the use of the house, the automobiles, and all other equipment and durable goods. At this point management will be seen to be associated with real income because the usefulness of certain items will depend upon the use made of them as well as their kind, quality and amount. If a washing is not use efficiently or if part of the house is closed off, the potential service of these items will not be fully realized.

Another important part of real income is the knowledge contributed and services rendered by members of the family as specially the women home maker. Valuable also is the ability of members to use their dollars to good advantages. Few realize the economic worth of such knowledge, for plan and control the use of money how to care for and use all type goods in order to conserve the utility each can give. The knowledge of how to buy household linens, for instance, to get the best but for the dollars spent, and to follow up the purchase with the knowledge of how to care for the articles in order to obtain long wear from them, constitutes a significant part of the family's real income. With such knowledge and ability considerable amounts of money can be saved to use for other pressing needs. Any family can develop such ability and talent, and can there by materially increase its realized income.

Families are often unaware of the vital part played by these services. This is where the quality of management is revealed, both the management contributed by the wife alone and that contributed by husband, wife and children jointly.

The community provides yet another from the real income for family use through its public schools, libraries, television programmes, parks, fire and police protection and so forth. The family that make use of these facilities can increase realized income markedly without an expenditure of money.

The potent quality of real income available for any family is impressive. The way families make use of all forms of real income, thus materially increasing the sum total of realized income is dependent primarily upon the managerial ability of the husband and wife and the magnitude and drive of their philosophy and goals in living.

Wherever goods forms a part of family living, the worth of the family's real income can be determined only with considerable care. The farm family, for instance, can show its true value of living only if takes into account the goods furnished by the farm for family use. Although it is not hard to estimate the money value of such goods as food or fuel, the worth of services rendered the family by its members is more difficult to compute, however, such services play an important role in increasing the total value of the family's living.

Psychic income is that flow of satisfactions that arises out of everyday experience derived largely from the use of money and real income and making for psychic and physical well being. It is intangible and subjective but the most important income of all in terms of quality of living.

Although the amount of money income for most families is based mainly on the earning capacity of its members, the quantity of real and psychic income depends largely on the skill that is exercised in management of everyday living.

Decisions as to the manner in which income shall be used to satisfy the family's needs, desires and responsibilities collectively and individually become a major family function. Income management is a family responsibility which can cause considerable tensions and much worry and resultant unhappiness. On the other hand satisfaction and accomplishment for each members of the family can be realized throughout life if income is managed with thoughtful patience, justice and understanding of needs of all.

Thus, while we see that the quality of income management effects individual and family achievement it is difficult to make a fair appraisal of it interms of dollars and cents. Nevertheless the abilities of both home makers to use all available money and real income wisely should be recognized as part of the family's value of living. Since it is difficult to place a money value upon services of family members such real income is usually overlooked or underestimated.

Economy is a sub-system within social system. Sociologists consider it as the adaptive sub-system which produces generalized facilities. Economics studies the production and distribution of goods and services which are used by the government, various groups, families and other agencies. Within a society, Talcott persons has conceptualized a economy as a functional system. Thus it not conterminus with business sector, although there is a fit between the two the functional significance of business sector for a society is primarily adaptive.

Santhal economy is based on agriculture. Collecting, hunting and fishing are subsidiary. Though important sources of living. Animal husbandry has a minor place.

Three classes of land are cultivated:

1. Barge or the land about the dwelling, especially in the near.
2. Gods or highland fields at a little distance from the dwelling.
3. Khet or rice field.

The most important crop cultivated on bargo is jondra, *i.e.,* maize or Indian corn (Zee-May L). Other crops cultivated on barge include jari (Hibiscus cannbinus L). Bajra (sorghum vulgare para) certain winter legumes beans, vegetables such as eggplant, gourd, pumpkin and oilseeds bearing plants. Goda or hilly fields produce about seven varieties of jungle-millets, the principle one being iri (panicum Crusgalli L), Gundli (penicum miliara Lamarck) and Janhe (pespalum scrobicumletum L), several kinds of cotton plant, especially Gosspicum L and Gosspicum arboreum L, are also cultivated for weaving.

Khet or rice field are terraced on the hill slopes. These kinds of *Khet* are distinguished by different names, according to their position. Of these, the fields lowest down on the slopes are regarded as the best. Rice is the taple crop with one exception, all rice is transplanted. There are numerous varieties of transplanted rice. The only variety that is sown broadcast is cultivated not on a khet but on gods and hence called gods here or high lana rice. Rice is generally planted toward the end of the May and the beginning of June. The best rice Bihar hero ripens in November and December.

Ploughing is done by cows and buffaloes. Cowdung and ashes are used as manure. Cultivation is mainly dependent on rainfall, but the Santhal have also devised a system of artificial irrigation. Bandha or embankments are constructed across revines, hollows or other natural depressions in order to retain natural moisture. Both men and women take part in agricultural operations. There is a division of labour on the basis of sex, however, in accordance with which the heavier work such as cleaning forests or ploughing and constructing a bandh, is done by men and women help in constructing a bandh.

Some idea of the place of collecting in Santhal economy can be obtained by indicating the number of varieties of different kinds of forests plants that are gathered and eaten, either crew or cooked. About eighty two varieties of wild plants, seventy varieties of fruits, seven varieties of resins, thirty one varieties of mushrooms and seven varieties of jungle millets are gathered at some time or other. Matkom or mahua (Bassia Letifolio Romb) met or bamboo and serfom or sal (shores robusta) are very important trees which not only supply the Santhal with food in the form of flowers, fruits and young shoots (in the case of bamboo) but also, as has been said, serve many other purposes such as providing medicines, yielding wood for building and forming the base for liquor. Wild plants, roots, fruits and flowers of the forests also insure against the recurrent scarcities of the summer season and help in warding off the famines that result from crop failure. Wild foods are collected by women who work together in groups.

All Santhal economic activities are characterised by a strong co-operative spirit. We recall, for example, how the construction, maintenance and repairing of large bandhs or embankments for irrigation. Purposes is performed by the men of an entire village. The height of Santhal co-operative organization is seen in their annual hunt. The dihri who leads the hunt fixes the time and place, send message to all the villagers under his jurisdiction by means of branches of sal leave. The number of leaves on a branch indicate the number of days that must lapse before the hunt takes place. On the appointment day all adult men of the countryside assemble in a certain forest. For two or four days they hunt in the daytime and spend the evenings in an open space clear the forest where after cooking and eating their game, the group forms itself into a Lobour or Hunt Council, whose functions will be discussed later.

Labour is regarded as the main source of property rights since, according to Santhal tradition. Those who clear the forest for village sites and cultivation have the right to the land. As clearing used to be made not individually, but by collective effort, individual ownership of land as not recognised. Land belonged to the village community and individual redistribution of land, which prevented the monopoly of good land by a few individuals. The duty of the allocation and redistribution of lands was entrusted to the paranik (a member of the Panchayat) who may be said to have been economic head of the village.

As far as is known, individual ownership of houses, domestic utensils, ornament, tools and weapons and cattle has always been recognized. There are well established rules of inheritance for all these and for land we well. In the case of land one could inherit the use frustuary right only. Otherwise, a men's property, movable as well as immovable is divided equally among his sons, daughters have no right of inheritance, so that in the absence of sons, the belonging of a dead person go to the nearest male agnates.

Talking generally about Indian women Gandhiji once remarked women is the companion of man gifted with equal mental capacities. She has the right to participate in very minutes detail in the activities of man and she has an equal right of freedom and liberty with him. Here Gandhiji is talking about the expected role of Indian women, which is quite different from their actual role and position of the society. In the strongly patrilineal Indian society the women, in general, occupy a position lower than that of the men in all spheres of life, exceptions are in child-rearing and home management, their role and status are subservient to that of men.

There is however a basic contradiction between the concept of Indian womanhood and the actual position of women in Indian society. A women is the source of strength on object of purity and veneration. A virtuous wife is a satisavitri and she possesses great power. A mother is to be highly respected. Motherhood has been especially glorified in Indian literature. Sayings and thoughts so much so that she along with one's own country is considered better than heaven.

Whatever the social or historical reason may be for this apparent difference in the concept and actual role of women in India. It becomes clear that the early Hindu society realized the importance of the role of woman in the socio-cultural life of the community. Not being partilineal it regarded her to a second position. The loss is position was aptly compensated and established by glorifying womanhood, particularly the motherhood.

It is against the social backdrop that we are to see how womanhood is conceived in tribal a societies in India. My special effort will be to look for the basis contradiction in the tribal societies. If any, between the concept and role as has been noted in the Hindu society. Unfortunately, there is hardly any study which deals exclusively on the tribal woman of India. The best source of data is the anthropological monographs on the tribes which invariably contain reference to women's activities in various socio-economic spheres of the community. It is from these records one has to reconstruct the picture of a tribal women in the various stages of her life.

The tribals from about seven per cent of the total Indian population. They are distributed almost all over India in varying degrees of concentration. The north-eastern states of India, Orissa, Bihar, Madhya Pradesh and parts of Rajasthan and Gujarat contain a heavy concentration of tribal population. There are more than 400 tribal groups and the number of women to per 1000 men is 982. Culturally these tribal communities also show considerable divergence. The range spreads from primitive hunters and food-gatherers, such as Onga and Birhor to settled cultivators like the Munda, Oraon, Santhal and Bhil.

Unlike the Hindu, the tribes do not have any marked preference for boys over the girls. As a matter of fact girls are as welcome as the boys if not more. Even in the strongly patrilineal tribal societies with few minor exceptions the girl receive as much attention as the boys do, in fancy and childhood. This may be because of the important economic role in the women play in these societies.

From early childhood to begin with she is trained to various domestic chores. As soon as girl is old enough to play, she is regarded old enough to work. Who may be following her mother in all her domestic works including bringing firewood from the forest, water from the well in small pots or look after small babies. In the early years of her life she is very much dependent on her mother and gradually picks up different kinds of work. A tribal mother is often very permissive and seldom an occasion arises to take the daughter to task.

The first crisis in a girl's life with the on set of menstruation. A girl becomes impure and unclean at this point of time. She is debarred from continuing her normal activities like cooking, fetching water or serving food. In some extreme cases separate huts are built where manstriating women are segregated from the rest of the family. Menstruation signifies that a girl is ready to enter of the family. Menstruation signifies that a girl is ready to enter into full womenhood. Among a number of tribes there are formal puberty rites to signify the maturity of a girl. A nubile organ girl is rubbed with oil, her hair is combed and a wooden comb is inserted into it. She then only along with other such young boys and girls dance and are treated with a drink by the village headman.

The relatively uninhibited life of freedom and joy continue for a girl till she is married. It does not course means that she has assigned duties in her home. She has to do all kinds of work—cooking, bringing fuel and water, serving food to the members of the family and working in the field. Among the tribes of north-east India weaving is an essential art for the girls is acquire. These activities are interspersed with songs and dance, love making and sexual play. Marriage is universal in our tribal societies. A tribe if he or she is physically normal can not conceive of remaining a bachelor or spinster.

After a girl is married she embarks upon a new life. She is now the wife and the prospective mother of the children. She was to assume her role in right earnest and vigour. A good hard working wife is considered an assets. But she also enjoys considerable freedom in her movement. Within the confines of her home she enjoys an almost equal position with her husband. There is a invariably clear-cut division of labour between a man and a women. The women are to work at home attending to all the domestic chores and in the field. Even among the very primitive hunting and food gathering communities the women go out in the forest to collect fruits, roots, tubers, bark fuel etc. Hunting is considered as a mainly duty.

A women collects fire-wood, cook, do the sowing transplantation, harvesting and weaving. An ideal wife is she who provides the family with most food. It is therefore, not surprising that a tribal wife is considered as an asset, a kind of valuables property which has been acquired by proper payment of bride price.

Motherhood confers a special status to a tribal women. She is life a fruit bearing trees and she must be treated with care and respect. As soon as a child is born the marriage between a man and women is considered successful. It proves the virility of the man fertility of the women. A sterile woman is not looked upon with favour and in such a case the man is free to marry again even without divorcing the barren wife.

But motherhood also puts additional burden of work and responsibility on the mother. She has to resume her normal duties shortly after the birth and take care of child. A women carry her baby to the field allowing it to suckle from time to time.

As she grows in age and the children become old enough to take care of themselves, she probably gets a little breathing time. She has become a mature and full-fledged woman. Perhaps at this period of life she reaches the renith of her glory and poser. Even in the patrilineal societies, a mature women has a lot of say in family matters, selection of mates for her sons and daughters. Cultivation and procurement of food for the members of the family.

Tribal women enjoy considerable right to dissolve a marriage. If the husband ill treats her, if he is important or can not provide her with food she may divorce him.

The principle behind this almost universal right of tribal women to dissolve a marriage is that marriage is considered more a social contract in which the husband and wife should behave properly than a sacramental affair as conceived by the Hindus.

Widowhood in tribal societies in India is not at all severely looked upon as it is viewed by most of the Hindu castes. A widow is free to re-marry and if she is young and industrious she has hardly any difficulty to find a moto. A widow is not debarred from any activity normally done by a married women. She works in the field, raises her own family and exercises all the authority of a women of her age. The place of aged women in tribal India is not altogether enviable. She losses her physical strength and capabilities to work. Due to hard work and lack of proper food the women aged quickly.

But the old women continue to work for their family as best as their physical abilities allow. They look after a small babies cook and do such odd jobs as may be possible. The old village women is the symbol of the courage, devotion and the will to preserve the characteristics of her race. Upon her falls the heavy burden of work of an ever growing household. She is expected to be present and to help at the confinement of every one of her descendents. She constantly has to care for her grand children and may even be called on to provide milk for them from her withered.

Though the existing ethnographic literature on Indian tribes written mostly by male anthropologist do not give sufficient insight into the world of the women we get, nonetheless, a broad picture of their life from infancy to old age.

There is no marked preference between a boy and girl in tribal societies. Both are almost equally wanted, exceptions are in few societies, but then in some situations, a girl is more preferred then a boy (Garo, Khasi). She receives as much a care and attention as a boy gets. But she is more dependent on her mother from whom she receive the early training in household duties.

A woman is considered an economic asset and considerable value is placed on a hard working industrious and dutiful wife. There is a clear division of work between a men and women. Her life is spent in working in the field, raising the children and attending to all domestic chores. But her important economic role does not give her a very high position in the society at par with man. She can not fully inherit property except in marillineal societies, she has little religious duties and she can not hold any public office.

The emphasis on feminine roles has considerable effect on a girl's personality and identity. From early years of her life a girl is taught to be submissive to authority and this invariably her home world. In this respect, the tribal women are not better than other Indian women.

It is because of the role differentiation between a tribal man and women and secondary value ascribed to that she is more lagging behind her male counterpart in the changing face of tribal situation in India. An example may be given. According to 1971 census literacy among the tribal man is 17.83 per cent whereas it is only 4.88 per cent among the women. But in some categories of non-agricultural employment (mining, quarring, household industries) they are equal with their men. As agricultural labourers they out number the men, 490 per 1000 of women as against 273 per 1000 of men. It may be said the economic importance attached to tribal women continues in the emerging situation but jobs requiring technical skill and education are fewer for them (than their man folk).

The relative backwardness of the tribal women is primarily due to the attitude and conception of the menfold towards their women.

But then, is it not true for all societies dominated by men? To bring a radical change in the life of tribal women it is necessary to bring a radical change in the views and attitudes of men towards their women.

Ethnographers have consistently reported on the involvement of the Santhal women at various stages of agricultural operations. A large number of Santhal population from the main bulk of the agricultural labour force. The Santhal also work as share coppers. The Santhal women labourers are very casually referred to as Kamin. The Santhal women work in the agricultural operations like transplanting, weeding, harvesting and thrashing. All through the year there is a steady demand for the agricultural labourers and the Santhal women are specially preferred for transplanting and weeding. These tasks are performed by them very efficiently. The Santhal women have emerged as the potential economic partner for their families specially after the introduction of improved cultivation. Paddy cultivation has increased in various varieties and their high yielding seeds require more manpower in transplanting, weeding and harvesting. Besides working in the agricultural field, it was observed, the Santhal women collect dry leaves and twigs for fuel, they also collect the seasonal crops which are left in the field after the harvest. Sometimes some of them rear-up pigling. Collection of snails is still another task with them.

In the domestic life the Santhal women share the burden of boiling the paddy. They shoulder the responsibility of cooking and of child rearing. Even in the field some of them breed feed at the interval of their work. They also decorate the walls of their houses with indigenously prepared colours. The common preference by the Santhal man for able bodies girls as housewife, indicates her indispensability for hard work in life. The custom of presenting cow as bride price in a marriage perhaps and as a kind of compensation for a girl in a Santhal family. It may be assumed that the cow which occupies important role in an agricultural family replace the labour unit of a Santhal working girl.

Socially they are jolly, cheerful people, contended with their lot, so long as they have enough to eat and drink and to spend on religious and social ceremonies. As he is unfettered with caste, the Santhal enjoys existence in a far greater degree than does his neighbour, the priest ridden and caste-crushed Hindu. The Santhal eats his buffalo-beef, his kids, poultry, pork or pigeons, enjoys a hearty carouse enlivened with the spirit "pachwai" and dances with his wives and comrades to express his joy and thankfulness. Hard drinking is a peculiar failure of the Santhals who enjoy nothing so much as a course, but so far the physique of the race does not seem to be impaired. Their fondness for drink may be gathered from the attitude of an old people to get drunk twice, a week. When he heard the horrified answer of the missionary, he simply replies "Then touch our boys and girls, but leave us alone". Rice is their chief food but they are able to live on all sorts of roots and vegetables, when food is scarce, they will have recourse to other fare. They will for instance eat two kinds of Snake (the Dhamin and rock-snake) a few kinds of rats, one kind of frog, one lizard etc., the lizard is considered excellent eating, but the rest are generally only partaken of by children, especially shepherded boys. Though living mostly on vegetables, they enjoy animal food when they can get it and nothing so much so pig carry. Except at certain sacrifies they never eat cows, buffaloes, unless they die from disease or have to be used as draught cattle. They rather enjoy chewing the tough most but certain kinds of most they abhor, *e.g.*, horse-flesh.

Their food may be divided into two main classes *viz.* (1) cereals, prepared as bhat, with curry of some kind added and (2) other food eaten raw or roasted but without cereals. A list prepared by Mr. Bodding gives the following details—Cereals (19 kinds) besides a large number of varieties of rice, vegetables curries compound of (a) leguminous plants, (b) cultivated vegetables (18), and (c) leaves of wild plants and trees (59), mushrooms (24), resins (10), fruits (wild or cultivated) (65), tubers (25), all domestic animals except dogs, horses and cats and wild animals including tigers, leopards, jackles, foxes, five kinds of rats etc. (30) snakes (2) lizards (1) tortoises and crocodiles (6) birds with the eggs of every bird eaten (72), fishes (at least 30), wild grains, fruits etc. eaten during time of scarcity (21), oil seeds and karnals (16) and the ordinary Indian spices. A ground and could not wish for more miscellaneous material, and it is not certain that the list is quite complete.

It is probable that the social system of the Santhals was originally communistic and if their conditions are to be believed they are formerly a self-contained nation having very few social relations with other races. It is impossible to trace, even at the present time, distinct idea among them that a Santhal has a right to possess and appropriate any part of nature not previously in the occupation of anybody else. Land is common property till it has been held under a little, or at least, "trampled round". All forests and forests produce are considered free to all if they have not been definitely occupied by others Any wild animal is also lawful prey, but belongs to the man who first wounded it, not to the man who kills it although the latter and the village headman get portions of the animal as determined by customs. River fish belong to anybody and if a man some up a water course or has a natural pond, he does not enjoy the fish alone, but on some day or other invites the villagers and neighbours to catch all the fish there. They give the owner of the water-course a small share and the bigger fish are also divided, the idea of public property is thus apparent. This does not of course apply in the case of fish stocked in a tank, a very innovations with the Santhals. As soon as anyone takes possession of anything with the comment of the village, he is treated as the owner.

It is possible that the name feeling may partially explain the sexual relations of the people. As long as the girls are not owned by anybody, it does not much concern anyone that is done with them or what they do as long as they are not spoilt. But if they are anybody's property, it is different. If anything goes wrong, it is the wrong, it is the male who suffers, the female is regarded more or less as domestic animal—formely she might even be killed. It is a curious fact that the adulterer is called a thief in their legal phraseology further, that the people say that in olden times theft was unknown among the people the only exceptions being that they might occasionally kill and eat by stealth a stray goat or sheep. They have, they say, learnt to a teal and to lie from the Hindu eats, as they call them.

Under such conditions it will easily be understood that the Santhal in the old day did not and could not have any regular business transactions among themselves or with outsiders, they grow or made or found what they needed. They manufactured their weapons, implements and utensils. If any one wanted a cow, or a wife, they were obtained by barter. The old "gurus" any that to this day a mixed most and oil, used for culinary purposes, is never called anything also than "barter oil".

As the forests have been thinned and the Santhal have come into contact with other races, their circumstances have greatly altered. They may almost be said that they know the worth of a piece but not yet of a rupee. They namker after the finarios of others and will give away their substance to obtain them. Under the influence of Hindu caste ideas they are gradually developing into a kind of cultivator costs, whose real occupation is agriculture of an inferior kind and whose leisure time is spent idleness. There is no doubt that the Santhals are not as yet equipped to take up the struggle wit outsiders, if they are not helped, they will go to the wall. Their ideals are not the past, not in the further and another great draw backs is that they are liable to hopelessness as to their future as a people. But let them see a thing succeed and they are quick enough to adopt it. The Santhals are at sometimes rigid formalities. They do not go outside the old forms and regard any omission or aberration therefrom as serious faults. This love of ceremonial formalism is another obstacles to their development. As to personal characteristic the Santhal are easy going and on the whole easily contended.

With a view to study the household economy of the Santhal the respondents of this study which included only the female members were asked questions related to the various aspects of their household economy. The first question asked to the respondents was about the sharing of the major responsibility in household economy. Generally, in a role dominated society the major economic partner appears to be the husband or the male members of the family. The Santhals are not exception to the general perception. But when the question of the management of the family economy comes the responsibility of the women can not be ignored. This share the major responsibility of running the family. In almost all cases, the family resources are not enough to cover the necessary requirements. In this situation the skill for household management becomes very significant and this is possessed in most cases by the female members of the households.

In this study the respondents when asked about the sharing of major responsibility in household economy 42.75 per cent said that the women take the major responsibility. This included 58.53 per cent of the respondents who were below 35 years of age, 48.88 per cent belonged to the age group of 35 to 40 years, 44.00 per cent of those who were between 40 to 50 years. And 35.82 per cent in the age group of 45 to 50 years and 42.55 per cent of the respondents who were above 50 years of age. The respondents belonging to the lower age group were more amphatic about sharing the higher responsibilities by the women. 40.34 per cent of the total respondents were gave negative answers. This included 46.80 per cent of the respondents who were above 50 years of age and 16.89 per cent could not give any specific answer.

Table 5.1: Age and Question No. 22

Response/Age	*Yes*	*No*	*Don't know*	*Total*
Below 35 years	58.33	25.00	16.66	8.27
35 to 40 years	48.88	33.33	17.75	15.15
40 to 45 years	40.00	40.00	30.00	20.68
45 to 50 years	35.82	41.79	22.38	23.10
Above 50 years	42.55	46.80	10.63	31.41
Total	**42.75**	**40.34**	**16.63**	**290 (100.00)**

Apart from sharing the responsibility there is also a question of efficient management of family affairs. The family life has got many types of problems and solution of those problems requires efficiency on running the family. In almost all the societies with few exceptions of the matrienchal families the women since their childhood are specialized in the art of running the family. This training is important through the process of socialization. Moreover, as per the sexual division of labour which exists on almost all the societies of the world the women are assigned with the task of family management. There is also an old saying that men are for the field and the women are for the kitchen. The man earns money by toiling in the fields and the women is supposed to spend his income efficiently so that the maximum benefit can be derived out of the limited income. In this study the respondents were asked whether they thought that the male members could run the family affairs as efficiently as female members. In reply to the question 74.20 per cent were of the view that the men were not supposed to run the family affairs as efficiently as the female members. This included 75.00 per cent, 60.00 per cent, 82.08 per cent and 80.85 per cent of the respondents in the different age groups respectively, 23.79 per cent of the respondents however gave affirmative replies.

Table 5.2: Age and Question No. 23

Response/Age	*Yes*	*No*	*Total*
Below 35 years	25.00	75.00	8.27
35 to 40 years	40.00	60.00	15.15
40 to 45 years	25.00	75.00	20.68
45 to 50 years	17.91	82.08	23.10
Above 50 years	19.14	80.85	32.41
Total	**23.79**	**76.20**	**290 (100.00)**

In our contemporary urban society there have been lot of changes in the family including its size structure function as well as the interrelationship among the member of the family. The concept of male dominance is gradually receeding and the idea of equal partnership among the husband and wife is gradually emerging. In our contemporary society the spread of female education as well as women in many cases, going for jobs out of the family have made them more confident and also assertive to some extent than their mothers or aunts. In such a situation they feel that the burden of family life should be distributed equally between the husband and the wife. Those days when women used to remain confined within the fareneless of the family looking after the household work and corning for the comfort of the husband are gradually being replaced by a new style of living where the wife performs her role both inside and outside the family. This dual responsibility became quiet heavy for them and they naturally demand co-operation of their husbands on the performance of domestic role. In this study there respondents were asked whether they would prefer the idea of sharing the household works equally between male and female? The answers given by the respondents clearly painted out that these tribal women who

Table 5.3: Education and Question No. 24

Response/Education	*Yes*	*No*	*Don't know*	*Total*
Illiterate	28.77	62.58	8.63	47.93
Literate	31.46	53.93	14.50	30.68
Less than Matriculate	26.19	53.38	21.42	14.48
Matriculate and above	65.00	35.00	—	6.89
Total	**31.72**	**56.55**	**11.72**	**290 (100.00)**

constituted the sample of this study are opposed to the non-tribal urban family those of sharing of household works between male and female. 56.55 per cent of the respondents did not approve the idea of sharing the household works, 32.72 per cent were however expressed their opinion in favour, that included 65.00 per cent of the respondents who were matriculates and above, 11.72 per cent were undecided.

Another crucial question which is facing the families in most of the development countries and to some extent in the developing countries is the contribution of the women to the household economy through their services. The women liberation movement in many developed countries of the world are of the view that the house wives should be paid by the husband for the works which they perform at home. Their demand is based on the ground that women contribute to the household economy through their services equally with the man in developing countries also this trend is gradually emerging. The different women organisaitons in our country have demanded the recognition of the services tendered by the women to the family in terms of their monetary worth. The tribal societies as reported earlier are not at all sophisticated and tradition is more powerful than the forces of change. But in tribal societies the women enjoys a better status than the societies dominated by feudal ethos. The women in tribal society are in most cases work as the bread earner's of their family and as such their contribution to the family is treated as equal to those of the males. In this study in reply to the question whether they thought that women contributed to the household economy through their services equally with the men, 48.27 per cent expressed their opinion in favour of the view, 39.65 per cent did not agree with the view and 12.06 per cent were undecided.

Table 5.4: Education and Question No. 25

Response/Education	*Yes*	*No*	*Don't know*	*Total*
Illiterate	46.76	41.00	12.23	47.39
Literate	44.94	42.69	12.35	30.68
Less than Matriculate	47.61	35.71	16.66	14.48
Matriculate and above	75.00	25.00	—	6.89
Total				**290(100.00)**

Family is an institution has undergone various changes from time to time and also has faced with many problems. In no society of the world family is completely free from problems confronting them. Moreover the problems facing family in different societies are not equal in nature. They differ from the society to another on the basis of the socio-cultural and economic structure of the society. The tribal society has various problems and the most prominent among them in the poverty and economic backwardness. Most people believed that the miseries of the tribals are due to the exploitation of the non-tribals. But looking clearly at the tribal society it becomes clear that some of the habits and practices of the tribals themselves are responsible for the unhealthy state of affairs in tribal society. One of such habits is alcoholism. The tribals particularly the Santhals both male and female very much fond of alcoholic drinks. This habit combined with low income of tribal family create serious problems to the tribal families. In this study the respondents were asked what according to them was most difficult problem facing the tribal families. In reply, 39.31 per cent of the respondents including 60.00 per cent of the matriculates and above said that alcoholism was the most difficult problem, 11.37 per cent mentioned discord between husband and wife as the difficult problems. This showed that the conjugal difference or discord is not a problem in most of the tribal families, which was just appositive to the trend in the non-tribal societies in developed and developing countries. 38.27 per cent of the respondents mentioned low income as the most difficult problem and 11.03 per cent mentioned factors other than those as problems facing the tribal families. Those included ill health etc.

Table 5.5: Education and Question No. 26

Response/Education	*Alcoholism*	*Discord between husband and wife*	*Low income*	*Any other*	*Total*
Illiterate	38.84	11.51	35.97	13.66	47.93
Literate	38.20	13.48	42.69	5.61	30.68
Less than Matriculate	33.33	11.90	35.71	19.04	14.48
Matriculate and above	60.00	—	40.00	—	6.89
Total	**39.31**	**11.37**	**38.27**	**11.03**	**289(100.00)**

While talking about the household economy it becomes quite imperative to find out whether there is a balance between the income and expenditure of the family. In most cases the balance is not satisfactory and this can be described as the situation of poverty. An individual finds himself as a poor man when he can not maintain a satisfactory balance between the income and the expenditure require for meeting the basic needs of the members of the family. This also become a source of frustration as well as irrigation which tells upon the enter personnel relations of the members of the family and particularly between the husband and the wife. Here comes the question of efficient management of the family resources. In these cases were in some falls short of expenditure the family has to decide its priorities for spending the limited resources and to derive maximum benefit out of it. The Santhal are poor people and in most cases Santhals families do not have adequate income to meet the necessities of the families. But in spite of this quite a large members of respondents appeared to be contended with whatever income of their families had. In reply to the question they felt that they could run the household smoothly out of the total income of their families. 42.41 per cent gave affirmative answer, that included 60.00 per cent of the respondents who belonged to the families having income of more than Rs. 3,500 per month, 57.58 per cent of the respondents included 60.90 per cent of the respondents having an income of less than Rs. 1,000 per month and 63.33 per cent having an income between Rs. 1,000 and Rs. 1,500 however gave negative answers.

Table 5.6: Family Income and Question No. 27

Response/Income	*Yes*	*No*	*Total*
Less than Rs. 1000 per Month	39.09	60.00	37.93
Rs. 1000 to 1500	36.66	63.33	41.37
More than Rs. 1500	60.00	40.00	30.63
Total	**42.41**	**57.58**	**290 (100.00)**

In Tribal societies the movement of the women outside the family is not very much restricted and in majority of the cases the women in addition to their domestic works in labour hard to supplement the income of their families of course in recent decades the urban women of the non-tribal communities are also entering into the gainful employments outside the family in order to supplement the income of the families. The tribal women are in larger number of cases compelled to work for earning breads of their family and in case of urban women the prospect of a comfortable living all them to enter into jobs. Of course among the poorer section even in urban areas, the job for women becomes a necessity. In this study the respondents were asked whether they were making any effort to supplement the resources of their families. In reply 63.79 per cent of the respondents including 56.18 per cent of the illiterates 61.79 per cent of the literates, 66.66 per cent of the respondents who were less than matriculates and 50.00 per cent of the matriculates and above gave affirmative replies and the remaining 36.20 per cent gave negative replies.

Table 5.7: Literacy and Question No. 28

Response/Literacy	*Yes*	*No*	*Total*
Illiterate	66.18	33.81	47.93
Literate	61.89	38.20	30.68
Less than Matriculate	66.66	33.33	14.48
Matriculate and above	50.00	50.00	6.89
Total	**63.79**	**36.20**	**290 (100.00)**

One interesting feature which the analyzing revealed that the matriculates and above were in less of number working or making efforts to supplement the resources of their families. This was probably due to the fact that the women who were illiterate or literate as well as less than matriculate could work either as manual labourers or petty traders. But the matriculates and above adverse to those type of activities they preferred job in the government, semi-government or private institutions.

The following eight questions were related to several types of effort which were possible for the tribal women to do in order to supplement the resources of their families. At the first instance the respondents were asked whether they were maintaining any kitchen garden? This is a practice which is followed by the women since the early days of human civilization. In fact the pre-agricultural economy. The kitchen garden is more frequently found in the rural areas. The householders plant various types of vegetables in different seasons as well as fruit bearing trees in an around their homes. This is the practice of utilizing a portion of home stand land for meeting the needs of green vegetables. Such gardens are generally looked after by the women members of the family income substantially. In tribal societies particularly among the Santhals the women earn money by marketing the products of their kitchen garden in local markets. In this study 52.75 per cent of the respondents reported maintaining kitchen garden, 47.24 per cent were not maintaining any such garden.

Table 5.8: Literacy and Question No. 29

Response/Literacy	*Yes*	*No*	*Total*
Illiterate	56.11	43.88	47.93
Literate	53.93	46.06	30.68
Less than Matriculate	45.23	54.76	144.48
Matriculate and above	40.00	60.00	6.89
Total	**52.75**	**47.24**	**290 (100.00)**

Another very popular way of supplementing the resources of the family is to keep domesticated cattle. This practice has also come down since the beginning of the agricultural economy. The usual practice is to sell the milk, fish and hides of the domesticated cattle. In our country the cow-dung is used as a sources of fuel and as such the cow-dung cakes are also sold in the market. The Santhals unlike the caste Hindus do not observe any ban on leaf eating. Therefore, the cattle become their sources of money as well constructed to ghee or cured. Moreover, the cattle also helps them in their agricultural operation. The bullock are used for dealing the land as well as for drawing the carts. The Santhal treat their domesticated cattle as one of their protection and welfare of their domesticated cattle. But keeping cattle is also expensive and as such many people can not maintain cattle for use of proper land for grazing and non-availability of fodder. In this study 45.51 per cent of the respondents including 59.16 per cent of those who were not engaged in any job, 35.00 per cent those who were service holders, 37.20 per cent of the business women and 41.75 per cent of the manual labourers reported that they were keeping demesticated cattle, 54.48 per cent however, give negative replies.

Table 5.9: Occupation and Question No. 30

Response/Occupation	*Yes*	*No*	*Total*
Service	35.00	65.00	6.89
Business	37.20	62.79	29.65
Manual Labour	41.75	58.24	31.37
Not earning	59.13	40.84	32.06
Total	**45.51**	**54.45**	**290 (100.00)**

In the next question the respondents keeping cattle were asked specially the type of cattle or animal were keeping. The importance of cattle in tribal economy can be assessed from the fact that the Govt. have started the practice of providing loans to the tribals through the nationalized banks for purchase of cattle. The loan is not limited to just the cattle like cow and with view of increase the economic condition of the tribunals. For this purpose pigs have been imported from Australia and other parts of the world which can provide proteaneous food to the tribal people. As a result the number of piggeries have registered on improvement. The respondents in this study relied that they were keeping cows, buffaloes, pigs and goats in order to supplement their family income. 15.90 per cent of the respondents reported keeping cows, 21.21 per cent were keeping buffaloes, 37.12 per cent were keeping piggeries and 25.75 per cent were keeping goats. The pigs and goats are generally looked after by the females whereas the men are entrusted with the work of grazing the cows and buffaloes.

Table 5.10: Occupation and Question No. 31

Response/ Occupation	*Cow*	*Bufallow*	*Pig*	*Goat*	*Total*
Service	28.57	42.85	—	28.57	5.30
Business	15.62	21.87	37.50	25.00	24.24
Manual Labour	15.76	21.05	76.84	26.31	28.78
Not earning	14.54	18.18	41.81	25.45	41.66
Total	**15.90**	**21.21**	**37.12**	**25.75**	**290 (100.00)**

Another source of supplementing the family income is to keep poultry. It is quite common for the tribal families to keep poultry consisting of few birds which provide them eggs for consumption as well as marketing. The chickens are the familiar birds but in some cases where there is a pond or any other sources of water they also keep ducks. The chickens are sacrificed. On the alter of their traditional Gods or Goddess during the time of religious festivals. Therefore the chickens have those gold cetilities for the tribal peoples, namely: money earning by selling the chickens per cent of the total respondents including 56.25 per cent of the Christians, 44.00 per cent of the respondents who were following bongaism and 42.55 per cent of the Hindu gave affirmative replies the remaining 52.41 per cent were not keeping any poultry.

Table 5.11: Religion and Keeping Poultry

Response/Religion	*Yes*	*No*	*Total*
Hindu	42.55	57.44	32.14
Christians	56.25	43.74	33.10
Bongaism	44.00	56.00	34.48
Total	**47.58**	**52.41**	**290 (100.00)**

Similar was the case about basket making which is a form of cottage industry among the tribals. 47.24 per cent of the respondents in this study reported that they were making baskets with the purpose of supplementing their family income. Of course the percentage was higher in the higher age groups compared to the women belonging to lower age groups. This was probably because of the decline of the basket making trade due to the non-availability of raw material as well as lack of interest in the traditional expertise among the women belonging to younger generation. 52.75 per cent however were not engaged in basket making.

Table 5.12: Age and Weaving (Question No. 33)

Response/Age	*Yes*	*No*	*Total*
Below 35 years	29.16	70.83	8.27
35 to 40 years	42.22	57.77	15.51
40 to 45 years	33.33	16.66	20.68
45 to 50 years	34.32	65.67	23.10
Above 50 years	38.29	61.70	32.41
Total	**40.34**	**59.65**	**290 (100.00)**

Like basket making wearing is also done in many tribal families Homespun clothes are popular among them because of their low cost as well as durability. Normally the Santhals are using coarse clothing because they can not afford to buy the finer varieties from the market of course, the women who can afford to buy finer varieties from the market like to wear colourfull dresses, 40.34 per cent of the total respondents in this study reported that they were wearing the cloths at home, the remaining 59.65 per cent gave negative replies.

Table 5.13: Age and Basket Making

Response/Age	*Yes*	*No*	*Total*
Below 35 years	41.66	58.33	08.27
35 to 40 years	42.22	57.77	15.51
40 to 45 years	50.00	50.00	20.68
45 to 50 years	44.77	55.22	23.10
Above 50 years	51.06	48.93	32.41
Total	**47.24**	**52.75**	**290 (100.00)**

Women in tribal societies do not practice puradah or seclusion to the extent which is found in the non-tribal societies and many of them are found engaged in petty tradings. They go to the hatia or the local markets which are held weekly by weekly or every tri-weekly at places adjacent to their villages. The women as well as the men in Santhal villages are fond of visiting the hatia for the sake of recreation, Fua and also earning. In this study 52.75 per cent reported that they used to the hatias for marketing the commodities produced by themselves or by their family members.

Table 5.14: Age and Question No. 35

Response/Age	*Yes*	*No*	*Total*
Below 35 years	50.00	50.00	08.27
35 to 40 years	48.88	51.11	15.51
40 to 45 years	53.33	46.66	20.68
45 to 50 years	52.23	47.76	23.10
Above 50 years	58.31	44.68	32.41
Total	**52.75**	**47.24**	**290 (100.00)**

Though the tribal societies have left behind the good gathering stage of economy still in money cases the tribal women supplement their family income by gathering tubers, roots, fruits, mahua flowers fruit, from the jungle. In this study 51.37 per cent of the respondents including 56.11 per cent of illiterates and 55.09 per cent of the literates reported that they were collecting those articles for supplementing their income. The percentage of respondents practicing good gathering was much lower among those who were less than matriculates and the matriculation and above. The reason though they were not regular food gatherers but they did not mind collecting food occasionally and remaining 30.10 per cent remaining reported that were not engaging themselves in food gathering.

During the post-independence period various attempts have been made for the improvement of the tribals. The top most priority have been given to the programmes related to the augmentation of their family resources. In order to assess the awareness about those programmes the respondents in this study were asked whether they were aware of any scheme started by the government in their areas which could argument their family resources.

In reply 42.75 per cent of the total respondents including 75.00 per cent of the matriculation and above, 59.52 per cent of the less than matriculates and 30.21 per cent of illiterates reported their awareness, the remaining 57.24 per cent were unaware. Table 5.15, 5.16, 5.17, 5.18 states the answer of question no. 38, 39 and 40.

Table 5.15: Literacy and Question No. 36

Response/Literacy	*Yes*	*No*	*Occasionally*	*Total*
Illiterate	55.11	24.46	19.42	47.93
Literate	55.09	31.46	13.48	30.68
Less than Matriculate	38.09	38.09	23.80	14.48
Matriculate and above	30.00	45.00	25.00	06.89
Total	**51.37**	**30.00**	**18.62**	**290 (100.00)**

Table 5.16: Literacy and Question No. 37

Response/Literacy	*Yes*	*No*	*Total*
Illiterate	30.21	69.78	47.93
Literate	47.19	57.80	30.68
Less than Matriculate	59.52	40.47	14.48
Matriculate and above	75.00	25.00	06.89
Total	**42.75**	**57.24**	**290 (100.00)**

Table 5.17: Literacy and Question No. 38

Response/Literacy	*Yes*	*No*	*Don't Know*	*Total*
Illiterate	54.57	28.17	23.74	47.93
Literate	53.93	31.46	14.60	30.68
Less than Matriculate	52.38	33.33	14.28	14.48
Matriculate and above	60.00	40.00	—	06.89
Total	**54.46**	**31.03**	**14.48**	**290 (100.00)**

Table 5.18: Literacy and Question No. 39

Response/Age	*Yes*	*No*	*Don't Know*	*Total*
Below 35 years	58.33	41.66	—	08.27
35 to 40 years	44.44	37.77	17.77	15.51
40 to 45 years	55.00	36.66	08.33	20.68
45 to 50 years	52.23	32.83	14.92	23.10
Above 50 years	58.91	37.23	06.38	32.41
Total	**53.44**	**36.55**	**10.00**	**290 (100.00)**

In the next question an attempt was made to assess the hold of traditional belief on the Santhal women. They were asked whether thy did agree with the view that God created women for the kitchen and man for the field. In reply 54.48 per cent of the respondents expressed their acceptance of the view, 31.03 per cent disagreed. They were asked whether it was correct to say that inspite of hard labour and contribution to the household economy they were neglected by the male. In reply, 53.44 per cent of the total respondents considered that is correct, 36.55 per cent did not accept it and 10.00 per cent were undecided.

Table 5.19: Age and Question No. 40

Response/Age	*Yes*	*No*	*Don't Know*	*Total*
Below 35 years	70.83	29.16	—	08.27
35 to 40 years	48.88	37.77	13.33	15.51
40 to 45 years	33.33	58.33	08.33	30.48
45 to 50 years	59.70	25.37	14.92	23.10
Above 50 years	65.95	23.40	10.63	32.41
Total	**55.51**	**33.89**	**10.68**	**290 (100.00)**

55.15 per cent of the total respondents reported that even if they were given an opportunity they would not like to give up their domestic liability and that led to another question on which they were asked whether they agreed with the view that women were born with an instruct for household works. Replying this questions 58.27 per cent said 'yes', 32.06 per cent said 'No' and 9.65 per cent said 'do not' know.

Table 5.20: Literacy and Question No. 41

Response/Age	*Yes*	*No*	*Don't Know*	*Total*
Illiterate	55.39	33.81	10.89	47.93
Literate	62.92	30.33	06.74	30.68
Less than Matriculate	54.76	28.57	16.66	14.48
Matriculate and above	65.00	35.00	—	06.89
Total	**58.27**	**32.06**	**09.65**	**290 (100.00)**

Thus, based on the review of literatures and observations some of the important conclusions on women's status and contribution in agriculture/household economy may be drawn as under:

1. The role and status of women in rural societies is more concerned with sex-based division of labour.
2. The stage of agricultural development and the socio-economic status of family influences women's contribution in agriculture sector.
3. The women have been assigned lower status than that of men in Indian Rural Society.

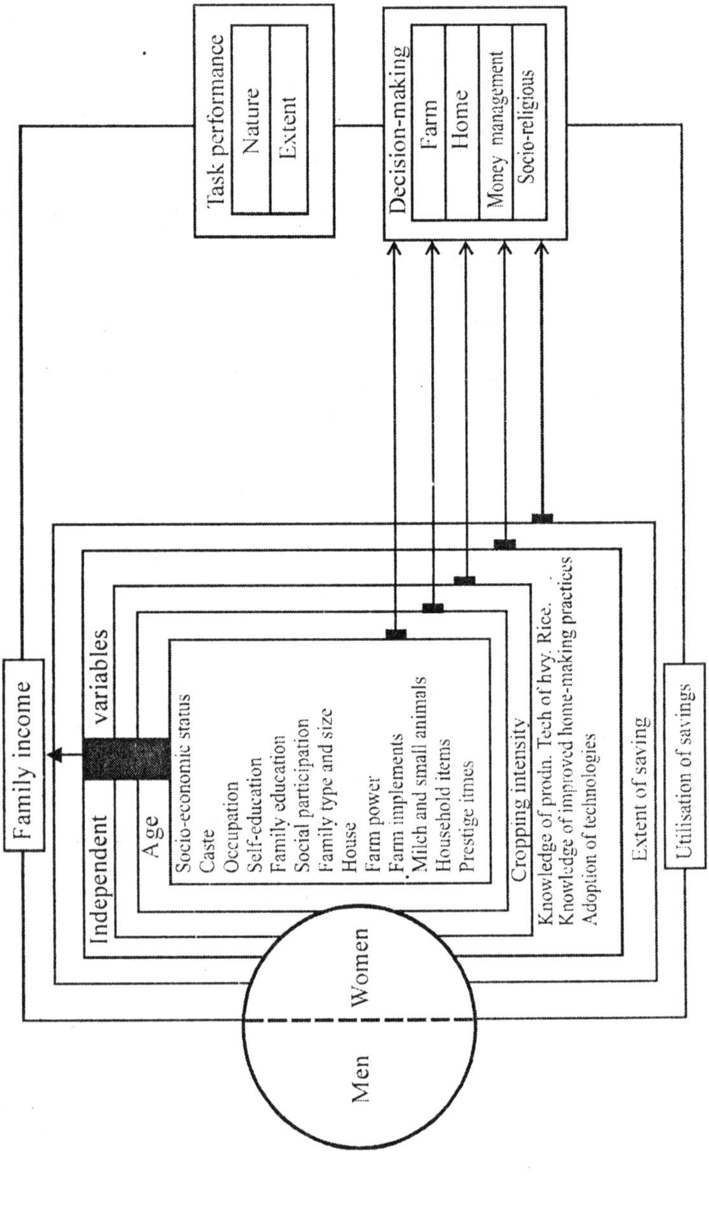

Fig. 5.1: A Framework

4. In the perspective of women's participation in agriculture, the sex-based division of labour and inequality between man and women are due to the combined effect of biological as well as culture factors.
5. Women's role in household decision-making has been found more prominent than other categories of work.
6. The division of labour in agriculture is not strictly on gender basis. However, division of labour is certainly influenced by the gender. Some tasks are generally performed by women whereas others are rarely performed by them.
7. Women's participation in farm activities is dependent of their status in social set up.
8. Cultural factors are very important not only at the participation level but also in performance of activities. The psycho-cultural environment in rural areas acts as an inhibiting factor in minimizing women's potentialities.
9. Irrespective of the geographical location and time period, women have been the major contributors of labour in the agricultural sector.
10. The technological changes have bypassed women by denying them to knowledge, training and extension services.

The foregone discussion indicates the existence of varied patterns of norms of female behaviour, sex-based division of labour and women's role in decision-making and physical participation in farm and home activities. The socio-cultural and regional factors affect the female input in decision-making process as well as women's economic participation. The women's decision-making in the household is positively correlated with the nature and extent of women's participation in market and non-market economy. A number of socio-cultural and economic factors at the individual and household levels influence women's decision-making and physical participation in home and farm activities. An attempt to conceptualize the way various factors combine to affect women's contribution to agricultural production and home-making directly or indirectly. The operational model is still very simple and only a tentative approximation of the reality which has been set out in a short-term perspective. Because the interaction or casual relationship among the factors are extremely complex.

REFERENCES

Bodding, P.O.: *How to Santhals Live,* p. 434.

Chakravarti, Satyabrata: *Santhal Women in Agriculture: Observations in a Burdwan Village.*

Choudhary, N.C.: *Women in Tribal India.*

Gocharane, N.W. and Caroy Shaw Bell: *The Economics of Consumption,* New York, McGraw Hill, 1956, Chap. pp. 33–35.

Gross, I.H. and E.W. Crandall: *Management for Modern Families,* New York, Appleton-Century-Crofts, 1963, p. 338.

Knoll, Marjorie: Economic condition to and from individual members of families and households, *Journal of Home Economics,* Vol. 47, No. 5, May 1955.

Mazumdar, Datta, N.: *The Santhal: A Study in Cultural Change,* Govt. of India Press, Calcutta, 1956.

Nickell, P. and Dorsey, J.M.: *Management in Family Living,* Willey Eastern Ltd., New Delhi.

O'Malley, L.S.S.: *Bengal District Gazetteer, Santhal Praganas,* Logos Press, New Delhi, pp. 102–04.

Prevey, Esther, E.: Developing Good Habits in the Use of Money, *Journal of Home Economics,* Vol. 38, Feb. 2005.

Ruth, C. Freeman: Spending and Saving Patterns of Illinois Farm Families from 1933 to 1950, University of Illinois, Agriculture Experiment Station, *Bulletin 592,* Sept. 1955.

Sherwill, W.S.: *A Tour Through the Rajmahal Hills,* Jan. 13, 1851.

6

Women and Decision-making Management

The concept of decision-making involves defining the problem, finding, comparing and choosing a course of action. Thus decision-making is the process of selecting one course of action from a number of possible alternatives in solving a problem or in meeting a situation. From these alternatives actions, only one can be chosen that will actually be carried out. The final selection should be one that further a definite purpose or creates a desirable situation.

The solution of any problem is made up of steps or phases. The number of steps or phases proposed by different writers varies, but they all have elements in common with the three steps suggested by John Dewey: (1) What is the problem? (2) What are the alternatives? (3) Which alternative is best? The steps or phases in the mental process of decision-making are:

1. Identifying the problem.
2. Obtaining information and formulating possible course of action.
3. Considering the consequences of each alternative, that is making an evaluation.
4. Selection the course of action that seems best. Brim points out that:

"...the conception of phases is suitable for use in analyses of decision ranging in scope from solving a mathematical or chess puzzle to the choice of a college or a husband or wife. In fact it is just this type of formal analysis of the basic phases of the process, which permits one to see the similar nature of all decision problem.

The first job in decision-making is the recognition that a problem exists and that finding and defining it is important one authority has pointed out that all problematic situations must be carefully searched out and often constructed: another also considers such processes as intelligence activities. The evidences of the problem may first appear as symptoms. The most discernible of these frequently hide the depths of the problem. To make the mistake of attacking symptoms instead of analysis the total situation may lead to false conclusions and the creation of even larger problems in the futures.

In the solution of a problem, two things are essential, first, a desire to find the causes leading to the problem and second, an unemotional and unprejudiced view of all the circumstances within the situation. The society's value system is an importance shown that recognition of problems is influenced by the degree to which the problems involve the unconscious components of personality. A person's defence against such a situation may be deny the existence of any problem or to identify the problem incorrectly. Age difference also seems to be factor of concern with problem definition.

Once the problem of situation that calls for change has been identified, all available knowledge plus information must be used to formulate possible courses of action. Imagination has been defined as the mental process that synthesizes new ideas from experiences. It is often described as making something ideas from experience. It is often described as making something from nothing, "Imagination is rather a process of making new wholes out of familiar parts".

The different task at the information gathering stage is allowing facts and imagination to incubates while giving attention to them and the problem. It is at this point that anyone having to make a decision may be faced with considerable confusion. Facts may come in pell-mell while imagination gives the image of the whole. The job here is to hold off from selecting a course of action until all aspects of the information sought have been appropriately weighed and organized.

The development of some frame of reference that will serve as a background against which the problem can be examined and the various alternatives can emerge is a valuable aid to a decision-maker. Such a framework entails an organized body of information, experience and opinions. It is mental storage for future use. When

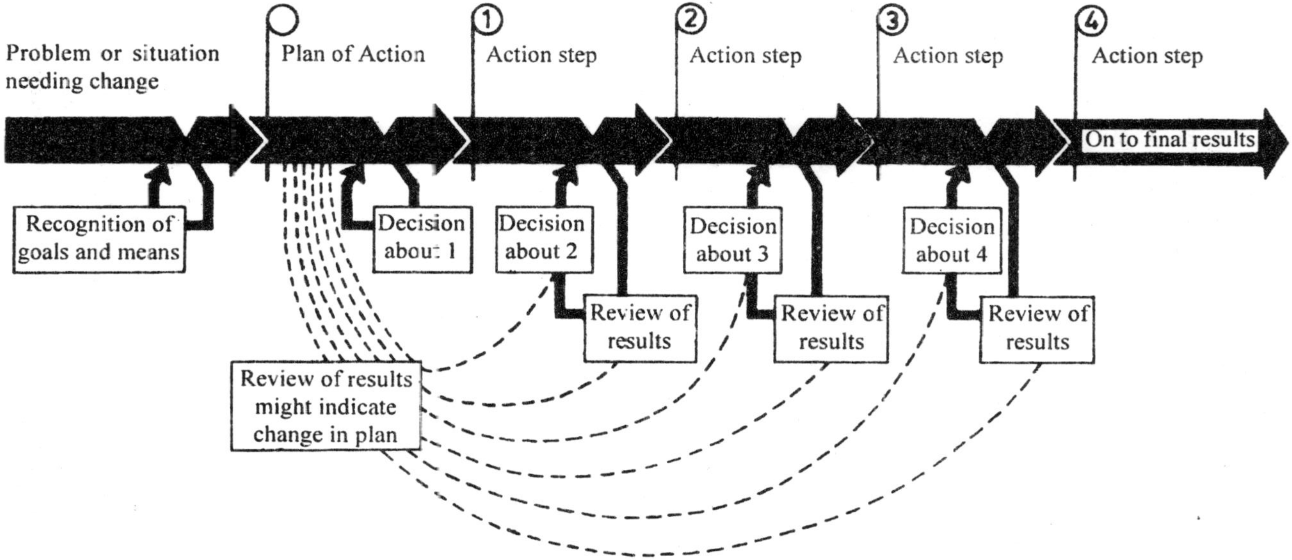

Integration of decision-making into management. (Adapted from a diagram by Kurt Lewin, "Group Decision and Social Change", in *Readings in Social Psychology,* E.E. Maccoby, T.M. Newcomb and E.L. Hartley, Editors, New York: Hol. 1958, p. 462).

Fig. 6.1: Action Steps in Organizing, Controlling and Evaluating

the need arises to consider ways of solving problems, the decision-maker draws from this storage that which is related to the problems.

The decision-maker having examined all the information relative to the problem, must next probe the future in his attempts to choose one alternative course over another. His objectives at this stage is to consider the most promising alternative among all the others, the one that seems likely to bring about the greatest number of wanted consequences.

Make a list and comparing wanted and unwanted consequences from different courses of action is a way of arriving at a basis of choice. The alternatives should serve as the best means of furthering immediate and means and goals with the least infurious effects on long-term goals. It is well to remember that the decision should always be made between acceptable alternatives, that is between courses of action any one of which would adequately solve the problem. Difficult situation often arises that demands a careful review of consequences of choosing between alternatives courses of action.

How can we judge the worth of different courses of action? or how can we choose from among the most promising alternatives the one or ones that will result in the greatest number of wanted and the smallest number of unwanted consequences?

No usually make a choice by imagining in detail what the result of an alternative would be. This imaginative process leads to deliberation or the weighting of values to discover and choose the best course under the circumstances. Only through such deliberation can be decide which of several conflicting course we want to take. Deliberation is actually an imaginative rehearsal of various courses of conduct. We give way, in our mind, to some impulse, we try in our mind some plan. Following its career through various stages we find ourselves in imagination in the presence of the consequences that would follow, and as we than like and approve, or dislike and disapprove, these consequences, we find the original impulse or plan good or bad. ...The advantage of a mental tribal, prior to the overt tribal (for the act after all is itself tribal, prior to the proving of the idea that lies back of it) is that it is retrievable, whereas overt consequences remain. They cannot be realized. Moreover, many tribals may actually be made in short time. This process calls for evaluation, because each alternative course of action possesses a unique set of consequences.

The concept of decision-making is considered by some to be synonymous with management, because at the moment of choice, the images of the decision-maker and manager have much in common. Others would not agree, maintaining that the relationship is close but not identical or the same. Although Simon treats the two as synonymous, he does not refer to the final choice alone, but to the whole process of decision-making.

Another approach suggest that decision-making represents one of the steps in management, which means it is a part of the process. This would place decision-making with planning, organizing controlling the plan in action evaluating the results and any other similar steps as parts of the management process. Decision-making permeates all of management and flows among in each step and through time in such a way that decision-making may be considered the control activity, the core activity, the core activity in the management process. Gross and Crandall have called decision-making the heart or crux of management. These two generalizations are in essential agreement because both mean it is dynamic power at the center. It indicates action. Thus we may think of decision-making as resembling the parts of a motor. When the motor is started by the ignition, the machine is ready for action, as long as the fuel supply lasts and the power is there, it will keep running. The conceptual framework of the management process involves decision-making yet goes beyond it. As the management of resources available for family use proceeds through its sequences of managerial activities or steps planning, organizing controlling, and evaluating—we must choose between desires and attainments and the number of choices may be malnutritions. At each step, we must face problems and situations that call for decision. We will sometimes find that the pollution or choice we had thought to be the best alternative at the time it was made has proved inadequate or deficient. Then before moving on to the next step, new decisions must be made. Thus, management is diffused with decision-making at all times and through time.

Decision-making forms the core or central part of the management process as one is faced with management problems or situations that need to be changed in the light of available resources. Our plans an action, or a series of actions and puts them into operation as the works towards the results anticipated. In carrying out the plan a decision for each action step must be made as one goes along and reviews progress towards results. Sometimes this review is made almost unconsciously, particularly if one is familiar with the situation. At other times it is made quite consciously. If the problem is simple the results may be reached in one or two action steps as with "think as you go" decisions. Value judgment are make as each action step leads to the next. When the problem is complex or leads to attaining a long-term goal, a number of steps are needed, each demanding decisions. Such steps may take a considerable amount of time. Evaluation of the results of any one-action step may show that unwanted consequences outweigh those that are wanted. Under such circumstances out a new plan may have to be make or the original one revised, whether of which may call for one or more new action steps. This is natural, for prediction of the future, involves risk, error, or faulty judgment. Somewhere along the way one may find a new step and may then fit it into the plan or even let it replace the first choice. In the latter event, a whole new plan must be made.

Decision-making is important in management, because it is the way we make things happen instead of just letting them happen. Decision-making forms the central activity pattern or core of the management process as resources (means) are used to attain goals (ends) in living day-to-day, year and for a life time.

In meeting management problems we are constantly faced with situations requiring decisions and actions. Some decisions related to our activities are routine and repetitive. For many of these, behaviour patterns are so well established that decision and action result almost immediately. They have become habitual acts carried out unconsciously and are not usually considered true decisions.

Making coffee is an example of such a habitual act. Water and coffee are measured into the percolator and the cord plugged into the electric socket without much thought, for instant coffee may be measured into a cup and hot water poured over it. Little conscious thinking about these things is called for, because the decision and problem solving steps have been telescoped into a habit of action.

Each day brings numerous problems that conscious decision-making. They are the ones that flow along as part of daily management and will be discussed later. Many of these are think as we go decisions. The non-routine, larger and more important decisions that are made within a long time span, call for more deliberations by one or more persons or the group.

In addition to the decisions described above there are the "unprogrammed" or emergency situations that call for decisions that are more complex in nature and require more time and considerations. As an example of such an emergency situation let us take the same case of a family who have lost their home and all their possessions in a disastrous flood. Their plans for personal and family life have been literally washed away. To meet the need for reconstruction or relocation, the family will have to reconsider their use of available money and plans for investment. The orientation of the family's life may call for complete readjustment depending on the crippling effect of the castrough. This complex situation requires unending decisions making on the part of the family and they may require help from some outside source as well.

When a problem is a new one or when because of changes, a previous solution is no longer useful, an individuals choice of action can not be routine. The new problem however, may be similar to one that has been solved before and learning from the previous experience may be the basis for the decision in solving the new one.

Difficult and complex problem must be studied carefully and possible ways sought to solve them before a decision can be made on the most suitable solutions. Seeking all the facts pertinent to a situation will help in making a more rational judgment.

For sometimes writers on the family and those engaged in home management research have been concerned with the question of who makes decisions in the family. The problem of who made the decisions who has the largest share in the processes husbands or wives the kinds of decisions made and how patterns of decisions-making change throughout the stages in the family life cycle have been investigated. A review of some of these studies will help to show the roles of family members in decision-making.

A Michigan survey of furniture and equipment buying paracices showed that both husband and wife participated in most of the planning and that they made many purchased together. In another study of the purchase of household goods and furnishings home improvements, handling the money and bills and savings, joint responsibility of husband and wife was shown. The husband made most plans for their purchasing. A Detroit study showed that the choosing of a new residence was most likely the responsibility of both spouses. The husband usually made the final decisions on buying the car and life insurance for family members. Contrary to that might be expected, the wife did not completely dominate family decisions with respect to food expenditures. No more that 54 per cent of the wives usually bought the groceries. According to Pansylvania study almost 100 per cent of the husbands and wives considered joint decision-making a desirable practice and 86 per cent were in favour of allowing children to share in decision-making.

A study of teenager perception of family decision-making showed the extent to which decision were made by parents and children in 1548 Florida families. The families were in either the pre-launching or launching stage of the family life cycle. In addition to the question of who made decisions in the family the respondents were asked which family member helped to decide. Who would participate in forty-three activities of which nine were concerned with income production and use eighteen were countered in the household maintenance area and sixteen were concerned with the care and control of children. The teenage responses to the question of who generally made the decisions in the family indicate that the children saw their parents as jointed their parents as part of family decision-making team in an additional 11 per cent the father was reported to the decision-maker in 15 per cent and the mother in 10 per cent. Thus this data supports the general opinion that decision-making is a joint in today's families as far as the mother and fathers are concerned.

Deciding who was to participate in the nine activities concerned with income production and use was found to be shared in 31 to 54 per cent of the families whereas in the eighteen activities concerned with household maintenance decision-making was found to be shared in 11 to 13 per cent. In the children the control are the range of shared decisions was from 14 to 67 per cent. For only two items, selecting large households equipment and shopping for furniture and furnishing, was decision-making found to be shared in more than half of the families. Plan for family savings were shared by 45 per cent shopping for a new car by 42 per cent and shopping for groceries by 35 per cent.

Another brief report dealing with teenager perception of decision-making in the social activities area of family living was made by the same authors. This data showed that teenager shared more in making decisions in this area than the areas previously reported. The findings gave some support to the idea that men and women have areas in which they are more apt to be concerned, for example, fathers and sons are apt to be more concerned with the family car and mothers and daughters with the entertainment of guests.

A recent study by Zunich shows the extent to which teenagers make buying decisions with respect to personal and family items.

The subjects of this investigation consisted of 294 teenagers between the age of fourteen and sixteen. About one-half were male and one half female. They were asked to reply to a questionnaire on which there was a list of various items such as clothing, furniture, jewellery, records and toothpaste. Differentiation was made to indicate whether the item was a personal or family one. The teenagers were asked to check one of the following:

1. Having all the influence.
2. Most of the influence.
3. Some of the influence.
4. Do not have any influence.
5. Others have all the influences.

These teenagers thought they have considerable influence towards purchasing personal items such as clothing, jewellery, record, sports equipment and watches. On the other hand, they reported that other family members had a great influence on the purchasing decision of such items as toothpaste and vaccination. Sixty per cent believed that they had complete influence on the purchase of clothing. Most of the teenagers believed that they had very limited influence on the purchase of the family car and furniture. However, they did have considerable influence in the selection of a Television set.

When the teenagers have asked to indicate whether they spent their own money entirely mostly or partially or their parent's money when buying the items under study, they said that they mostly used parent's money in purchasing toothpaste and watches. In buying jewellery, records and sports equipment they mentioned using their own money to greater extent. In the purchase of clothing the teenagers indicated that they usually spent their parent's money.

An analysis of the replies indicated that the teenagers in this study influenced the buying behaviour of their parents. Their influence is evident if we consider that many thought they had complete influence in the purchase of such personal items as clothing and records. The teenager's influence on the consumption patterns of parents in the alteraction of family income is attracting the attention of many home economists parents and marketing facilities.

In an article in Look magazine on children and money Gereon Zimmerman, senior editor, reported that teenagers have arrived as an economic force in the purchase of foods, beverages, clothing, entertainment, transportation and grooming aids. Their influence on family buying decisions can not be ignored.

A study of twenty five married couples all under graduate students at Iowa State University, was made with regard to the manner in which influence in family decision-making were distributed between husband and wife. It showed that 48 per cent expected the husbands have a greater share of the influence and 10 per cent expected the wives to have either most or somewhat more influence. Twenty eight per cent of the husbands had a higher degree of influence than wives and 16 per cent of the wives had a higher degree than husbands. Sixty four per cent of the husbands contributed a greater share of ideas as opposed to 8 per cent of wives, but 80 per cent of the wives made more or most of the contribution in the social emotional areas as opposed to 16 per cent of the husbands.

Another investigation was concerned with the development of the decision-making relationship of college educated couples in advancing states of marriage. It attempted to measure how the subjects perceived decision-making. The major independent variable of this study was the stage of the family life cycle. Data were also analysed in terms of home management, child rearing, money management and leisure time activities. Twenty couples in each of the six stages of the family life cycles participated and were selected on the basis of the age of the family life cycle, number of years married and ages of oldest children.

In the areas under study joint decision-making appeared to be at its peak in beginning families (Stage 1). The higher level of satisfaction and the largest amount of consultation in decision-making also occurred at this stage. Families with teenager children (Stage 5) exhibited the least co-operation, the lowest level of satisfaction and the smallest amount of consultation in decision-making. The data indicated that when families reached the launching stage (Stage 6) there was a return to about the same pattern of decision-making participation in the four stages of the families life cycle in which there were children (Stage 2–5). Women appeared to be most active in home management and men in money management. Women reported that they become more emotionally involved in decision-making discussion than men.

Decision-making was also the subject of large-scale investigation at the Minnesota Family study center, at the University of Minnesota. Judgment and consumership in the management of family resources was the first report released. Four components of consumership-planning, "planfulness" as indicated by actions preceded by plans, efficiency of decision-making designed as judgment and risks involved as drawn from volume of action taken were surveyed from ways of interviews with 300 urban Minnesota families.

The findings indicate that of these the judgment component (efficiency of decision-making) is most highly associated with consumer satisfaction with action taken. Consumership of this order is found most developed among the better educated, younger marriages with high residential mobility, who share a developmental modern manipulative, prudential, optimistic out look with high role consensus and good skills of communication.

Although Hill's study is not directed specifically at the question of who makes decisions, it is a significant one in decision-making and management in family living. The findings have therefore been reported along with other research in decision-making.

In male dominated societies the process of decision-making is normally dominated by the male members. There is a belief prevailing in a male dominated societies that women are inferior creatures incapable of lacking decisions as properly as the male members. In tribal societies, particularly among the Santhals the women are allowed more freedom and equality with the men in matters of economic activities and also in domestic management. But still in decision-making process they are playing a subordinate role. In this study the women were asked whether they considered male members as better decision-makers than the women. In reply 38.27 per cent of the respondents expressed their agreement with that view. The analysis of the data however revealed that the women belonging to the lower age group were less inclined to accept the males as better decision-makers than those in higher age groups. That was because of the growing self-confidence amount the women in tribal societies as a result of various reforms as well as spread of education. 38.96 per cent of the total respondents didn't accept this idea and 22.75 per cent were undecided.

Table 6.1: Age and Question No. 42

Response/Age	*Yes*	*No*	*Don't know*	*Total*
Below 35 years	25.00	37.50	37.50	08.27
35 to 40 years	17.77	53.33	28.88	15.15
40 to 45 years	4.00	40.00	20.00	20.68
45 to 50 years	41.79	35.82	22.38	23.10
Above 50 years	47.87	34.04	18.08	32.41
Total	**38.27**	**38.96**	**22.75**	**290 (100.00)**

In the following question the respondents were asked whether they were entirely free to take decision regarding matters relating to their personal lives. As said earlier in tribal societies the women are enjoying more freedom than the non-tribal people living in rural areas as well as in urban areas in most of the cases. In cases of urban areas small section of people who have become more sophisticate and westernized give their women more freedom compared to others who are still largely fettered with traditional ideas. But in tribal societies which is also true in case of Santhals the community norms exercise more pressure as well as strict vigil on the behaviour and movement of the women. It is very difficult to delay those norms which are in most cases, sanctioned by their religious beliefs. Therefore, it can be said that within the limits prescribed by the community norms. Women in tribal societies are allowed freedom to take decision regarding matters related to their personal lives. However, in case of elderly women the area of freedom is more extended than the younger one's. In the present study 50.68 per cent of the total respondents including 57.44 per cent in the age group of above 50 years, 58.20 per cent in the age group of 45 to 50 years said that they were free to take the decisions regarding matters relating to their personal lives. The remaining 49.31 per cent which included 58.33 per cent,

55.55 per cent and 60.00 per cent of the respondents in the age group of below 35 years, 35 to 40 years and 40 to 45 years respectively gave negative answers.

Table 6.2: Age and Question No. 43

Response/Age	*Yes*	*No*	*Total*
Below 35 years	41.66	58.33	08.27
35 to 40 years	44.44	55.55	15.15
40 to 45 years	40.00	60.00	20.68
45 to 50 years	58.20	41.89	23.10
Above 50 years	57.44	42.55	32.41
Total	**50.68**	**49.31**	**290 (100.00)**

The next question was a covallary to the previous one in which the respondents were asked whether they were free to more about as they like. Normally the Santhal women do not observe any seclusion from the males and in most cases the women are permitted to go outside the family without any male escort. The elderly women however, enjoy more freedom of movement than their younger one's. In this study 36.89 per cent of the respondents including 49.25 per cent of those who belonged to the age group of 45 to 50 years and 41.40 per cent of those who were above 50 years of age said that they were absolutely free to move, about 43.44 per cent said that they were free to more as they liked to a great extent and the remaining 19.65 per cent including 45.83 per cent of those who were below 35 years of age said that their other tribe the women before their marriage enjoy more freedom of movement than the period when they got settled in life after marriage.

Table 6.3: Age and Question No. 44

Response/Age	*Absolutely free*	*To a great extent*	*Restricted*	*Total*
Below 35 years	16.66	37.50	45.83	08.27
35 to 40 years	26.66	44.44	28.88	15.15
40 to 45 years	31.66	43.33	25.00	20.68
45 to 50 years	49.28	38.80	11.94	23.10
Above 50 years	41.48	47.37	10.63	32.41
Total	**36.89**	**43.44**	**19.65**	**290 (100.00)**

The next question was about the process of taking major decisions in families of the respondents. In case of any family it is true that not all decisions taken by the family are major in nature. But at times when the family is to take a serious decision having significant implications for consequences the task is given to some particular member or members. Such decisions may include the questions related to the family economy, marriage of the children, or religious observances etc. In the patriarchal family the male head of the family or the father is entrusted with the power of taking major decisions. In recent years however, in some cases the major decisions are taken by all the neighbour of the family together. In other words, it is a collective process of decision-making. The person behind the emergence of collective process appears to be the increase in employment of women etc. In this study 22.41 per cent of the respondents said that major decisions being taken in their families by their father-in-laws, 13.10 per cent reported that the major decisions being taken by their mother-in-laws, 50.00 per cent of the respondents informed that the major decisions being taken by their husbands and 14.48 per cent informed that the collective process of decisions making *i.e.*, decisions of all family members were practiced in this families.

Table 6.4: Education and Question No. 45

Response/Education	*Mother-in-law*	*Father-in-law*	*Husband*	*All member together*	*Total*
Illiterate	23.74	15.82	47.48	12.94	47.93
Literate	17.97	4.98	58.42	14.07	30.68
Less than Matriculate	28.57	11.90	42.85	16.66	14.48
Matriculate and above	20.00	15.00	40.00	20.00	06.89
Total	**22.41**	**13.10**	**50.00**	**14.48**	**290 (100.00)**

The respondents were also asked whether their opinion were sought while a decisions is taken in their families. Normally in our society the women are not always consulted while taking any decision by the family. If we look at the rural society we find that the males often considered it derogatory to act according to the opinion of their wives. Even those who are dominate by their wives or considered it prudent to consult their wives while taking any decision he situate to disclose it before others. In urban areas also this is true to a great extent. In some cases however, the women are sufficiently educated enlightened and holding responsible positions capable enough to enforce their opinion or to give necessary advice while any decision is taken by the males and the women are treated as equal partners. They are very often consulted while the decision are taking in their families. Particularly, the educated women in larger numbers participated in decision-making process in their families. In the present study 45.17 per cent of total respondents including 65.00 per cent of the matriculates and above said that their opinion were sought while the decisions were taken, 19.31 per cent give negative replies. And 35.51 per cent said that though their opinions were not sought on all occasions but at times they were asked to give their opinion in certain issues.

Table 6.5: Education and Question No. 46

Response/Education	*Yes*	*No*	*At times*	*Total*
Illiterate	37.41	23.74	38.84	47.93
Literate	42.69	20.22	37.07	30.68
Less than Matriculate	66.66	11.90	21.42	14.48
Matriculate and above	65.00	—	35.00	06.89
Total	**45.17**	**19.21**	**35.51**	**290 (100.00)**

At the next place the respondents were asked whether they thought that the opinion of female members should be given equal consideration with male members while the family decision was taken. In case of illiterate respondents include in this study 40.28 per cent were undecided, 34.53 per cent were in favour of it and 25.17 per cent did not think it as necessary. Among the literates, the percentage of 'yes', 'no' and 'undecided' answers were 50.56 per cent, 39.32 per cent and 10.11 per cent respectively. 59.52 per cent of those who were less than matriculates were in favour of giving equal consideration to the opinion of the female members, 28.57 per cent gave negative replies. 10.00 per cent gave negative and 25.00 per cent were undecided. Out of total respondents 45.17 per cent opposed to the idea of equal consideration and 28.27 per cent were undecided.

Table 6.6: Education and Question No. 47

Response/Education	*Yes*	*No*	*Undecided*	*Total*
Illiterate	34.53	25.17	40.28	47.93
Literate	50.56	29.33	10.11	30.68
Less than Matriculate	59.52	11.90	28.57	14.48
Matriculate and above	65.00	10.00	25.00	06.89
Total	**45.17**	**26.55**	**28.27**	**290 (100.00)**

There is a common belief that the working women enjoy more significant status in their families than those who are not working. The working women are assets for their families and the husbands take more care of their working wives and treat them more respectfully. Consequently their opinions are given more consideration than that of non-working women in their family while making a decision. In this study the respondents were asked whether they agreed with the view that in most cases the opinion of working women was given more considerations while making a decision than that of non-working women in their families. In reply to these questions, out of the total respondents who were service holders, 30.00 per cent agreed with the view, 50.00 per cent disagreed and 20.00 per cent were undecided. Among the respondents who were engaged in business or petty trading 50.00 per cent, 41.86 per cent disagreed and 20.00 per cent were undecided. Among the respondents who were engaged in business or petty trading 50.00 per cent, 41.86 per cent and 8.13 gave 'yes', 'no' and 'don't know' answers. In case of manual labourers 40.65 per cent agreed with the view but 40.65 per cent did not accept it, 18.68 per cent were undecided. Among these respondents who were not earning 56.98 per cent agreed with the view could not give any specific answer. The analysis of the data, therefore revealed that the women as a whole, whether earning or non-earning did not necessarily believed that the opinion of working women was given more consideration whole making any decision. In the overall analysis it was found that 47.92 per cent of the total respondents believed that the opinion of the working women are given more weight age than that of the non-working women, 38.96 per cent did not accept the view and 13.10 per cent were unable to give any specific reply.

Table 6.7: Occupation and Question No. 48

Response/Occupation	*Yes*	*No*	*Don't Know*	*Total*
Service	30.00	50.00	20.00	06.89
Business	50.00	41.86	8.13	29.65
Manual Labour	40.65	40.65	18.68	31.37
Not earning	56.98	32.25	10.75	32.07
Total	**47.94**	**38.96**	**13.10**	**290 (100.00)**

Though apparently the women either educated or uneducated or working and non-working do not figure as the principal decision-makers of their families. They exercise equal significant influence on the decision-making through their husbands. In most cases opinion of the female members prevail in decision-making because the male act necessary according to the advice of their female counterpart. Infact their position is like that of a back seat driver of a vehicle. This is however, not true only in case of the Santhal families but this found in almost all the societies whether urban, rural or tribal. Women experts their opinion on the decisions taken by the family not directly but of course indirectly through the male members over who they exercise control. In the present study the respondents were asked whether they accepted it as correct. In reply, 49.31 per cent of the total respondents which included 40.00 per cent of the service holders 46.51 per cent of those who were engaged in petty trading or business, 58.24 per cent of the manual labourers and 45.16 per cent

Table 6.8: Occupation and Question No. 49

Response/Occupation	*Yes*	*No*	*Don't Know*	*Total*
Service	40.00	35.00	25.00	06.89
Business	46.51	43.00	10.46	29.65
Maual Labour	58.24	41.75	—	31.37
Not earning	45.16	40.86	13.97	32.06
Total	**49.31**	**41.37**	**09.31**	**290 (100.00)**

of those who were not earning accept it as correct. The analysis therefore clearly pointed that in majority of the cases women, either earning or non-earning, exercise their control over their husband as well as other members of the family. In other words, they are the real conscience keepers, 41.37 per cent of the total respondents however, did not accept the idea as correct, 9.31 per cent were unable to give any specific reply.

Women all over the world are subjected to the male domination. In many few cases they are given freedom to take decisions on matters related to their personal lives. From time to time society relaxes its grip over the women and that is generally followed by the socio-economic changes. Since the beginning of the industrialization society in different parts of the world have witnessed. The gradual emancipation of the women from the drackanian laws of ethics and morality of the medieval era. But still the masculine instinct of possessiveness and jealousy are still persisting and the women are treated as commodities, possessed by their husbands. The position of women in respect of freedom differs in the different types of society having three district type of economy, namely industrial feudal or agricultural and the tribal. So far as the industrial societies are concerned people are more realistic in their attitude because of the impact of science and technology and as a result the women in these societies enjoys more freedom than the feudal societies which are characterized by orthodox belief and norms. In tribal societies as said earlier the women enjoy a position of equality with men because of their economic potentiality as working partners of their husbands. As such, it is expected that they should enjoy more freedom to take decisions on matters relating to their private lives. In this study 45.17 per cent of the total respondents including 61.90 per cent of the non-matriculate and 60.00 per cent of the matriculate and above were of the view that women should be given freedom to take decisions in matters related to their personal lives. 29.13 per cent were opposed to this idea and 25.51 per cent were undecided.

Table 6.9: Education and Question No. 50

Response/Education	*Yes*	*No*	*Don't Know*	*Total*
Illiterate	35.25	27.33	37.41	47.93
Literate	49.43	34.83	15.73	30.68
Less than Matriculate	61.90	26.19	11.90	14.48
Matriculate and above	60.00	25.00	15.00	06.89
Total	**45.17**	**29.21**	**25.51**	**290 (100.00)**

The respondents were also asked whether it was correct to saw that in most cases the female members are reluctant to take part in decision-making. It often happens that the women if they are asked to express their opinion regarding matters of significance for the family they remain non-committal. Because of the responsibility involved in the process of decision-making. They generally leave it to the elderly male members of the family. In this study 52.06 per cent including 55.39 per cent of the illiterates, 49.43 per cent of the literates, 52.38 per cent of the non-matriculates and 40.00 per cent of the matriculates and above agreed with the view, 36.20 per cent expressed their disagreement and 11.72 per cent could not give any specific answer

Table 6.10: Education and Question No. 51

Response/Education	*Yes*	*No*	*Don't Know*	*Total*
Illiterate	55.39	32.37	12.23	47.93
Literate	49.43	41.57	08.98	30.68
Less than Matriculate	52.38	35.71	11.90	14.48
Matriculate and above	40.00	40.00	20.00	06.89
Total	**52.06**	**36.20**	**11.72**	**290 (100.00)**

Females in most cases are threatened as inferior creatures by the men. Though, it is purely based on the male idiosyncrasy. The women are not supposed to have high level of intellect and incapable of taking any serious decisions. This is one of the reasons why the males don't consider the opinion of females in the process of decision-making. In tribal societies also this idea prevails and as such the women are excluded from taking part as members of the village council as well as in the process of decision-making. But this view is not accepted by women in general. In this study the respondents were asked how far they did agree with the view that female were capable of taking any serious decision as considered by the males. In reply to this question 45.51 per cent of the respondents including 58.33 per cent in the age group of below 35 years and 35.55 per cent who were between 35 to 40 years of age, expressed their disagreement with the view, 37.58 per cent however considered the view of correct. In that case percentage of the elderly respondent was definitely higher than those belong to the lower age groups, 16.89 per cent were undecided.

Table 6.11: Age and Question No. 52

Response/Age	*Agree*	*Disagree*	*Undecided*	*Total*
Below 35 years	29.16	58.33	12.50	08.27
35 to 40 years	26.66	55.55	17.77	15.15
40 to 45 years	33.33	40.00	26.66	20.68
45 to 50 years	41.89	44.77	13.43	23.10
Above 50 years	44.68	41.48	13.82	32.41
Total	**37.58**	**45.51**	**16.89**	**290 (100.00)**

In the next question the respondents were asked whether they are agreed with the view of that acceptance of decision taken by the male members of the family had become a matter of habit for the women members. This is a psychological phenomenon. The persistence of the male dominance for a very long period of the time has made the women to accept the superiority of the males. That is more a matter of habit than conscious acceptance. This also shows the impact of custom or tradition on the process of thinking of individuals. In present study 57.58 per cent of the respondents including 50.00 per cent, 48.88 per cent, 60.00 per cent, 64.57 per cent and 57.44 per cent of the respondents in the different age groups respectively expressed their agreement with the view, 27.93 per cent however disagreed and 14.48 per cent were undecided.

Table 6.12: Age and Question No. 53

Response/Age	*Agree*	*Disagree*	*Undecided*	*Total*
Below 35 years	50.00	33.33	16.66	08.27
35 to 40 years	48.88	40.00	11.11	15.15
40 to 45 years	60.00	33.33	16.66	20.68
45 to 50 years	64.17	22.38	13.43	23.10
Above 50 years	57.44	27.65	14.89	32.41
Total	**57.58**	27.93	**14.48**	**290 (100.00)**

The trend of modernization however has created some of change in the families and in modern household women are increasingly participating in decision-making compare to the traditional homes.

The women in modern home are generally more educated and possess self-confidence than the women of traditional homes. Moreover, as said earlier, the concept of husband domination over the wives is gradually replaced by a concept of equal partnership between husband and wife.

Table 6.13: Education and Question No. 54

Response/Education	*Yes*	*No*	*Undecided*	*Total*
Illiterate	54.67	34.53	10.89	47.93
Literate	49.43	37.07	13.48	30.68
·Less than Matriculate	47.61	28.57	23.80	14.48
Matriculate and above	60.00	15.00	25.00	06.89
Total	**52.41**	**33.10**	**14.48**	**290 (100.00)**

Further, it can be pointed out that in modern homes the collective process of decision-making in which all members of the family capable of taking any decision is being more popular than the old process of decision-making only by elderly male members. In the present study 60.34 per cent accepted that in modern households women were increasingly participating in decision-making compared to the traditional homes, 37.58 per cent did not accept the view and 12.06 per cent were undecided.

Table 6.14: Education and Question No. 55

Response/Education	*Yes*	*No*	*Undecided*	*Total*
Illiterate	50.35	37.41	12.23	47.93
Literate	51.68	37.07	11.23	30.68
Less than Matriculate	47.61	33.33	19.04	14.48
Matriculate and above	50.00	50.00	—	06.89
Total	**5.34**	**37.58**	**12.06**	**290 (100.00)**

57.58 per cent of the respondents including 50.00 per cent of the service holders, 60.81 per cent of the women engaged in business, 62.63 per cent of the manual labourers and 55.91 per cent of the women who were not earning reported that they were participating in decision-making about the family budget of course, in most cases, the Santhal families are poor and they could not have a balanced budget for the family. But still as in case of other people, they too had certain priorities, which were to be given more consideration than the other items. In that case the women were better persons than the men to take a decision. Moreover, analysis of the data pointed out that in matters related to family particularly the crucial matters like budget making the women were not discarded by the males. Their opinion was given proper consideration.

Table 6.15: Occupation and Question No. 56

Response/Occupation	*Yes*	*No*	*Don't Always*	*Total*
Service	50.00	25.00	25.00	06.89
Business	55.81	10.46	33.72	29.65
Maual Labour	62.63	10.98	26.37	31.37
Not earning	55.91	14.28	30.76	32.06
Total	**57.58**	**12.75**	**29.65**	**290 (100.00)**

Regarding the family property 52.06 per cent of the respondents said that they were participating in making decisions. 20.34 per cent gave negative answers and 27.58 per cent of the respondents said that though they were not participating in making decisions regarding family property all the times but sometimes they used to be involved in it. Thus, it can be said that the decisions regarding the family matters like family budget or property were not solely taken by males. The females are also allowed to participate in different process of decision-making.

Table 6.16: Occupation and Question No. 57

Response/Occupation	*Yes*	*No*	*Don't Always*	*Total*
Service	40.00	30.00	30.00	06.89
Business	48.83	27.90	33.25	29.65
Maual Labour	57.14	09.89	32.96	31.37
Not earning	52.68	21.50	25.80	32.06
Total	**52.06**	**20.34**	**27.58**	**290 (100.00)**

Marriage is an essential part of the family institute. The Santhal have elaborate form of marriage ceremonies. Though the young boys and girls are allows sexual freedom to a great extent compared to a non-tribal society the marriage is solemnized on the basis of socio-religious rites. And after marriage the women and also the male are supposed to remain faithful to each other. Extra marital sex is not supported by the society. The marriages are not also self-selected. They are arranged after a good deal of negotiations between the families of the bride and the bridegroom. In this study the respondents were asked whether in majority of the households the mothers had a grater say in the matter related to their children. In reply, 41.72 per cent of the respondents gave affirmative replies, 43.44 per cent gave negative replies and 14.82 per cent were undecided.

Table 6.17: Occupation and Question No. 58

Response/Occupation	*Yes*	*No*	*Don't Always*	*Total*
Service	30.00	45.00	25.00	06.89
Business	44.18	44.18	11.62	29.65
Manual Labour	35.15	50.54	14.28	31.37
Not earning	48.38	35.48	16.12	32.06
Total	**41.72**	**43.44**	**14.82**	**290 (100.00)**

In the next question the respondents were asked who took decisions about the marriage of the children. In reply, 19.31 per cent of the respondents mentioned the father of the children as the person who was taking the decision 14.82 per cent reported that the mother of the children was taking the decision. But the larges number that is 41.37 per cent said that the elderly members of the family has the privilege of negotiating marriages of their children. The remaining 24.48 per cent said that the decision was being taken by all the members collectively.

Table 6.18: Occupation and Question No. 59

Response/Occupation	*Father*	*Mother*	*Elderly members*	*All together*	*Total*
Service	20.00	15.00	50.00	15.00	06.89
Business	25.38	16.27	44.18	13.95	29.65
Manual Labour	15.38	13.18	41.75	29.67	31.37
Not earning	17.20	15.05	36.55	31.18	32.06
Total	**19.31**	**14.82**	**41.37**	**24.48**	**290(100.00)**

In the following the respondents were asked about the person in the family playing the major role in decision-making in matters related to the religious aspects of the family. This was quite significant because the tribal families are run according to various religious norm. In other words, like the non-tribal societies of our country, in tribal society also religious aspects terms a major part of family life. In reply to the question 40.68 per cent said that the privilege of decision-making was with the male members. 25.17 per cent named the female and 34.13 per cent reported that male and female together took the decisions.

Table 6.19: Education and Question No. 60

Response/Education	*Male*	*Female*	*Both*	*Total*
Illiterate	42.44	26.61	30.93	47.93
Literate	41.57	28.08	30.33	30.68
Less than Matriculate	38.09	16.66	45.23	14.48
Matriculate and above	30.00	20.00	50.00	06.89
Total	**40.68**	**25.17**	**34.13**	**289 (100.00)**

Since the independence of the country and an introduction of adult franchise the women in tribal society along with the males have been given the right to vote generally it is believed that the women seldom exercise their discretion, while casting their votes in favour of any party or candidate. They are supported to abide by the decision taken by the male folk of their community. In this study, it was found that though majority of the respondents *i.e.,* 56.65 per cent admitted that they were not taking any independent decision about to right of franchise at the time of election, 40.34 per cent expressed an opposite view, they said that the women used to take independent decisions, while exercising their right to franchise.

Table 6.20: Education and Question No. 61

Response/Education	*Yes*	*No*	*Total*
Illiterate	33.81	66.18	47.93
Literate	39.32	60.67	30.68
Less than Matriculate	47.61	52.38	14.48
Matriculate and above	75.00	25.00	06.89
Total	**40.34**	**59.65**	**290 (100.00)**

The following was about the participation of daughter-in-law in decision-making in her law's family. They were asked in case they had a daughter-in-law, would they like her to participate equally with their members in decision-making in their families. In reply 36.20 per cent said 'yes' 43.10 said 'No' and 20.68 per cent were undecided.

Table 6.21: Age and Question No. 62

Response/Age	*Yes*	*No*	*Undecided*	*Total*
Below 35 years	50.00	16.66	33.33	08.27
35 to 40 years	04.00	40.00	20.00	15.15
40 to 45 years	48.33	38.33	13.33	20.68
45 to 50 years	20.89	56.22	23.88	23.10
Above 50 years	34.04	45.74	20.21	32.41
Total	**36.20**	**43.10**	**20.66**	**290 (100.00)**

Lastly, they were asked about the possible barrier to the participation of women in decision-making. In reply, 38.27 per cent of the respondents mentioned the traditional norm of male dominance in their community, 17.58 per cent mentioned reluctance of women for fear of being criticized, 13.10 per cent mentioned incapability on the part of women to take serious decisions and 11.03 per cent considered the tendency of avoiding responsibility by the women as the possible barrier to the participation of women in decision-making process.

Table 6.22: Age and Question No. 62

Response/Age	*(a)*	*(b)*	*(c)*	*(d)*	*Total*
Below 35 years	41.66	25.00	12.50	20.83	08.27
35 to 40 years	10.00	17.77	08.88	33.33	15 11
40 to 45 years	33.33	21.66	11.66	33.33	20.68
45 to 50 years	41.89	13.43	08.95	35.82	23.10
Above 50 years	37.25	15.95	19.14	27.65	32.41
Total	**38.27**	**17.58**	**13.10**	**11.03**	**290 (100.00)**

(a) Traditional norm of male dominance.
(b) Reluctance of women for fear of being criticised.

(c) Incapability of taking serious decisions.
(d) Avoidance of responsibility.

Thus, in decision-making process by Santhal revealed that the majority of respondents are putting in on an average of 8 to 12 hours of work/day. Women attended activities like cooking, fetching water, washing clothes, upkeep of house, collecting fire-wood, collection of vegetables and fruits from forest, caring children, agriculture, feeding animals, preparation of rice beer, and social visits. Average workload (hour/day) of respondents hovered around 12 hours/day. There are minor variations in workload across districts of Santhal Parganas. As regards exchange labour, majority of respondents reported that there is a need for it. On an average 4.5 days of advance notice is required for getting such labour. Factors like number of Jhum plots, number of animals, years of schooling, and index of awareness are found to be positive and significant. Decision-making in important activities is by husbands, while decision associated with responsibility and duties of use value are left to women. There is a positive change among younger generations and they are actively participating in making variety of decisions.

REFERENCES

Cooper, Joseph, D.: *The Art of Decision Making,* Double Day and Co. Inc., 1961.

Cella Van Sackle: *Consumer Use and Purchase of Furniture in Flint,* Michigan, 1951, p. 4.

Dewer, John and Tuffs James, H.: *Ethic,* Macmillan, New York, 1938, p. 303.

Diesing, Paul: *Reason in Society, Five Types of Decision and Their Social Conditions,* Urbena, Illinois, 1962, p. 108.

Dowey, John: *How You Think,* D.C. Health and Co., New York, 1910, p. 8.

East Lensing: Conceptual frame works, Process in Home Management, Home Management Conference, Washington, 1964.

Elizabeth H. Wolgest: Consumer De Husbands or Wives make the purchasing decisions, *Journal of Marketing,* Vol. 23, No. 2, pp. 151–58.

Harry Sharp and Paul: Consumer Decision in the Metropolitan Family, *Journal of Marketing,* Vol. 23, No. 2, pp. 1 149–156.

Hebert, A. Simon: *Administrative Behaviour,* New York, Macmillan, 1961, p. 88.

Herbert, A. Simon: *New Science of Management Decision,* New York, Harper and Row, 1960, p. 2.

Honey, R. *et al.*: *Decision Making in the Use of Family, Financial Resources*, 1939, pp. 5–6.

Irma, H. Grass and Elizabeth, W. Crandell: *Management for Modern Families*, Appleton Century Crafts, New York, 1963, p. 63.

Kekel, W.F.: *Influence of Differentiation in Family Decision Making Sociology and Social Research,* Vol. 42. No. 1. (Sept-Oct.).

Michael Zunich: Teenagers Influence on Personal and Family Purchases, *Journal of Home Management,* Vol. 58, No. 6. June, 1966, p. 483.

Nickell, P. and Dorsey, J.M.: *Management in Family Living,* Walley Eastern Ltd., New Delhi, 1967, pp. 60–76.

Orville, C. Brim: *Personality and Decision Processes,* Stanford University Press, California, 1962, pp. 10–11, 12

Overstreet, H.A.: *The Mature Mind,* W.W. Norion and Co., New York, 1949, p. 64

Reuben Hill: Judgment and Consumership in the Management of Family. *Resources, Sociology, and Social Research,* Vol. 47, No. 4, (July 1963) pp. 446–60.

Schlesinger, Benjamin.: A Survey of Methods Uses to Study Decision Making. In the Family, *The Family Life Coordinator,* Vol. 11, No. 1, Jan. 1962, pp. 8–14.

Theodere, B. Hohannis: Teenager perception of Family Decision Making, *The Family Life Co-ordinator,* Vol. 4, pp. 70–74.

Theordore: *Op. cit.* pp. 59–60.

Zimmermen, Gerepon: Kids and Money. *Look,* Nov. 2, 1965, p. 49.

7

Women and Leisure Time Management

At the present time there is no more confused or confusing term in common usage that of "leisure". Leisure should be life, declares Novelist John Horsey but August Heckscher has said that "leisure" means time off from the job. Heckscher refers to time and means hearsey to activities and ends, and usage to the term tends to polaries at either recreation or "free time" but as noted a qualitative distinction is also sometimes drawn. The term can refer to an informed "use of free time and when the notion of creative leisure is employed all distinction between work and free times becomes blood. In any event, either activity, free time or creativity is meant, leisure by no one who uses the term refers to unemployment, under employment or forced retirement. Whatever all leisure may mean the term refers to a condition that is for the most part voluntarily.

Leisure time is an important part of the total pattern of living as the time studies reported. In his study of time, work and leisure, Edgrazia, divided 24 hours a day into four categories of time: work related, work, subsistance and free time. Subsistence time include sleeping, eating, cooking, shopping, health care, housework and maintenance. Free or leisure time usually considered as time free from the demands of work or duty and the activities of leisure are those are done for their own sake. In discussing the family function of consuming and recreation Vinsaint point out: It is quiet possible (but almost impossible to measure) that today's family spent for more time not only but also in producing own recreation than the family of 50 or 100 years age.

The way in which the individual or families spent their leisure time shows a variety of leisure activities. These activities has been classified in a number of different ways by various writers. According to Kapplan, they can be categorized as: (i) sociability including social activities, feasts, conversations, visiting friends, (ii) Association: religious activities, community meetings, hobbies etc. (iii) Games and sports including spectator, sports active sports, other games, playing cards etc. (iv) Art including artistic activity, attending musical concerts, watching drama or theatre, music and dancing, (v) mobility, including travel in car and bus, boat trips walking, shopping trips etc., and (vi) immobility, including resting, or adding, radio, television etc.

Recreation policy is determined in part by age, occupation, income and amount of leisure time available. Plan that included a variety of leisure time activity helps come to enjoy and develop new interests, skills and abilities.

In his book "Sociology": Themes and Perspectives, Michel Heralambos writes, "ever since Adam and Eve were expelled from the Garden of Eden, Man has had to work for his deliberate. As a part of the punishment for original sin he must earn his living by sweat of his brow. Any time left over from his daily toil may be sent in leisure but leisure must first be earned.

A variation of the Christian theme was provided by Calvinists in the 17th Century Europe. They show work as religious calling to be pursued with single minded determination. Success of work meant that the individual had not lost grace and fovour in the sight of the Lord. Leisure as normally defined by the standards of the day, way attacked as free volcus and time wasting, drinking, dancing, going to the theatre, recreation and sports, gossip and the pleasures of the flash were condemned.

In traditional black American sub-culture the work is defined at best as an unfortunate necessity. Life, in the title of a song by the Joys is "Living for the weakened, work heging on Blue Money" where barks in low income gnetto areas have "Blue Monday" parties to cheer people up after the worst day of the week.

The three views briefly described above are based on attitudes towards on evaluation of work and leisure. They are not objective view, they are not neutral observations. Many, if not all of the views of nocioulogists on work and leisure have a similar basis. They are influenced by the particular sociologists beliefs about what work and leisure ought to be like. They are coloured by his evaluation of the work and leisure, activities. In fact sociologists who are strongly committed to an idol of work and leisure often produced the most interest the most interesting and influential view on the subjects.

Stanley, Parker, argues that "leisure activities are conditioned by various factors associated with the people's work. In particular, he suggests that the amount of freedom to take decisions and organize their work, the degree of involvement they find in work and their levels of intrinsic job satisfaction are directly related to the leisure activities. He sees the relationship between work and leisure falling into these main patterns: the extension pattern, the neutrality pattern and the opposition pattern.

In the extension pattern work extend in leisure. There is no clear dividing line between the two. Activities in both spheres are similar, and work is central life interests rather than family and religion. Time for activities, which can be defined exclusively as leisure is short and is used mainly for the development of personality.

In the neutrality pattern a fairly clear distinction is made between work and leisure. Activities in the two spheres different family and leisure rather than work, form the central life interests. This pattern is associated with occupations providing a medium to low degree of autonomy, which required the use of only some of the individuals abilities and where satisfactions is with pay and conditions rather than work. Leisure is often family centered.

In the opposition pattern work is sharply distinguish from leisure. Activities in the two areas are very different and leisure forms the central life interests. The pattern is associated with the low degree of autonomy which require the use of only a limited range of abilities and which often produce a feeling of hostility towards work. Hours of leisure are long and used mainly to compensate from work. The opposition pattern is typical by of unskilled manual work and mining.

In the present study it was found that Santhals because of the remoteness of their habitation, absence of the proper means of communication, their love for cultural traditions, the leisure time activities of these people are centered round the traditional folk songs and dances. The penetration of electronic media has not yet taken place. Television is yet to replace their traditional leisure time activities of course in some of the households the transistors, radios and television are found in some cases the tribals are shown films by the public relation department of the government. Sometimes back the improvement organize the "Modmandialies" to visit the tribal villages in order to provide them with healthy recreation, but they have not been very effective.

The fairs and markets known as hatias also provides some relaxation to the tribal people. One of the most important fairs is the "Hajla Mela" of Deoghar. The staff from All India Radio, Bhagalpur Ranchi, Patna and Darbhanga stage emateur plays in the mela which are educative cum recreational in nature. But in most cases the leisure time activities of the people centered round the songs and dances in which the members of both section of the people participated.

It is however, necessary to point out the place that the film songs particularly made a dent in the traditional pattern of their leisure time activities. Many of the Santhals boys and girls are very found of films and they particularly those from the adjoining areas of the cities often go to the cinema halls in cities for recreation.

Hunting can also be said to be one of the foremost leisure time activities and so also in the fishing. The Santhal boys knows and very expert in playing on flutes. In many cases they are found carrying flutes all the times and whenever they go.

The dance, says Curt Sacha, author of the monumental work "History of Dance" is the mother of the arts. Music and poetry exist in time, painting and architecture in space. But the dance lives at once lives in time and space. "The tribals are poor and economically backward. Even though they may have no instrument or materials for other arts, the rhythemic pattern of movement of the body can itself be a source of joy. Among Indian tribals there is little of graphic or plastic art they do not have tools for painting or sculptures. Nature has endowed him with a fine body. Music and poetry are in his soul.

Dance and song have an important role in the socialisation of the tribal child. Children sit between their father's knees their tiny hands strike the symbols and or mental keys are hold the drumsticks. It also seems that they absorb the rhythm and postured of the dance. There is appropriate music and dance for every occasion, birth and weddings, for purification, feasts for driving away diseases and demons.

An exploration of the hidden springs of music and dance in tribal life is rewarding. The tribals live, move and have their being among the sights and sounds of nature. The murmur of a forest streamlet, the sight of a water falls, peacocks playing its multicoloured feathers, a herd of goats or sheep grazing quietly, a bell thinking here and there, trees laden with flowers and fruits swell the spring of music. A tribal youth tending cattle in a lonely valley or on a hill top beguiles his solitude with melodies produced by the plate. Wherever he is, the tribal gives vent to this emotions of joy or sorrow without any inhibition. His feelings find an easy expression. They are spontaneous and charged with deep emotions. A moment of joy is enjoyed with complete abandon, an occasion of grief is full of poignancy. Music and dance mark these occasions and through them the tribal expresses himself. His numerous festivals and Jatras give him repeated opportunities for the display of music and dance for long periods. On these occasions there is free flow of the native tribal drink, a kind of home brewed been prepared from rice, mahua etc. Besides supplying many nutrients which the tribal looks in his diet, the drink act a stimulent and gives him so much energy that even a whole night's dancing does not tire him out. For the time being he forget all his troubles, economic and otherwise. He has no emotional tension, no mental reservations and the only restraints on his behaviour are those prescribed by the social code. Dance and song supplement each other. The full-throated melody and the equisetic foot work are vitally connected.

Songs give expression to the inner feelings and thoughts of human beings. Among all types of songs the folk-song represents the most natural style. The folk-songs are neither composed after a long deliberation nor are they attached to the name of any particular composer. They can be based on any incident or phenomenon.

The folk-songs of any county exposes the thought, feelings and emotion of the people as well as provides understandings of the history and culture of new experience. The folk-songs of our rural society are based on various objects and social problem *viz.* increasing price level, communal tensions, Gandhi's contribution to the freedom struggle, Satyagraha movement, Freedom movement, significance of khadi, price control, innovations and so on. The folk-songs are not confined to any age group. There are different songs meant for young boys and girls as well as for the ages and old people. However, the folk songs are not restricted to an professional groups. People belonging to different occupational groups, people belonging to different occupational castes and categories like the peasants, washerman, the pedestrians, the religious mendicants, the cattle grazers and also the beggars sing these songs. The folk-songs are also not restricted to a particular session. In the Indian villages there are some types of folk-songs which the people sing throughout the year, but along with these songs there are songs meant for specific periods of the year, *e.g.* songs of the rainy seasons. Peoples sing the folk-songs most enthusiastically during festivals and fairs like Holi, Deepawali or marriage ceremony etc. Life in villages is not so fact as we find in cities and in order to make their slowly moving life little colourful, the village women sing folk-songs along with their daily choices and chours. They sing melodious songs while grinding the corn, going to fetch drinking water while taking bath or brooming the courtyard of their houses and also at many other times. In this manner the folk-songs present a most vivid picture of the daily routine of the people. To explain and also present comments on the different types of behaviours of the people and different incidences of their lives. Through the medium of folk-song are the individual can express his reaction toward any act or phenomenon.

The folk-songs are closely related to folk life. Folk is the societal composite product of associational processes integrated in the cultural and real setting. Folk is the heart of society. It is the universal societal constant in a world of historical variables. The concept of folk many variables:

1. The folk as bearers of culture: While the folk connotes the people, the two terms are in no way synonymous. The people constitute the population in terms of the measurable units. The folk, on the other hand represent the composite essence of the mental and cultural interaction nearest to the primary associational level. The folk, at any time and in any place, approximate the product and process of the people in their associations interactions among each other and their interactional among each other and their interactions between their regional physical environment and their cultural development.

   Thus, as bearers of culture the folk represent a general term, applying to the mode of the people in any given area and time which conditions and determines the culture of people at that time. Illustrations are abundant in the history of civilization and culture reflecting situations in which within a single great civilization, it was peaceful to observe different folk societies within the major society. This is clearly the case in such great aggressive aggregate societies as those of India, Russia etc.

2. Folk as a substitute for race? This meaning of the folk as being the societal composite product of the associational processes in balance with regional, physical and cultural environment makes it the correct designation of an entity frequently miscalled "race".
3. The folk universal not primitive only? The chief value of this, general concept of the folk is to divorce it from the pure ethnological concept and the popular interpretation which made the folk synonymous with the primitive as only early society. This larger meaning is still accurate as applied to the literacy and technical use with reference to folklore, folk-songs and the like as distinguishing the unwritten and written culture.
4. The folk is contract to the state? This meaning of the folk and folk society is of importance further more in the definition of the state society and of the corresponding terms, stateway and technical ways which are in contradiction to the earlier accept organic folkways and norms.
5. Folk culture in contract to civilization? This concept of folk also provides base for the measurable distinction between the folk society as culture and civilization as the specialized culture of state-urban technological society. That is, culture represents the total processes, products and development, whereas civilization represents a special advanced cross-section of culture in the higher brackets of technological and organizational achievement.

In folk songs the singer represents the folk. Some sociologists, in course of their investigation of the primitive social thought consider proverbial literature as an authentic source but they should also take the folklore and folk-songs into considerations. In folk-songs one can witness the environment of the community life quite vividly. The folk-songs at times represents a particular class and on other occasions he presents the feelings of a particular community. The songs composed on village damsale or the married women do not describe the sorrows and joys of any particular girl or women but they expose the feelings of all the girls and women. This way the folk-songs are of eternal significance. The feelings or thought contained in folk-songs can be seen at any place or at any time. They are composed by anonymous or unknown comparers but in spite of their repetition from general to generation each singer folk the songs as his own composition. This is the speciality of the folk-songs.

The folk-songs not only tell us about the sacraments and rituals of the people, but also acquaint as with their moods and feelings. The folk-songs cover all the occasions of our lives from birth to death, but the folk-songs related to marriage ceremony are most poignant and full of entertainment. Indians being a religious people prefer to worship various Gods and Goddesses along with their every day activities. This has caused the composition of numerous folk-songs based on religion. These folk-songs based on religious ethos or mythology are very popular with the people living in villages. The religion practiced in villages resembles the primitive religion. Nature worship occupies a very significant position and thus there are numerous folk-songs related to rivers, mountains, trees and different animals.

The folk-songs are do not require much of training to sing. It can be sing quite easily. The singers do not necessarily know the intricacies of classical music but inspite of their ignorance the singers produce high melody at the time of singing. This is because of the fact that these songs are sung on certain occasions when the melody of the singers is affected by the emotionally charged situation.

Lucidity is another characteristic of folk-songs. These songs always providing recreation to the people. Ralph, S. Williams is of the opinion that the folk-songs are never old or new. Like a tree in the forest the roots are buried in the distant past but the branches spread with new leafs and fruits.

Folk-songs move from one place to another within a short period of time. The expedition is quick and defies the barriers of villages, cities or even states. Folk-songs of different languages bear similarities with each other and this is because of the expansion of the folk melodies to other places from the places of their origin.

Folk-songs are passed from generation to generation and along with their movement to different generations the folk-songs often change their forms. If any folk-songs relates to incident of the past, it may change its form in order to suit itself with similar incidents of the present time. For example, the folk-songs Tange Wale Tu Le Chal Resine Mujhe has changed into several forms like more Moula Bula Le Madine Mujhe or Lake Bula Le Madine Ise or Mere Shambhu Bula Lo Kailash Mujhe.

Lastly it should be pointed out that the folk singer represents the common people. Folk-songs are the manifestations of the culture of the people. The folk-songs manifest such feeling and sentiments as are universal in nature. The folk-songs of India, for instance, manifest our feelings as out of singer.

An analysis of the characteristics of folk-songs also throw light on their significance. The significances also have social, cultural and functional significance. Though the medium of folk-songs every new generation learns about the traditional ethics religion and ideal behaviour pattern. According to Fletcher Scout the folk-songs of any people race are more significant than their legal system.

Folk-songs are the mirrors of folk life. They manifest the different rituals, religious rites, beliefs and practices prevailing in the society. They provide the knowledge of folk behaviour. According to T.A. Matkin, if some one has knowledge about the folk-songs of any society it should be equivalent to knowing the society. Folk-songs therefore, are considered as rich treasures by sociologists, social psychologists and anthropologists.

The cultural significance of folk-songs is no less significant than their social significance. Folk-songs enrich the culture of a society. In the majority of cases the folk-songs are related to religion, worship religious faith and customs of the people on different occasions. These songs provide a glimpse of these cultural phenomena.

The folk-songs also have functional significance. They enrich the feelings of the people and also bring modifications. In rural society as well as among the tribal the folk-songs are used to make the people aware of certain social problems. In the words of Shyam Parsai, "song, music and drama are the manifestations of the folk mind". Folk-songs provide healthy recreation to the people and are capable of removing various unwanted feelings from their minds. They also encourage liberal ideas tolerance and sense of social service among the common people.

T.A. Lewin and E.C. Man sensed the importance played by poetry in Santhal life: There is a dash political feeling of in the composition of the Santhals which shows itself in their traditions. Their songs generally allude to birds and flowers and unlike the lyrics of their neighbours are remarkably free from obscenity. The tune also which they play on their flutes are often attempts at an limitation of the notes of birds or have a wild melancholy codence, which heard in the depths of the jungle, sounds pleasing to the ear. The following is the song of a love-sick girl:

The osprey's voice is heard on the mountain
Then the people's feel pity
Oh, mother, at midnight, the peacock's tail
Can be seen on the top of the hills and
In the valley,
My brother observes the white flower
Upon the dried up tree
The parrot has her young ones
Oh, aunt, when will you dandle my children?
When will you, my aunt?
The cock crows in the morning
The turtle-dove hilds its must in the garden
Oh, my mother, come and see it
From the sleep sides of the mountain
I hear a pair of flutes
And below the valley
The beating of a drum.

This was not the only song than men accord. During a camp at Simra he attended a Santhal wedding and as a consequences passed a sleepless night. The full meeting of these song was not perhaps realized by men and it is also obvious that a whole category of Santhal Poetry—the Bir-soren or forest songs accepted him referring to a dash of political feeling in the composition of the Santhal, he had made a crucial point.

Majority of the Santhal songs are ancestral, but it is part of the vitality of Santhal poetry that new songs are sometimes made up on the spur of the moment. There is no special class or part singer or band and the songs are accordingly communal in origin and inspirations.

All Santhal songs whether 'forest' or 'village' have certain characteristics. Shyme is not employed and the form of the song, the length of the lines and indeed its whole structure is determined to a great extent by the tune or melody. Few song have more then 10 or 12 lines, any that are longer here usually a ritual purpose. In some cases the fourth line respects the record but more normally every line is different rhythm and imagery. In one important respect the use of unemployed unexplained symbols Santhal poetry is very close to that of the Ursons.

Among the dental 'rar' is a term used for melody and "ror" for the ordinary human speech or voice. The distinction between "ror" is, however, not very sharp because the letter is conceived as "a continuous" of the former as obvious from their aphorism—rorak tage rorak (melody is the prolongation of ordinary human speech). The Santhal divides the melodic sound into low and high (mots and nanha). The low pitched melody is mota rar and the high pitched melody is the nanha rar. Another onomatopoetic expression of the low pitched melody is "nere nere" and for the high pitched ones "naron naron or murun nurun". The Santhal do not however consider the sound of the percussion instruments melodic. They equate the sound with noise *i.e.* sade.

"Melody" forms the bais of Santhal, "seron" (song). The Santhals thus have a variety of seron (songs) associated either with rituals and festivals or with the dances that fellow the ritual celebrations. While classifying them oxroding to their nomenclature. Beeding gave a list of the Santhal songs forms. The folk-songs included in the list are Bapla (marriage songs), Bir (forest songs), Bente (songs containing traditional and similar matters some very old, Dorom (a hymn), Gam (songs in connection with a folk tale), Horo Nohoo (songs of planting paddy), Jharni (song sung by ojhas when practicing jhar), Jan (an incentation used by the witch finders), Mantar (a chant used by ojhas), Morna (a dirge further connected with dances), Beha (songs of the flower festivals), Bhinsar (songs sung at Bhinsar), Dahar (songs sungs at Dehar dancing), Dasse (song sung by the ojha's disciples when they go out for begging. Don (songs sung at Dhunger dance that are full of obsecue contents), Gilwari (sung at Gilwari dances), Humti jhike (songs sung at the jhike dance performed during the jatra festivals), Lagger (song sung at the large dance), Loboe (the same as dance), Binje (songs sung at Rinja dance) and Dehrae (songs sung during the sohras festivals).

The Santhals however do not consider the sound of drums as musical but non-musical. This observation of the Santhals also parallels the scientific character observation in relation to the sound quality of membranophone. As Jeans pointed out the vibrations of stretched membranous as in a drum usually show no simple relations between their frequencies, so the sound they omit are discordant musically. However, the case of stretched strings is totally different were the frequencies of vibrations stand in the simple ratio 1 : 2 and 3 : 4. Here in either case the harmonies are natural and hence concordant musically.

This study aimed at on the point investigation of the leisure time activation of the leisure time activities of the Santhal women in their villages and with this aim in view included several question the respondents were asked whether the women enjoyed the same amount of leisure time as the males. In reply to the question 64.48 per cent of the total respondents which included more than 62.00 per cent of the respondents in the different occupational categories gave negative replies which showed that the women were sharing more burden in running the household compared to the males, 35.51 per cent of the respondents however thought that women were enjoying same amount of leisure time as of the males.

Table 7.1: Occupation and Question No. 64

Response/Occupation	*Yes*	*No*	*Total*
Service	35.00	65.00	06.89
Business	30.23	69.76	29.65
Manual Labour	38.46	61.53	31.37
Not Earning	37.63	62.36	32.06
Total	**35.51**	**64.40**	**290 (100.00)**

In the following question they were asked whether they were getting time to take part in community activities outside their families.

In reply 55.51 per cent gave affirmative replies, 25.86 per cent gave negative replies and 18.62 per cent said that seldom they used to take part in such activities. The data, thus revealed that the women were in general very much enthusiastic about participating in community activities. Whatever little leisure was available to them they enjoyed it by taking part in community activity. Another significant features which came out of this analyzing was that educated among the women were less enthusiastic about those the women were less enthusiastic about those activities compared to the illiterates.

Table 7.2: Occupation and Question No. 65

Response/Occupation	*Yes*	*No*	*Seldom*	*Total*
Service	40.00	20.00	40.00	06.89
Business	55.81	25.58	18.60	29.65
Manual Labour	57.14	18.68	24.17	31.37
Not Earning	56.98	34.40	8.60	32.06
Total	**55.51**	**25.86**	**18.62**	**290 (100.00)**

Dancing being one of the major leisure time activities among the Santhal the respondent were asked whether they were taking part in dancing with other women of their villages? In reply, 51.03 per cent of the respondents which included 56.83 per cent of the illiterates, 55.05 per cent of the literates, 23.80 per cent of those who were less than matriculates and 50.00 per cent of the matriculates and above reported that they were taking part in dancing quite frequently, 33.44 per cent were taking part in frequently and the remaining 15.51 per cent informed that they were sometimes taking part in dancing with other women of their villages.

Table 7.3: Education and Question No. 66

Response/Education	*Frequently*	*In-frequently*	*Rarely*	*Total*
Illiterate	56.83	34.53	08.63	47.93
Literate	55.05	28.08	16.85	30.68
Less than Matriculate	23.00	33.33	42.85	44.48
Matriculate and above	50.00	50.00	—	06.89
Total	**51.03**	**33.44**	**15.51**	**290 (100.00)**

Like dancing gossiping is one of the favourite pastime of the women. The tribal women are not exception to this. Therefore, the respondents were asked whether they joined their neighbourhood during leisure time for gossip? In reply to this question 50.66 per cent of the total respondents including 53.23 per cent of the illiterates, 60.67 per cent of the literates, 33.33 per cent of those who were less than matriculates and 20.00 per cent of the matriculates and above informed that they used to join the women of their neighbourhood for gossip during the leisure time quite frequently, 39.65 per cent of the respondents said that they indulged in gossiping in frequently and remaining 9.65 per cent rarely joined other women for gossiping.

Table 7.4: Education and Question No. 67

Response/Education	*Frequently*	*In-frequently*	*Rarely*	*Total*
Illiterate	53.23	39.56	07.19	47.39
Literate	60.67	31.46	07.86	30.68
Less than Matriculate	33.33	54.76	11.90	14.48
Matriculate and above	53.00	45.00	30.00	06.89
Total	**50.68**	**39.65**	**9.65**	**290 (100.00)**

Another form of recreation for the tribal women is to visit places outside their village for a change. They sometimes visit their relations in other villages as well as the leisure places were important melas, are held. One of such males is the Hijla Mela of Dumka, the divisional headquarter, which is visited by thousands of Santhal men, as well as children. This mela is held during the month of February-March every year in a place adjoining the hill known as Hijla pahar. The respondents in this study were asked whether they are visiting places outside their villages for a change? In reply 52.75 per cent of the total respondents including 61.66 per cent in the age group of 40 to 45 years, 53.73 per cent in the age group of 45 to 50 years, 50.00 per cent in the age group of above 50 years and 37.30 per cent among those who were below 50 years of age said that they were visiting places outside of their villages occasionally for a change. 23.10 per cent reported that they use to visit places quite often and remaining 24.13 per cent reported that they were visiting places outside their villages quite rarely.

Table 7.5: Age and Question No. 68

Response/Age	*Quite often*	*Occasionally*	*Rarely*	*Total*
Below 35 years	20.83	37.50	41.66	08.27
35 to 40 years	17.77	53.33	28.88	15.51
40 to 45 years	23.33	61.66	15.00	20.68
45 to 50 years	23.88	53.73	22.38	23.10
Above 50 years	25.53	50.00	24.46	32.41
Total	**23.10**	**52.75**	**24.13**	**290 (100.00)**

In the following question which was an alternation of the previous question the respondents were asked whether their relatives or acquaintances visiting their places frequently. In reply 58.62 per cent said that those people were visiting rarely, 30.68 per cent informed that they were visiting infrequently and only 10.06 per cent said that they were receiving visitors quite frequently.

Table 7.6: Income and Question No. 69

Response/Income	*Frequently*	*In-frequently*	*Rarely*	*Total*
Less than 1000 P.M.	08.18	32.72	59.09	37.93
Rs. 1000 to 1500 P.M.	08.33	27.50	64.16	41.37
More than Rs. 1500 P.M.	20.00	33.33	46.66	20.68
Total	**10.68**	**30.68**	**58.62**	**290(100.00)**

The respondents were also asked whether they were visiting melas or hatias for recreation? In reply 54.40 per cent of the total respondents including 53.93 per cent of the illiterates, 60.67 per cent of the literates, 52.38 per cent of those who are less than matriculates

Table 7.7: Education and Question No. 70

Response/Education	*Yes*	*No*	*Sometimes*	*Total*
Illiterate	53.93	36.61	19.42	47.39
Literate	60.67	25.84	13.48	30.68
Less than Matriculate	52.38	28.57	19.04	14.48
Matriculate and above	35.00	40.00	25.00	06.89
Total	**54.48**	**27.58**	**17.93**	**290 (100.00)**

and 35.00 per cent of the matriculates and above reported that they were visiting melas or hatias for recreation, 27.56 per cent gave negative replies and 17.93 per cent said that they used to visit hatia and melas sometimes.

Among various forms of leisure time activities story telling, particularly by the elderly women to the young boys and girls is very significant to because by means of such stories the children are taught the feds and fabuls of their society. In this study 62.57 per cent of the respondents including 48.20 per cent of the illiterates, 55.05 per cent of the literates, 61.90 per cent of the matriculates and above reported that they were telling the stories to children or grand children, during the leisure time, 21.03 per cent replied in negative and 26.20 per cent reported that they were telling such stories sometimes.

Table 7.8: Age and Question No. 71

Response/Age	*Yes*	*No*	*Sometimes*	*Total*
Below 35 years	54.16	45.83	30.93	08.27
35 to 40 years	62.22	37.77	30.33	30.68
40 to 45 years	53.33	46.66	24.28	14.48
45 to 50 years	46.26	53.73	23.80	23.10
Above 50 years	46.80	53.19	—	32.41
Total	**51.03**	**48.96**	**26.20**	**290 (100.00)**

The activities of knitting falls completely under the domain of the women's activity. In this study the respondents were asked whether they had any taste of knitting during their leisure time. In reply 51.03 per cent of the total respondents including 54.46 per cent of those who were below 35 years, 60.22 per cent in the age group of

Table 7.9: Education and Question No. 72

Response/Education	*Yes*	*No*	*Sometimes*	*Total*
Illiterate	48.20	20.86	30.93	47.39
Literate	55.05	14.60	30.33	30.68
Less than Matriculate	61.90	23.80	14.28	14.48
Matriculate and above	55.00	45.00	—	06.89
Total	**52.75**	**21.03**	**26.20**	**290 (100.00)**

35 to 40 years 53.33 per cent in the age group of 40 to 45 years, 46.26 per cent in the age group of 45 to 50 years and 46.80 per cent of those above 50 years gave affirmative replies and 48.96 per cent were not having taste for knitting.

Asked about the functioning of Adult Education Centre in their locality 27.93 per cent reported the presence of such centre in their locality, 35.51 per cent said that no such center was functioning and 36.55 per cent could not give any specific answer.

Table 7.10: Source of Income of Family and Question No. 73

Response/Source	*Yes*	*No*	*Don't Know*	*Total*
Service	30.00	25.00	45.00	06.89
Business	30.23	41.86	27.90	29.65
Manual Labour	25.27	32.96	41.73	31.37
Agriculture	27.95	34.40	37.63	32.06
Total	**27.93**	**35.51**	**36.55**	**290 (100.00)**

The next question was meant only for those respondents who had the information about the adult education center in their localities. In this question they were asked whether the women of their villages were going their for learning something? In reply 27.16 per cent which included 50.00 per cent of the women who were service holders, 34.61 per cent of those who were engaged in small trading, 17.39 per cent of the manual labourers and 23.05 per cent of those who were having agriculture as the source of family income gave positive reply. 49.38 per cent of the total respondents in this category gave negative answers which included 50.00 per cent of the respondents among both the service holders and those who were

Table 7.11: Source of Income of Family and Question No. 74

Response/Source	*Yes*	*No*	*Don't Know*	*Total*
Service	50.00	50.00	—	70.40
Business	34.61	50.00	15.38	32.09
Manual Labour	17.39	39.13	43.47	28.39
Agriculture	23.07	57.69	19.23	32.09
Total	**27.16**	**49.38**	**23.45**	**290 (100.00)**

engaged in small trading 57.69 per cent of those who were dependent on agriculture and 39.13 per cent of the manual labourers, remaining 23.45 per cent could not give any specific answer.

Sometimes it is said that the educated women are not so laborious as the uneducated. There is a presumption that the educated women enjoy more leisure time than the illiterate or uneducated women. In this study the respondents were asked whether they thought that educated women enjoy more leisure in their lives than the uneducated or illiterates women. In reply 51.37 per cent including 56.11 per cent of the illiterates, 53.93 per cent of literates, 35.71 per cent of those who were less than matriculates and 40.00 per cent of the matriculates and above said 'yes' 33.79 per cent of the total respondents did not agree with the view and 14.82 per cent has no specific information.

Table 7.12: Education and Question No. 75

Response/Education	*Yes*	*No*	*Don't Know*	*Total*
Illiterate	56.11	11.65	12.23	47.39
Literate	53.93	31.46	14.60	30.68
Less than Matriculate	35.71	42.85	21.42	14.48
Matriculate and above	40.00	40.00	20.00	06.89
Total	**51.37**	**33.89**	**14.82**	**290 (100.00)**

Asked about their activities during leisure time 23.79 per cent of the total respondents reported and they work in kitchen garden. Among the Santhals kitchen garden is an important source of green vegetables for the family. At times they also earn some money by marketing the products of their kitchen garden, 23.44 per cent reported that they spend the leisure time in cleaning and washing. The Santhals are widely known for their clean living as well as artistic temperament. The huts in which they live are tidy and clean. Cleaning as well as washing is exclusively a female job and in this matter the Santhal women scales many others, 33.46 per cent reported that they were enjoying the leisure time in gossiping with other women and 19.31 per cent said that they were taking part in singing and dancing during their leisure time.

Table 7.13: Education and Question No. 76

Response/Education	*(i)*	*(ii)*	*(iii)*	*(iv)*	*Total*
Illiterate	25.89	28.05	30.21	15.82	47.39
Literate	22.47	20.22	37.07	20.22	30.68
Less than Matriculate	19.04	19.04	33.33	28.57	14.48
Matriculate and above	25.00	15.00	40.00	20.00	06.89
Total	**23.89**	**23.44**	**23.44**	**19.31**	**290 (100.00)**

(i) Work in kitchen garden;
(ii) Gossiping with other women;
(iii) Engaged in cleaning and washing;
(iv) Take part in singing and dancing.

In the next question the respondents were asked whether they agreed with the view that the women given more leisure indulge more in quarreling with other women. In reply to this question 43.44 per cent of the respondents agreed with the view. That showed that even the women admitted the frequent quarrels taking place among them 40.00 per cent of the respondents disagreed with the view and 16.55 per cent were undecided.

Table 7.14: Age and Question No. 77

Response/Age	*Agree*	*Disagree*	*Undecided*	*Total*
Below 35 years	29.16	50.00	20.83	08.27
35 to 40 years	44.44	35.55	20.00	15.15
40 to 45 years	43.33	36.66	20.00	20.68
45 to 50 years	50.74	35.84	13.43	23.10
Above 50 years	41.48	44.68	13.82	32.41
Total	**43.44**	**40.00**	**16.55**	**290 (100.00)**

Asked about the leisure time activities of women in recent time. The respondents answered the question, which is given in Table 7.15:

Table 7.15: Age and Question No. 78

Response/Age	*Yes*	*No*	*Don't known*	*Total*
Below 35 years	54.16	25.00	20.83	08.27
35 to 40 years	71.11	15.55	13.33	15.15
40 to 45 years	53.33	25.00	21.66	20.68
45 to 50 years	35.82	35.82	28.35	23.10
Above 50 years	37.23	44.68	18.08	32.41
Total	**46.89**	**32.41**	**20.68**	**290 (100.00)**

Further they were asked about the factors responsible for change. In reply 16.17 per cent of those respondents who believed that changes taking place in leisure time activities attributed the changes to growing education, 14.70 per cent mentioned female employment as the reason for change. According to 38.97 per cent the change were brought by the urban mode of recreation like cinema and 30.14 per cent attributed the changes by mass media like radio, T.V. etc.

Table 7.16: Age and Question No. 79

Response/Age	*(i)*	*(ii)*	*(iii)*	*(iv)*	*Total*
Below 35 years	15.38	—	61.53	23.07	09.55
35 to 40 years	15.62	15.62	37.50	31.25	23.52
40 to 45 years	18.75	21.87	31.25	28.12	23.52
45 to 50 years	20.83	16.66	33.33	29.16	17.64
Above 50 years	11.42	11.42	42.85	34.28	32.41
Total	**16.17**	**14.70**	**38.97**	**30.14**	**290(100.00)**

(i) Growing education;
(ii) Female employment;
(iii) Urban mode of recreation like cinema;
(iv) mass media like radio, T.V.

25.17 per cent respondents which included 33.33 per cent of those below 35 years and also the same percentage of in the age group of 35 to 40 years, 32.85 per cent in the age group of 40 to 45 years 17.02 per cent of the respondents who were above 50 years of age reported possessing radio or transistor sets. Remaining 74.82 per cent said that they had no radio, transistor in their possession.

Table 7.17: Age and Question No. 80

Response/Age	*Yes*	*No*	*Don't known*	*Total*
Below 35 years	33.33	66.66	—	08.27
35 to 40 years	33.33	66.66	—	15.15
40 to 45 years	20.00	80.00	—	20.68
45 to 50 years	32.85	67.14	—	23.10
Above 50 years	17.02	82.97	—	32.41
Total	**25.17**	**74.82**	—	**290 (100.00)**

Asked about the source of recreation they prefer most? 28.27 per cent of the respondents said that they prefer 'jatra' more than source of recreation, 31.37 per cent mentioned dance and 40.34 per cent preferred cinema as the best source of recreation. The overall analysis pointed out that 66.66 per cent in the age group of below 35 years, 51.11 per cent in the age group of 35 to 40 years, 40.00 per cent in the age group of 40 to 45, 4.29 per cent in the age group of 45 to 50 years mentioned cinema as the most preferred source of entertainment.

Table 7.18: Age and Question No. 81

Response/Age	*Jatra*	*Dance*	*Cinema*	*Total*
Below 35 years	08.33	24.99	66.66	08.27
35 to 40 years	17.77	21.11	51.11	15.15
40 to 45 years	26.66	83.33	40.00	20.68
45 to 50 years	25.37	34.32	04.29	23.10
Above 50 years	41.48	29.78	20.72	32.41
Total	**28.27**	**31.37**	**40.34**	**290 (100.00)**

The respondents were asked about the frequency of visiting the cinema shows. In reply only 15.51 per cent reported that they were visiting cinema shows gradually. In this category the highest percentage was of those who were below 35 years of age 32.41 per cent of the respondents said that they were visiting sometimes and 52.06 per cent said that they were visiting cinema shows rarely.

Table 7.19: Age and Question No. 82

Response/Age	*Frequently*	*Sometimes*	*Rarely*	*Total*
Below 35 years	33.33	41.66	25.00	08.27
35 to 40 years	22.22	42.22	35.55	15.15
40 to 45 years	20.00	26.66	53.33	20.68
45 to 50 years	07.44	26.59	65.95	32.41
Above 50 years	41.48	29.78	28.72	32.41
Total	**15.51**	**32.41**	**52.06**	**290 (100.00)**

In order to make further prove that the changing pattern of recreation the respondents were asked whether they fell that the composition of folk-songs in their society had been affected by the film songs. In reply 34.20 per cent gave affirmative replies, 31.72 per cent gave negative and 32.06 per cent said that they did not know anything about it.

Table 7.20: Education and Question No. 83

Response/Education	*Yes*	*No*	*Don't Know*	*Total*
Illiterate	25.17	32.37	42.44	47.39
Literate	37.07	33.70	29.21	30.68
Less than Matriculate	52.38	28.57	19.04	14.48
Matriculate and above	75.00	25.00	—	06.89
Total	**36.20**	**31.72**	**32.06**	**290 (100.00)**

In continuation to the previous question the respondents were asked whether they agreed with the view that the people had developed preference for the Hindi film songs than their traditional folk-songs. In reply 58.62 per cent expressed their agreement with their view, 31.37 per cent disagreed and 10.00 per cent were undecided.

Table 7.21: Occupation and Question No. 84

Response/Source	*Yes*	*No*	*Don't Know*	*Total*
Service	70.00	30.00	—	06.89
Business	58.13	34.88	06.97	29.65
Manual Labour	61.52	24.17	14.28	31.37
Agriculture	53.66	35.48	10.75	32.06
Total	**58.62**	**31.37**	**10.00**	**290 (100.00)**

In the last question regarding the leisure time activities the respondents were asked whether they agreed with the view that people belonging to the youngest generation were drifting away from the traditional pattern of leisure which is closely linked with their traditional culture. In reply 52.06 per cent expressed agreement, 33.79 per cent expressed disagreement and 14.13 per cent were undecided.

Table 7.22: Age and Question No. 85

Response/Age	*Agree*	*Disagree*	*Undecided*	*Total*
Below 35 years	70.83	29.16	—	08.27
35 to 40 years	61.22	26.66	11.11	15.15
40 to 45 years	60.00	26.66	13.33	20.68
45 to 50 years	44.77	35.82	19.40	23.10
Above 50 years	42.55	41.48	15.95	32.41
Total	**52.06**	**33.89**	**14.13**	**290 (100.00)**

REFERENCES

Archer, W.G.: *The Hill of Flutes,* George Allen and Unwin, London, 1966.

Bodding, P.O.: *Santhal Dictionary,* Vol. I, Oslo, Aschehoug and Co., 1929.

Bodding, P.O.: *Santhal Folk Tales,* Vol. I, Oslo, Aschehoug and Co., 1929.

Fairchild, M.P. *et al.*: *Dictionary of Sociology,* Little Field Adams and Co. Peterson, New Jersy, 1962.

Green, A.W.: *Sociology: An Analysis of Life in Modern Society,* Macgraw Hill Book Co., New York, 1964.

Grazia, Sebastian: Of Time, Work and Leisure, The 20th Century Fund, New York, 1963.

Heralambos, M.: *Sociology: Themes and Perspectives,* Oxford University, Press, Delhi, 1980.

Jeans, W.J.: *Science and Music,* The University Press, Cambridge, 1961.

Kapplan, Max: *Leisure in America: A Social Inquiry,* New York, Willey, 1960.

Liwen, T.H.: *The Wild Races of South-Eastern India,* 1867.

Man, E.G.: *Sonthalia and the Santhals,* London, 1966.

Mukherjee, R.N.: *Samajik Manav Shastra Ke Ruprekha,* Vivek Prakashan, Delhi, 1983.

Nickel, P. and Doursy, D.M.: *Management in Family Living,* 4th Edition, Walley Eastern Ltd., New Delhi, 1967.

Parker, S.: Work and Leisure in (Bulletin) Butturworth and Weir, 1970, in the *Sociology of Leisure*, George Allen and Unwin, London, 1976.

Parsad, Onkar, : *Santhal Music*, Inter-India Publicatios, New Delhi.

Sachidanand: Profiles of Trible Culture in Bihar, Firma K.L.M, Calcutta, 1965.

Vinsaint, C. E. ...Familia Spoumia: The Adaptive Function, *Journal of the Marriage and Family*, Vol. 28, No. 1, 1966.

8

Women, Energy and Food Management

Chemically human body, if analysed is found to contain carbon, nitrogen, hydrogen, oxygen, calcium, phosphorous, magnesium, sulphur, sodium, potassium, cobalt, molybdenum, selenium, most of organic compounds. Though present in minute quantities of trace iron, copper, cobalt, codine, flourine, zinc, manganato, molybdenum, solonium, iodine play essential role.

Inorganic compounds are hydrochloric acid, ammonia and salts, *e.g.*, calcium, phosphates in bones, sodium chloride in blood, urine and gastric juice, ammonia in urine etc.

Organic compounds are nitrogenous *e.g.* proteins and non-nitrogenous *e.g.*, carbohydrates and fats. These inorganic and organic compounds of which the body is built enter the body in the food that we eat. Foods are changed by the process of digestion into suitable forms which enter the blood stream and are carried to all the cells of the body.

All physical and mental work and work in connection with life process of circulation, respiration etc. is done at the expense of breaking down of the body. This is done by the process of Oxidation (slow burning) of the carious compounds available in the tissues. Thus heat and energy for all the work is produced. The simpler compounds such as water, carbondioxide and urea results from the process of oxidation and are removed from the body through the sweet expired air and urine. Thus the body is growing burning and repairing throughout life for which food, water and air are essential.

Health depends to a large extent on nutrition and on food. Food in fact is the most important single factors in connection with the attainment and maintenance of health. Every drop of water and blood in the body is conditioned by the food we eat and it is in blood in the body is conditioned by the food we eat and it is in blood that every tissue, every organ, every gland and indeed every function of the body fundamentally depends.

By food is meant any material taken into the system that serves to sustain normal bodily processes. It is a fallacy of our times to regard that anything and everything called food is good for health.

For any subsistence to be properly regarded as human food, it must be capable of supplying the body with the material needed for the repair of body tissues and maintenance of various function, while at sometime doing no harm to the body and in no way interfering with its activities. Food in order to replace the body, therefore must be food so in selecting food make sure first that it is really food. We must live on truly nutritious food and not on anything generally considered as food.

To be healthy and in good conditions it is imperative to eat natural, wholesome food making sure that the food supply is in proper proportion and of a character or quality suitable for protecting the body.

By natural food we mean food as provided by nature containing all the elements and not flavoured or doctored or devitalised by mass. No form of life can be supported wholly upon laboratory products and man is not exception to the fundamental law.

Natural food properly selected scientifically combined and judiciously administered has true remedial value and can cure disease by supplying the proper saline elements in food preserve the tissues from disorganisation and from purification. These vitalising minerals, salts and vitamins are vital to health; ward off disease and premature old age.

The degeneration of the human race has been brought about by the departure from its natural foods. The only basis of possible regeneration is a return of it.

It is undoubtedly of the human race has been brought about by the departure from its natural foods. The only basis of possible regeneration is a return of it.

It is undoubtedly true that our eating habits depend upon our economic status as well as the availability of foods. But it is economically and equally that beliefs, customs, traditions and prejudices influence our food habits much more than we realise. The general found belief of any community is a social product deeply extended and entrenched in the minds of the community and practiced almost alike a faith. These beliefs, therefore, significantly influence the nutritional status of these population groups and become a force to reckon with in any nutrition programme.

Sir Robert Mc Carrison, who was for many years Director of Research on Nutrition in India, may be said to have summed up his many experience in nutrition that had special reference to India this vast country with its many varieties of climate, food, physical types, habits, etc. The single factor in the acquisition and maintenance of good health is perfectly constituted food which consists particularly of milk, milk products, whole grain, cereals, nuts, fresh fruits and vegetables. These are called protective foods as they product you against disease and epidemics. He adds that most people do not get enough of protective food and their diet is therefore incomplete and results ultimately in diseases.

The Santhals suffers from a perennial shortage of food supply because of the nature of the soil, unscientific mode of cultivation, due to the small size of the holding, exploitation of the traders and middlemen, etc. This has caused the problem of malnutrition as well as undernutrition. Of course, these problems are not exclusive for the Santhals.

It is said that a large proportion of humanity lives on a starvation diet. It is equally true that food has never been more abundant or a greater variety of food been available to the man or women in the street.

There are just as many overfed people as there are underfed. The temptations are so great with delicacies available in your round. In fact, disease which are gaining ground now a days have their root in unwise indulgence, unwise distetics, individual feds and notions apart from outside factors which we have at times no control.

In the strictest sense of the term, undernutrition means insufficient food, while nutrition implies the wrong sort of food.

An undernourished individual will almost invariably be malnourished also, since he will not obtain enough of the various food constituents needed for health. On the other hand, an ill balanced diet may be sufficient in quantity and yet lead to malnutrition, because of its qualitative defects. In practices undernutrition and malnutrition is often used with references to general inadequacy of the diet in both the nutritive and qualitative sense.

So malnutrition should be differentiated from undernutrition as the former is not so much due to shortage of food but from faulty food habits and conditions arising from social and cultural factors. The chief cause of constitutional deterioration or our state of health at present is to be found in the defective diet of civilised nations causing malnutrition.

Undernutrition is found amongst those belonging to the lower socio-economic groups as they are deprived of proper nourishing food due to poverty. There are two main factors respondiminution in the fertility of the soil apart from economic factors.

Malnutrition is a worldwide problem. A considerable portion of the world population today, whether rich or poor is suffering from various types of malnutrition because the main cause of it is a defective diet, over consumption of highly refined foods and drinks, adulteration and additives to food, living on artificial commercialized, denatured and devitalized foods with improper balance of diet consisting of processed foods and to the excessive consumption of proteins, carbohydrates which disturb them mineral and vitamin balance of a properly constituted diet and on top of it the raps of the soil with insecticides, pesticides and poisonous chemical sprayer on plants, vegetables and fruits is leading to nothing short of reination of health and premature death.

Inspite of all our cultural advancement progress of science and accumulated knowledge we have failed miserable in this most vital problem—malnutrition.

We have successfully eliminated a multitude of infectious diseases, but we are still a longway from realising the old fact that killing of insects with insecticides for increasing the production of food, is like poisonous drug. We can not expect to produce a healthy crop and vegetables on such soil.

People have starved through lack of proper food undernutrition leading to lethargy, lack of initiative and drive, falling an easy prey to infection and sickness but many have died of malnutrition through eating refined, rich died and poisonous adulteration denatured food.

So the diet of the poor is often seriously lacking in the growth promoting and protective foods, whereas the diet of the well-to-do. On the other consists of highly refined or preserved foods and to the excessive consumption of proteins, fats, sugars, which disturbs the mineral and vitamin balance of a properly constituted diet. It will these be seen that the diet of the well-to-do as well as that of the poor is likely to be defective, in different ways.

Malnutrition and even undernutrition are at times man-made. With notable exceptions the capitalists, traders, together with politicians and high ranking officials become greedy and unmindful of the obligations to the community, the nations and the country. They create an artificial shortage and swindle the consumers in price and quality.

These vicious and anti-social activities may be found elsewhere but in poor country like our with three forth of the population comprising of agriculturists, it is lamentable, to find that corruption, adulteration, hoarding and amassing of wealth by an artificial like in price and by other unscrupulous means are so much rampant and to an extent not to be found anywhere else.

We have been hearing of shocking and unbelievable things that during the food crisis, or so called food shortage, or even during genuine famine or strike people start concerning the market and make a profit out of it or hoarding sugar, grains, ghee, etc. to last them for a year. Besides for weddings, the supply and consumption of milk for guests and visitors go up to than 100 to 200 litres per day. Over and above levish dinner parties with criminal waste of food are conveniently overlooked whereas of that sometimes, poor and middle class mothers do not get even in iota of good wholesome milk or food for their babies and children because of the so called "short supply".

If it was mainly shortage of food due to over-population causing malnutrition then the rich countries with plenty of food resources and others in the world who are rich, should not suffer from malnutrition. It is the defective food of modern civilized nations, all over the world which is responsible for malnutrition and which is underlying causes of modern ailment, like heart disease, cancer, diabetes and other degenerative disease. Today people not only have strayed from a natural method of eating but are also refining, concentrating, preserving degeneration, pickling, colouring and processing foods then ever before.

Unless the modern artificial ways of living on denatured, adulterated commercialised, insecticides-processed foods, etc. are not seriously tackled the problem of malnutrition can never be improved.

If the majority of poor people in India are unhealthy or short lived, it is not because the diet is vegetarian in origin but because of undernutrition resulting from those economic conditions which compel them to consume foods highly deficient in certain essential elements.

The classes in the community which are particularly likely to suffer if their diet is defective are infants and growing children and expectant and nursing mothers.

So as undernutrition is more due to defective diets because of the lack of protective foods like milk, milk products, green vegetables, whole grain cereals etc. causing deficiency of vitamins, minerals, protein—our aim in public health nutrition, work in general and in planning well-to do 'diets' must be to increase intake of protective foods and not concentrate on more protein deficiency.

The food habit of the Santhals are more akin to the Bengalis of the adjoining districts of West Bengal. Rice, fish and meat with vegetables are the common food. The Maithil Brahmins are not strictly vegetarians. Plenty of fish used to be available in the tanks, ponds and rivers and most of the people take fish and rice. Wheat is tolerated but to not appreciated. The mode of cooking in lao much akin to the mode of West Bengal. Milk and milk products are in great demand, particularly by the well-to-do people. Chenna and Porha of this district two milk products are well noted.

Cooked rice is the staple food of the Santhals. The rice is usually "dhanki" husked. Their main edibles have also been motioned. It may be added that they take a lot of rice water (amnr) with salt. Mahua oil is the chief cooking medium, various kinds of pithas (cakes) are relished – the usual ingredients is the sun-dried rice ground to powder. Jil pitha is the (sun dried rice) delicacy and minute pieces of raw meat with condiments are put in. Dumu pitha is sharped like eggs with powdered rice, gur and salt. There are various leaves and flowers, bamboo shoots and wild fruits which are edible. They love jack fruit.

Rice bear or handia is a must in everyday Santhal homes whether as an offspring to the bongas or as a drink to go round in a social visit or as a part of the food. Mr. Charulal Mukherjee has mentioned the modusoperandi of the preparation of the handia.

Sun dried rice is first ground and mixed with a powdered root, called "ranu". The whole mass in then shaped into little balls. Next rice is boiled and spread out to dry and the balls and them powdered and mixed thoroughly with the rice. The next stage requires the mixture thus obtained to be kept in large earthen pots, covered with sal leaves for three or four days together, in course of which the rice is well fermented. The flued of the rice beer is often allowed to trickle down a bamboo sieve being pressed by the hand with a handful of fibres. Handia is drink from sal leaf cup.

Socially, they are a jolly cheerful people contended with their lot, so long as they have enough to eat and drink and to spend on religious and social ceremonies. As he is unfettered with cases, the Santhal enjoys existence in a few greater degree than does his neighbour the ridden and caste crushed Hindu. The Santhal eats his buffalo-beaf, his kids, poultry, park or pigeons, enjoys a hearty carouse onlivened with the spirit pachwai and dances with his wives and comrades to express his joy thankfulness. Hard drinking is a peculiar failure of the Santhals, who enjoy nothing so much as a carouse, but so far the physique of the race does not seem to be impared. Their foodness for drink may be gathered from the attitude of an old manjhi who asked whether the God of the Christian would allow old people to get drink twice a week when he heard the horrified answer of the missionary, he simply replied. Then teach our boys and girls, but leave us alone. Rice is their chief food but they are able to live on all sorts of roots and vegetables, when food is scarce they will recourse to other fare. They will for instance set two kinds of snake (the dhamin and rock snake) a few kinds of rats, one kind of frog, one lizard etc. The lizard is considered excellent eating but the rest are generally only partaken of my children especially shapped boys. Thus though living mostly on vegetables they enjoy animal food when they can get it and nothing so much as pigcurry. Except at certain sacrifices they never eat cows, bullocks or buffaloes, unless they can get it and nothing so much as pigcurry. They rather enjoy chewing the tough meet, but certain kinds of most they akhor *e.g.* horse flesh.

Their food may be divided into two main classes, *viz.*

1. Cereals prepared as "bhat" with curry of some kind added; and
2. Other food eaten raw or roasted but without cereals. A list prepared by Mr. Boding given the following detail—Cereals (19 kinds) besides a large number of varieties of rice, vegetable curries composed of (a) leguminous plants (14) (b) cultivated vegetable (18) and leaves of wild plants and trees (59), mushroom (24), resins (10), fruits wild or cultivated (65), tubers (25), all domestic animals, except dogs, horses and eats and wild animals including tigers, leopards, jackels, foxes, five kinds of rats etc. (30), snakes (2), lizards (1), tortoises and crocodiles (6) birds with the eggs of every kind eaten (72), fishes at least (30), wild gains, fruits etc. eaten during time of scarcity (21), oil seeds and karnels (10) and the ordinary Indian spices. A gourmand could not wish for more miscellaneous material and it is not certain that the list is quite complete.

It is probably that the social system of the Santhals was originally communistic and if their tradition are to be believed they were formally a self-contained nation having very few social relations with other races. It is impossible to trace, even at the resent time a distinct idea among them that a Santhal has arise to possess and appropriate any part of nature not previously in the occupation of any body also. Land is common properly till it has been held under a title, or at least trempled round. All forests and forest produce are considered from to all if they have not been definitely occupied by others. Any wild animal is also lawful pray but belongs to the man who first wounded it not to the man who kill it although the latter and the village headman get portions of the animal as determined by the custom. River fish belong to anybody and if a man dame up a water course or has a natural but on someday or other incites the villagers and neighbours to catch all the fish there. They give the owner of the water-course a small share and the bigger fish are also divided the ides of public property is thus apparent. This does not of course apply in the case of fish stocked in a tank, a very recent innovation with the Santhals. As soon as any one takes possession of anything with the consent of the village he is treated as the owner.

The principal diet of the Santhals is "daka utu" that is cooked rice, pulses and vegetables. In case of non-availability of pulses and vegetables they eat the cooked rice along with Mard *i.e.* the water which is left in the pot after the rice boiling is completed and a little amount of salt. The second important form of diet or food is called "Jaondra Daka" or Dalia *i.e.* boiled maize. Some people prefer maize more than the cooked rice. Millet is also taken in the form of dalia which is prepared in the shape of small balls after boiling the millet. They neither grind it to make it like flour for bread not they take it in form of "sattu". During festivals times, particularly, the Santhals like to take 'chura' (pounded rice) and "Murhi" (rice fried on sand). During the month of Falgun they take boiled mahua fruits and in the month of Ashadh they prepare "Lathy" from the mahua fruits for which they have a great taste.

Among the pulses kurthi is the main product. Among the vegetables the Santhals prefer brinjal, potato, gourd, pumpkin, bins, etc. and jackfruit. Among the leafy vegetables they prefer the leafs of the kutchnar, papal and munga. These do not require any plantation and grow abundantly.

The Santhals also prefers to eat fish, as well as different animals, birds and reptiles. Sauces pork and chicken are quite common elements of food. Among the spices they use haldi, dhania and chilly, onion and garlic are also used as a spice.

Maria is the most popular intoxicating drink among the santhals. It is less harmful than the alcoholic drinks. Maria is prepared by the process of fermentation of rice, millet, etc.

These people generally eat three or four times a day:

1. Daskayak (breakfast) at about 9 or 10 o'clock in the morning;
2. Majjan (kaleba) at about 2 o'clock during the day time;
3. Modok (Bualu) at about 8 o'clock in the evening. They generally take stale rice as their breakfast.

In the present study the researcher has attempted on the spot study of the food and energy problem by the Santhal families. And for this purpose the respondents were asked several questions related to the availability of food and energy in Santhal village. As we all know the economic condition of the tribal people in our country including Santhal is not at all encouraging. Most of the families suffer from shortage of food. They don't have sufficient earnings to buy food stuffs from the local markets. This is one of the major reason for indebtedness among the Santhals. They are to borrow money or to foodstuff from the non-trible traders on very unreasonable terms. In the past these traders managed to grab the lands of the tribals in lieu of meager amount advanced to them in the shape of loan. Moreover, most part of the area in which the Santhal live are not very fertile and the water resources for irrigation are scares. The structure of agriculture is most favourable for ingenic cultivations and adoptation of advanced technology. As a result the yield per acre of land is a also quite unsatisfactory. The tribals have no other avenue of employment because of the absence of industrialization and dacy of traditional cottage industries. Therefore, the shortage of food is not at all common among the Santhals. In such situation management of food assumes and important functions for the women who run their families because whatever quantity of food is available has to be consumed in the best possible manner.

Regarding the energy the position of its availability is no better than the food supply. The Santhals depend mostly on the forest for the supply of energy in the shape of wood. The women and children in Santhal villages are often found collecting firewood's for their own use as well as for selling it in the market. As a substitute for wood they use dry leaves of the trees and also the cow-dung cakes. In few cases the kerosene oil is also used as a source of energy. Only the comparatively affluent families and particularly those villages which is adjacent to the urban areas use coal as a source of energy.

In the present study the respondents were asked whether they get sufficient supply of fuel to run their kitchen, the answers were analyzed on the basis of the family income of the respondents. 66.20 per cent of the respondents which include 70.00 per cent of the respondents in the income group of less than Rs. 1000 per month 73.33 per cent in the income group of Rs. 1000 to 1500 and 43.66 per cent of those earning more than Rs. 1500 per month said that they were not getting sufficient supply of fuel, 33.79 per cent of the total respondents including 56.66 per cent in the income group of more than 1500 per month gave affirmative replies.

Table 8.1: Income and Question No. 86

Response/Income	*Yes*	*No*	*Total*
Less than 1000 P.M.	29.09	70.00	37.93
Rs. 1000 to 1500 P.M.	26.66	73.33	41.37
Rs. 1500 and above	56.66	43.66	20.68
Total	**33.79**	**66.20**	**290 (100.0)**

The most question was meant for those respondents who reported insufficient supply of fuel. They were asked about the member who took major share in fuel management generally. In reply 63.02 per cent of the respondents including 57.69 per cent, 65.90 per cent and 69.23 per cent of the respondents in the income groups of less that 1000 per month, 1000 to 1500 per month and more than 1500 per month respectively said that generally the women members were taking the major share of fuel management. 18.22 per cent said that the male members were taking the major share in fuel management and 16.75 per cent told that the children were taking the major share.

Table 8.2: Income and Question No. 87

Response/Income	*Men*	*Women*	*Children*	*Total*
Less than 1000 P.M.	16.66	57.69	25.64	40.62
Rs. 1000 to 1500 P.M.	20.45	65.90	13.63	45.83
More than Rs. 1000 to 1500 P.M.	15.38	69.23	15.30	13.54
Total	**18.22**	**63.02**	**16.75**	**290(100.00)**

As said earlier, the main source of fuel for the tribal including the Santhals is the forest. But in recent years this source appears to be dwindling because of the indiscriminate cutting of the failing of trees under the "save forest campaign". The receeding forest has also created some ecological problems and as such imposition of restriction became necessary. But still now the Santhals largely depend upon the forest for their female requirements, the respondents in this study were asked about the major source of availability of fuel and energy they were using. In reply 65.51 per cent of the respondents mention forest as the major source. In recent years discovery of large reserve of coal in the area adjacent to "Damin-i-koh" or the homeland of Santhal has opened up a new source of energy. The Santhal living in villages adjacent to coal mines area have started using coal as a source of energy. In this study 21.37 per cent of the respondents mentioned mines as the source of energy and the remaining 13.10 per cent of the respondents depended on market for their fuel supply.

Table 8.3: Income and Question No. 88

Response/Income	*Forest*	*Mines*	*Market*	*Total*
Less than 1000 P.M.	69.09	20.00	10.90	37.93
Rs. 1000 to 1500 P.M.	68.33	23.33	08.33	41.37
Above Rs. 1500 P.M.	53.33	20.00	26.66	20.68
Total	**65.51**	**21.37**	**13.10**	**290(100.00)**

With the change of time the Santhal not only learn the use of coal but also have started using kerosene oil as a source of energy. In this study the respondents were asked whether they are getting sufficient supply of home kerosene oil. They reply 64.82 per cent which included 67.27 per cent, 68.33 per cent and 53.33 per cent in the respective income group of the less than 1000 per month, Rs. 1000 to Rs. 1500 and above Rs. 1500 per month respectively said that there were not sufficient supply of kerosene oil. The remaining 35.17 per cent expressed satisfaction. The analysis of the data pointed out that the supply of kerosene oil was much less than its demands.

Table 8.4: Income and Question No. 89

Response/Income	*Yes*	*No*	*Total*
Less than 1000 P.M.	32.72	67.27	37.93
Rs. 1000 to 1500 P.M.	31.66	68.33	41.37
Above Rs.1500 P.M.	46.66	53.33	20.68
Total	**35.17**	**64.82**	**290(100.00)**

In the past next question the respondents were asked about the main type of fuel they were using. In reply 8.96 per cent including 20.00 per cent of the service holders said that they were mainly using coal as the main type of fuel. 46.55 per cent were using wood that included 40.00 per cent of service holders, 50.00 per cent of businessman, 41.75 per cent of manual labourers and 49.46 per cent of those who were not engaged in any type of job, 29.65 per cent of the total respondents mentioned cow-dung cakes as their main type of fuel. That included 30.00 per cent, 32.55 per cent, 28.57 per cent and 27.95 per cent of the respondents in the respective occupational groups. Remaining 14.82 per cent were using dry leaves of the trees. That included 10.00 per cent, 11.62 per cent, 19.78 per cent and 13.97 per cent of the respondents in the respective occupational categories.

Table 8.5: Occupation and Question No. 90

Response/Occupation	*Coal*	*Wood*	*Cow-dung cake*	*Dry leaf*	*Total*
Service	20.00	40.00	03.00	10.00	06.69
Business	05.81	50.00	32.55	11.62	29.65
Manu.. Labour	09.89	41.75	28.57	19.78	31.37
Not Earning	02.60	49.46	27.95	13.97	32.06
Total	**8.96**	**46.55**	**29.65**	**14.82**	**290(100.00)**

In Santhal village it is economically found that the women and also children and in some cases also go to the forest for cooking woods. It is no less essential than fetching water for drinking and washing. In this study respondents were asked about the frequency of their visit to the forests for picking woods. In reply 43.10 per cent including 57.14 per cent of manual labourers, 41.93 per cent of the not earning member said that they were going to the forest regularly for picking woods and an equal members of total respondents said that they were going to forest sometimes and the remaining 13.79 per cent were seldom going to the forest.

Table 8.6: Occupation and Question No. 91

Resonse/Occupation	*Regularly*	*Sometimes*	*Seldom*	*Total*
Service	10.00	20.00	70.00	06.89
Business	37.20	52.32	10.46	29.65
Manual Labour	57.14	35.16	07.69	31.37
Not Earning	41.93	47.31	10.75	32.06
Total	**43.10**	**43.10**	**13.79**	**290(100.00)**

In the following question the respondents were asked whether they did agree with the view that the use of wood as fuel causes the disappearance of forests. In reply to this 45.51 per cent including 48.92 per cent of the illiterates, 42.69 per cent of literates, 38.09 per cent of those who were less than matriculates and 50.00 per cent of those who were matriculates and above expressed their agreement with the view, 39.65 per cent expressed their disagreement. Those who disagreed were of the opinion the disappearance of the forest was caused mainly because of the illegal falling of trees by unscrupulous contractors in connivance with the officials of the forest department. Another reason they put forward was that the forest were being alarmed for the purpose of agriculture and also for building new habitations of the growing population in the tribal areas, 14.82 per cent of respondents however could not given any specific answer.

Table 8.7: Education and Question No. 92

Response/Education	*Yes*	*No*	*Can Not*	*Total*
Illiterate	48.92	33.81	17.26	47.93
Literate	42.69	44.94	12.55	30.68
Less than Matriculate	38.09	42.85	19.04	14.48
Matriculate and above	50.00	40.00	—	06.89
Total	**45.51**	**39.65**	**14.82**	**290(100.00)**

The respondents were also asked whether there had been any change in their society regarding the use of fuel for the domestic purposes. In reply to the question 37.58 per cent of the respondents including 52.68 per cent, 37.07 per cent, 42.85 per cent and 45.00 per cent of the illiterates, literates, less than matriculates and matriculates and above respectively spread agreed with the view, 51.27 per cent disagreed and 11.03 per cent were undecided.

Table 8.8: Education and Question No. 93

Response/Education	*Yes*	*No*	*Don't Know*	*Total*
Illiterate	52.68	53.95	18.79	47.93
Literate	37.07	55.05	07.86	30.68
Less than Matriculate	42.85	42.85	34.28	14.48
Matriculate and above	45.00	35.00	20.00	06.89
Total	**37.58**	**51.27**	**11.03**	**290(100.00)**

Out of the total respondents 67.93 per cent including 7.18 per cent of those having an income of less than Rs. 1000 per month, 60.83 per cent of the respondents in the income group of Rs.1000 to 1500 per month and 63.33 per cent in the income group of Rs.1500 per month and above reported that they were failing difficulty at times to prepare means for want of fuel. The analysis thus indicated the extent of fuel crisis in the Santhal household, remaining 32.06 per cent of the respondents however, had no complain about the shortage of fuel for preparing meals.

Table 8.9: Income and Question No. 94

Response/Income	*Yes*	*No*	*Total*
Less than 1000 P.M.	07.18	21.81	37.93
Rs. 1000 to 1500 P.M.	60.83	39.16	41.37
Above Rs. 1500 P.M.	63.33	36.66	20.68
Total	**67.93**	**32.06**	**290(100.00)**

The Santhal as said earlier are food of eating steel food particularly rice. Santhals are predominantly rice-eating people and the practice of eating cooled rice put in the water for sometimes in quiet common among them. In other words it is called "basi bhat". The respondents in this study was asked whether it was because of shortage of fuel that Santhal are used to take satisfied? In reply 53.79 per cent of the total respondents including 4.00 per cent of service holders, 48.83 per cent of the businessman, 63.73 per cent of manual labourers and 51.61 per cent of the agriculturists expressed their agreement with view, 37.24 per cent, however, did not agree with this view and 8.96 per cent were undecided.

Table 8.10: Main Source of Income and Question No. 95

Response/Source	*Yes*	*No*	*Don't Know*	*Total*
Service	04.00	35.00	35.00	06.89
Business	48.83	40.69	10.46	29.65
Manual Labour	63.73	30.76	05.49	31.37
Agriculture	51.61	40.86	07.52	32.06
Total	**53.79**	**37.24**	**08.96**	**290 (100.00)**

The respondents were also asked whether thought that the average Santhal family could meet the daily requirement of foodstuff? In reply to this question 56.89 per cent of the respondents including 50.00 per cent among the service holders, 56.97 per cent of the small traders, 59.34 per cent of the manual labourers, and 55.91 per cent of the agriculturists gave negative answers, 31.72 per cent of the total respondents including 25.00 per cent, 27.90 per cent, 32.95 per cent and 35.48 per cent of the respondents in respective categories given above said that average Santhal family could most the daily requirements of foodstuff. The remaining 11.37 per cent of the total respondents could not give any specific reply.

Table 8.11: Main Source of Income and Question No. 96

Response/Source	*Yes*	*No*	*Don't Know*	*Total*
Service	25.00	50.00	25.00	06.89
Business	27.90	56.97	15.11	29.65
Manual Labour	32.95	59.34	07.69	31.37
Agriculture	35.48	55.91	08.60	32.06
Total	**31.72**	**56.89**	**11.37**	**290 (100.00)**

In view of the prevailing shortage of foodstuff it was felt necessary to ask respondents about the main reason for the shortage of foodstuff. In reply 31.37 per cent of the respondents attributed it to the poor state of agriculture. According to 25.66 per cent small land holdings was responsible for the short supply of food. 36.09 per cent were of the opinion that explaining 5.86 per cent mentioned causes other than those, namely, alcoholism, lack of entertaining, lack of enterprising habit, absence of alternative employment etc.

Table 8.12: Education and Question No. 97

Response/Education	*Poor Agricul-ture*	*Small holing*	*Exploitation of daku mahajan*	*Any other*	*Total*
Illiterate	32.37	28.77	38.84	—	47.39
Literate	29.31	26.96	30.20	05.61	30.68
Less than Matriculate	35.71	16..66	28.57	19.04	14.48
Matriculate and above	25.00	20.00	35.00	20.00	06.89
Total	**31.37**	**25.66**	**36.09**	**5.89**	**290 (100.00)**

The acute shortage of food supply also motivated the research as ask the respondents who were all women that could they provide healthy food to their children with the existing source of food supply. In reply 62.41 per cent, which included more than 60.00 per cent of the respondents in each of the occupational group, said that they were unable to provide healthy food to the children, remaining 37.58 per cent however, gave affirmative answer.

Table 8.13: Source of Family Income and Question No. 98

Response/Source	*Yes*	*No*	*Total*
Service	40.00	60.00	06.89
Business	37.20	62.79	29.65
Manual Labour	39.56	60.43	31.37
Agriculture	35.48	64.51	22.06
Total	**37.58**	**62.41**	**290 (100.00)**

The Santhals are very much found of alcoholic drinks. Both male and female love drinking. In most cases the drinks are prepared from the fruits of mahua tree and also they are fond of taking brews made of rice. Some people are of the view that these drinks are alternative to food. Therefore, the respondents were asked whether they did agree with the view that mahua or handia (rice brew) are taken in most cases as alternatives to food. In reply 53.44 per cent of the respondents which included 50.00 per cent of the respondents or more of the respondents in each of the occupational categories expressed their agreement with the view, 36.89 per cent did not agree and 9.65 per cent were not able to give any specific answer.

Table 8.14: Source of Family Income and Question No. 98

Response/Source	*Yes*	*No*	*Don't Know*	*Total*
Service	35.00	50.00	15.00	06.89
Business	58.13	31.39	10.46	29.65
Manual Labour	50.54	42.85	06.59	31.37
Agriculture	52.68	36.55	10.75	32.06
Total	**53.44**	**36.89**	**9.65**	**290 (100.00)**

In a situation of food shortage people do not have any choice for food and this appears to be true in case of the Santhals. In reply to the question: Do the people in your society can afford to have food of their own choice? 30.34 per cent said 'yes', 58.96 per cent said 'no' this included 50.00 per cent of the service holders, 62.79 per cent of Businessmen, 62.63 per cent of manual labourers and 53.76 per cent of the agriculturists. Remaining 10.68 per cent of total respondents said that they did not know.

Table 8.15: Source of Income and Question No. 100

Response/Source	*Yes*	*No*	*Don't Know*	*Total*
Service	35.00	50.00	15.00	06.89
Business	27.90	62.79	09:30	29.65
Manual Labour	27.47	62.63	09.89	31.37
Agriculture	34.40	53.76	11.82	32.06
Total	**30.34**	**58.96**	**18.68**	**290 (100.00)**

Food gathering is an usual practice among the Santhals. But the quantity of food which they are able to gather is not sufficient even for few days consumption of the family. In this study the respondents were asked whether the women of their villages were able to gather sufficient food at least for few day for the family?

In reply 34.13 per cent gave affirmative answers, 54.13 per cent gave negative replies that included 70.00 per cent of the service holders, 53.48 per cent of the businessman, 52.74 per cent of manual labourers and 52.68 per cent of the respondents belonging to the families drawing their subsistence from agriculture, 11.72 per cent were undecided.

Table 8.16: Source of Income and Question No. 101

Response/Source	*Yes*	*No*	*Don't Know*	*Total*
Service	30.00	70.00	—	06.89
Business	34.68	53.48	11.62	29.65
Manual Labour	31.86	52.74	15.38	31.37
Agriculture	36.35	52.68	10.68	32.06
Total	**34.13**	**54.13**	**11.72**	**290 (100.00)**

The following question was about the availability of the green vegetables or fruit from the jungle was supplement for food supply. In reply 28.62 per cent said that they had sources of green vegetables and fruits from the jungle as supplement for food supply. But remaining 71.37 per cent denied that those who denied, including 80.00 per cent of the service holders, 74.61 per cent of the business women, 70.32 per cent of the manual labourers, and 67.74 per cent of those respondents who were not engaged in any type of profession.

Table 8.17: Occupation and Question No. 102

Response/Occupation	*Yes*	*No*	*Total*
Service	20.00	80.00	06.89
Business	25.38	74.61	29.65
Manual	29.67	70.32	31.37
Not Earning	32.25	67.74	32.06
Total	**28.62**	**71.37**	**290 (100.00)**

Enquiry was also made from the respondents about any governmental or semi-governmental agencies distributing food and nutrition among the Santhals. In reply 34.14 per cent gave affirmative replies, that included 54.76 per cent of those who were less than matriculates and 60.00 per cent of those who were matriculates and above, 37.50 per cent of the respondents had no knowledge about any such agencies and 28.27 per cent said that they were undecided.

Table 8.18: Education and Question No. 103

Response/Source	*Yes*	*No*	*Don't Know*	*Total*
Illiterate	31.65	37.65	38.93	47.39
Literate	22.47	41.57	36.95	30.68
Less than Matriculate	54.76	28.57	16.66	14.48
Matriculate and above	60.00	40.00	—	06.89
Total	**34.13**	**37.50**	**28.27**	**290 (100.00)**

Asked about the supply of food from Church 40.34 per cent of the respondents said that they were getting food supply from the

Church or Christian missions, remaining 59.66 per cent, however, gave negative answers.

Table 8.19: Source of Family Income and Question No. 104

Response/Source	*Yes*	*No*	*Total*
Service	35.00	65.00	06.89
Business	37.20	62.79	29.65
Manual Labour	46.15	53.84	31.37
Agriculture	38.70	61.29	32.06
Total	**40.34**	**59.66**	**290 (100.00)**

In the next question the respondents were asked whether they were supplementing the milk of the domesticated cattle as food for the family members? In reply 44.48 per cent gave affirmative reply and 55.51 per cent gave negative replies.

Table 8.20: Source of Income and Question No. 105

Response/Source	*Yes*	*No*	*Total*
Service	50.00	50.00	06.89
Business	44.18	55.81	29.65
Manual Labour	41.75	58.24	31.37
Agriculture	46.23	53.76	32.86
Total	**44.48**	**55.51**	**290 (100.00)**

33.44 per cent of the tribal respondents reported that the male members of their families went for fishing with a view to supplement food resources. 66.55 per cent, however, gave negative replies.

Table 8.21: Age and Question No. 106

Response/Age	*Yes*	*No*	*Total*
Below 35 years	37.50	62.50	08.27
35 to 40 years	35.55	64.44	15.51
40 to 45 years	30.00	07.00	20.68
45 to 50 years	32.65	67.14	23.10
Above 50 years	34.04	65.95	32.41
Total	**33.44**	**66.55**	**290 (100.00)**

As regards hunting by the male members of their families 13.44 per cent of the respondents gave affirmative replies, 71.72 per cent gave negative replies and 14.82 per cent said that male members were going for hunting out rarely.

Table 8.22: Education and Question No. 107

Response/Education	*Yes*	*No*	*Rarely*	*Total*
Illiterate	12.23	71.22	16.54	47.39
Literate	11.23	77.52	11.23	30.68
Less than Matriculate	21.42	64.28	14.28	14.48
Matriculate and above	15.00	65.00	30.00	06.89
Total	**13.44**	**71.72**	**14.82**	**290 (100.00)**

In the last question they were asked to support measures to remove the economic hardship of the Santhals. In reply 16.55 per cent suggested that modernisation of agriculture, 23.44 per cent suggested creation of alternative source of income 15.17 per cent suggested that avoidance of alcoholism and 34.82 per cent suggested return of mortgage land to Santhal by the 'Dikus' or the non-Santhals.

Table 8.23: Education and Question No. 107

Response/Education	*(a)*	*(b)*	*(c)*	*(d)*	*Total*
Illiterate	15.82	21.58	28.77	33.81	17.39
Literate	20.22	26.96	22.47	30.33	30.68
Less than Matriculate	11.90	23.80	19.04	45.23	14.40
Matriculate and above	15.00	20.00	25.00	40.00	6.89
Total	**16.55**	**23.44**	**25.17**	**34.82**	**290 (100.00)**

(a) Modernisation of agriculture
(b) Creation of alternative sources of income
(c) Avoidance of alcohol
(d) Return of land mortgaged to Santhal by the Dakus.

Thus, the concept of Food Management involves meeting and solving the constant managerial problems that have to do with feeding the family. The goal of food management is to provide food that will insure the physical and mental growth of the family for its social development and well being with a reasonable expenditure of available resources.

Many managerial decisions must be made in providing the family with adequate food, and in preparing and serving it. Decision begin with the setting of nutritional standards and the planning of meals to meet these standards. They lead to planning the amount that can be spent for food, planning for purchase, choosing the markets, buying and storing food supplies. Then comes planning for the preparation and serving of the meals. These are common to all stages of the family life cycle.

In addition to these management problems of supplying food to be eaten at home and sometimes preceding it are the decisions about the money the family will spend on eating away from home. With the modern school lunch programme, the earners working too far to return home for meals, the ever-present snacke bars and vending machines in schools, office buildings and on the corners plus the enticing drive-in a great deal of money can be spent on food eaten outside the home. Decisions on ways and means of meeting these demands and the amount a family can afford to spend for food away from home complicate food management in the home.

In stating the goals of food management, the phrase reasonable expenditure of resources was used. What constitutes a reasonable expenditure of a given family can be arrived at only through careful analysis and planning by the manager in her own home.

Both human and non-human resources are needed to solve these problems. Knowledge is one important human resource. It includes information on the amount of income available for food, nutrition, the different kinds of food and how to prepare and serve them, food prices, general market conditions and local shopping facilities. Other resources needed are abilities and energy of the homemaker to coordinate the flow of adequate supplies and their preparation into meals.

The effective use of time helps the homemaker to develop a smoothly operating household. The more she knows about the time required to do each task connected with food buying and preparation, the better will be the management of this resource.

The resource of money determines the types of food selected for the family, the markets used, the methods of buying and whether and to what extent other resources will need to be substituted for money when it is limited.

The solutions of food management problems vary from home to home because of the difference in the supply of these resources. If one or more of the resources is limited in amount, it may be a challenge to the homemaker to compensate for it in some other way. In food management, the more able a person is in using resources alternatively, the greater will be the returns in satisfaction. Because a large amount of the money income of the majority of families is spent for food, no area in homemaking demands more careful planning and organizing than food management.

REFERENCES

Choudhary, P.C. Roy: *Bihar District Gazetteer Santhal Parganas,* Secretriat Press, Bihar, 1965, pp. 946–47.

Ghei, Amarnath and Ghei, P.: *Text Book of Food and Nutrition,* Sagar Publications, Ved Mansion, Janpath, New Delhi, 1973, p. 3.

Jussawalle, J.M.: *Natural Dictetics, A Handbook of Food, Nutrition and Health,* Vikas Publishing House Pvt. Ltd., New Delhi, 1979, pp. 1–4.

Op. cit. Junawalla: pp. 31–34

O'Malley, L.S.S.: *Bihar District Gazetteer, Santhal Parganas,* The Bengal Secretariat Book Depot, 1910, pp. 102–03.

Shenwik, W.S.W.S.: *A Tour Thought, The Rajmahal Hills,* J.A.S.B. 1861.

Samir, Doman Sahu: *Santhal In Bihar,* K.C. Adivasi by L.P. Vidyarthi College Center, Patna, 2005, pp. 53–54.

9

Women Welfare and Social Development

The terms "Gender Justice", "Women Empowerment", "Women Welfare" are in limelight in the social and economic development analysis of both developed and developing nations. The debate on gender justice/women empowerment/women welfare was at the center stage in the international arena in 1994 UN Conference in Cairo; UN's Fourths International Conference on Women at Beijing in 1995 and UN's Social Summit Conference at Copenhagen in March 1995.

In UN International Conference on Population and Development (ICPD) 1994 in its guiding principles states "the human rights of women and girl child are an inalienable, integral and indivisible part of universal human rights. The full and equal participation of women in civil, cultural, economic, political and social life at the national, regional and international levels and the eradication of all forms of discrimination on grounds of sex are priority objectives of the international community".

Table 9.1: Number of Girls Enrolled in Schools and Colleges

Year	*Primary (I-V)*	*Middle (VI-VII)*	*Secondary (IX-X)*	*Colleges and University*
1950–51	39	20	15	14
1960–61	48	32	23	22
1970–71	60	41	35	34
1980–81	62	48	41	39
1990–91	70	60	51	53
2000–01	85	75	60	60

Source: Selected Socio-economic Statistics for India 2004 CSO, Ministry of Planning and Programme Implementation, Government of India, p. 59.

Indian women continues to languish in a patriarchal society and a colossal percentage of them largely belonging to traditional and religiously orthodox families are deprived of even social mobility and enjoy low social status.

The Government of India has taken numerous measures and making honest endeavours to hoist the status of women and establish gender equality. The constitutional obligations as well as different plans, programmes and policies have laid emphasis on women empowerment in order to bring them to the mainstream of development. Article 15 of the Constitution prohibits any discrimination on the grounds of sex while Article 15(3) clarifies that this provision will not prevent the State from making any special provision for women. Article 42 of the Constitution envisages that the State shall make provision for securing just and human conditions of work and for maternity relief. Besides, the Directive Principles of State Policy also urge that the State shall direct its policy towards securing an adequate means of livelihood for women and ensuring equal pay for equal work for both men and women. The Eighth Five Year Plan intends at enabling women to function as equal partners and participants in development by extending the services to women both qualitatively and quantitatively. Moreover, the plan also aims to effectively implement social legislation for women by formulating and strengthening grass roots level women's group. The Ninth Five Year Plan intends to empowering women as the agents of social change and development. Formulation of National Commission for Women (NCW) and idea of setting up of a National Council for Empowerment of Women are encouraging steps in this direction. Moreover, the effort to formulate the National Policy for Empowerment of Women and setting up a National Resource Centre for Women are other steps taken by the Department of Women and Child Development.

A recent UN report notes that India has improved its score in education, employment and per capita income of women, but has not improved women's representation in Parliament, removed their unequal wages or lessened their debt burden. Ironically, a Parliamentary Committee report depicts that as against a budget estimate of Rs. 231.40 crore for various schemes meant for women welfare in 1998–99, the figure came down to Rs. 167.61 crore in the revised estimate and actual expenditure stood at Rs. 141.26 crore. Similarly, the budget estimate for 1999–2000 stood at Rs. 24.06 crore only. The committee advocated the need for maximum and judicious expenditure of funds allocated for schemes for women welfare.

Table 9.2: Representation of Women in Lok Sabha

General election	*Year*	*Total no. of seats*	*Number of women members*	*Percentage of the total*
First	1952	499	22	4.4
Second	1957	500	27	5.4
Third	1962	503	34	6.8
Fourth	1967	523	31	5.9
Fifth	1971	521	22	4.2
Sixth	1977	544	19	3.5
Seventh	1980	544	28	5.1
Eighth	1984	544	44	8.1
Ninth	1989	517	27	5.2
Tenth	1991	544	39	7.2
Eleventh	1996	544	40*	7.4
Twelfth	1998	543	43	7.8

* One member was nominated by the President
Source: Times of India

Notwithstanding numerous welfare measures, the status of women has not been adequately hoisted and the women empowerment status varies from region to region, state to state, and even between rural and urban areas. Moreover it also varies from one community to the other. A colossal large percentage of women are engaged in the unpaid household activities and are largely employed in the informal and unorganized private sector. Only a meagre 14.01 per cent of women are employed in organized sector. In the organized sector, they are assigned unskilled activities requiring more physical labour for which they earn less comparatively to their male counterpart. In unorganized private sector, they become victims of wage discrimination by the employers and contractors of wage employment programme. Due to domination of patriarchy norms most of the women lack property rights and hardly one or two per cent of women enjoy the ownership of property. Moreover, women have lower accessibility to saving and credit facilities.

Since independence, there is snail pace rise in female literacy, as the percentage of male literacy has risen from 25 per cent to 64.13 per cent, the female literacy from 7.9 per cent to only 39.29 per cent. Further the literacy of rural women and women belonging to Scheduled Castes, Scheduled Tribes and orthodox Muslim monorities are astoundingly low.

The World Bank in its report on Improving Women's Health in India pointed out that India accounts for almost 25 per cent of world's maternal death and the number of pregnancy related deaths in rural areas are still among the world's highest. The National Prospective Plan (NPP) for Women 1988–2000 adopted by the Government of India also noted, "Women face a high risk of malnutrition, retardation in growth and development, diseases, disability and even death at three critical stages in their lives *viz.* infancy, early childhood and adolescence and the reproductive phase. In the old age they face threats of breast and uterine cancer and menopause related problem". They are largely denied their reproductive health rights in the conservative, traditional and religiously orthodox families.

Inadequate Representation

Women are not adequately represented in the legislative, executive and judiciary spheres of the government. It could be remarked that although the recent years have witnessed an increase in women voters, changes in voters, anticipation have not been accompanied by changes in similar magnitude in the number of women occupying decision-making positions. In India, women's representation in Parliament and in the State Assembly has never gone beyond eight and ten per cent respectively. In recent years due to reservation of seats, there have been increased participation of women at the grassroots democratic system. Not only in legislative sphere but also in the executive and judiciary sphere women are thinly represented. A meagre percentage of women are positioned in Indian Administrative Service (IAS), Indian Police Service (IPS) and also in Allied Services. As far as representation of women in judiciary is concerned, Supreme Court and High Courts have history of fewer number of women judges.

Table 9.3: Women Empowerment and Social Development
Part I

Sl. No.	*Women Empowerment Indicators*	*Socially Developed State (Kerala)*	*Socially Backward State (Bihar and Jharkhand)*	*All India*
1.	Women Literacy	86.20	22.90	39.30
2.	Non-enrolment of Girl Children	00.00	32.79	29.00
3.	Women Work-participation in Organized Sector	35.8	06.6	14.01
4.	Women Non-farm Employment	58.41	09.11	21.19
5.	Sex-ratio	1068	956	927
6.	Percentage of Women Voting in Parliament	72.59	47.89	55.00
7.	Life Expectancy at Birth (female)	73.80	57.00	59.40

In the social sphere there is "gender isolation" and "gender oppression". The UNFPA report on The State of World Population 1997 envisages that there has been an increase in violence against women in the past decade in India. In the traditionally and religiously orthodox societies women are not allowed to formulate Mahila Mandal and they silently bear the atrocities and become victim of "wife beating", "bride-burning", "molestation", "rape" and other types of physical and socio-psychological harassments. Being isolated from social sphere, women are less represented in sports and business because of "gender stereotypes". In equal terms, women are also less involved in trade unions and labour associations.

A society that has effectively implemented women welfare measures, has ensured gender justice and empowerment of women, has achieved greater social development.

Table 9.3: Part II

Sl. No.	*Social Development Indicators*	*Social Development in*		
		Bihar and Jharkhand	*Kerala*	*All India*
1.	Life expectancy rate	57.5	71.3	58.37
2.	Infant mortality rate	66	16	73
3.	Maternal mortality rate	813	234	555
4.	Literacy rate	38.48	89.81	52.21
5.	Percent below poverty line	40.8	17	29.9
6.	Human development index	0.14	.775	—
7.	Per capita state net	2650	4020	—
8.	Per capita income growth (in %) from 1981–91 to 1992–97	0.7	4.9	—

In India, Kerala is an outstanding example of socially advanced state and Bihar and Jharkhand is one of the socially backward states. A comparision of social development indicators *vis-à-vis* women empowerment indicators in both these states reflect faster social development in Kerala than that of Bihar and Jharkhand. Thus women are the vital human infrastructure and their empowerment economic, educational, social and political would hasten the pace of social development. Investing in women's "capabilities" and empowering them to achieve their "choices" and "opportunities" is the surest way to contribute to economic growth and overall development. Overlooking of empowerment of women means dispossession of half of human capital. It means an incomplete attempt for social development and a complete violation of Human Rights for All.

10

Women and Communication Need

Development thinking has a perceptible shift towards people centred programmer. All the Five Year Plans in India gave a special place to women ranging from welfare to development and now from development to empowerment. Empowerment and information go hand in hand. Without information no development can take firm roots. It is also essential that people and communities participate in the process of development and bring about desirable change. They should be in a position to take decisions concerning their lives. New opportunities need to be provided and all the information needs of the community ought to be met to stimulate their awareness and better their capabilities.

Communication needs in rural areas are different from the urban areas where awareness level is higher and access to information is smoother. Intelligent use of different methods of communication helps development and facilitates dialogue and debate which are essential in a democratic set up. These can provide people a voice to spell out their needs, problems they encounter and even to recount their success which is useful to other places in similar situations. Exchange of ideas and information will increase the level of awareness and empower them to take informed decision regarding matters affecting their lives.

Majority of rural women are illiterate and live in remote and inaccessible areas where flow of information is intermittent or little. They don't have mobility or access to outside world. They hardly get any trainers to train them in any skill.

Communication which is one way and top-down just transferring message is not conducive to development. Two-way communication that helps sharing and participation is essential for sustainable development. The Food and Agricultural Organization (FAO) consultation on one occasion defined communication for development as "a social process", designed to seek a common understanding among all the participants of a development initiative creating a basis for concerted action.

Communication technology and media which are steadily improving and expanding are to be treated only as tools and means and not an end in themselves. Messages and purpose should not be lost in the glitz. Development also means change and the change involves attitudinal and behavioural changes besides material and environmental changes.

The experts at FAO consultation indicated that sustainable development "can only realise its full potential if rural people are involved and motivated and if information and knowledge are shared. Sharing is not a one-way transfer of information; it implies rather an exchange between communication equals. On the one hand, technical specialists learn about people's needs and their techniques of production; on the other, the people learn about the techniques and proposals of the specialists".

When efforts are directed towards giving a voice to rural women and harnessing the potential of communication towards this end, media strategy has to be specific, goal-oriented and need-based keeping in mind local compulsions.

Rural women may be illiterate but they have wisdom and knowledge rooted in cultural norms, traditions and experience that gained over generations. Listening to rural women not only gives an opportunity to assess their needs but also to understand their aspirations. So communication strategies are to be developed keeping in mind women's perceptions and needs. Sharing experience is possible through group discussions, interpersonal communication, audio-visual media and local media like district newspapers or publications brought out by voluntary organizations because in villages we still have a tradition of one reading out to a group of listeners.

The objectives of media strategy for rural women should include the following:

(a) Rural women are to be made aware of the barriers to

their development and to occupy their rightful place in community.

(b) Promoting the abilities of rural women.

(c) Facilities should be provided to enhance their knowledge and skills.

(d) Those who provide facilities at local level should also be involved in the development process.

Though backwardness is a common feature among rural women because of lack of education, information and media reach, women belonging to Backward Classes, Scheduled Castes and Scheduled Tribes have many more barriers to overcome. Here governmental and non-governmental agencies can have active role in information, education and communication.

The Ninth Five Year Plan (1997–2002) spells out certain measures as means to women's empowerment. It seeks reservation of not less than one-third seats for women in Parliament and State Legislative Assemblies. Existing services, resources, infrastructure and manpower in women specific and women related sectors are to be converged. All scheme and projects of rural development have to women's component which is not less than 30 per cent. So also the benefits that accrue from the schemes should be for women. Economically and as development partners too gets priority in scheme of things.

Equipping women and girls with education and necessary skills and increasing access to credit for women entrepreneur are also among the strategies for women's development.

All these strategies and implementation require free flow of information, multi-directional communication by all possible means. Centralized, homogeneous and top-down communication does not serve the purpose. Though broad guidelines, methods, targets and goals are visualized centrally, specific target-oriented personalized communication has to take place at district, block and village levels. Democratization of information, education and communication are prerequisites of rural development, more so in the case women including poor, socially backward and tribal women.

There are a number of poverty alleviation programmes with specified women's component designed for rural areas because it is economic empowerment which is a first step towards a developed society. Broadly these programmes have following objectives:

(a) Self-employment through credit and training;
(b) Wage employment during lean agriculture season;
(c) Encouraging savings habit and facilitating revolving fund;
(d) Providing support services and meeting minimum needs like nutrition, health, sanitation, housing and education; and
(e) Awareness generation regarding status of women and girl child in society.

Self-employment programmes meant for rural people below the poverty line have 30 to 40 per cent component for women Swarnajayanti Gram Swarozgar Yojana (SGSY) covers all aspects of self-employment like self-help groups, training, credit, technology, infrastructure and marketing. Apart from exclusive women groups women are encouraged to be part of all self-help groups. Four or five activities will be identified for each block with the approval of Panchayat Samitis. Individual families are identified through a participatory process.

Employment Assurance Scheme (EAS) provides wage employment in unskilled manual works to the rural poor who are in need of employment and seeking it. The second objective is to create economic infrastructure and community assets for sustained employment and development.

Indira Awas Yojana (IAY) helps construction of new houses as well as conversation of "kuchha" houses to "pucca" houses or semi "pucca" houses by members of Scheduled Castes/Schedule Tribes, freed bonded labourers and also rural poor below poverty line by extending them grant in aid. It is beneficiary oriented programme for SC/ST households who are victim of atrocities, households headed by widows/unmarried women and other households who are below poverty line.

The National Social Assistance Programme (NSAP) seeks to provide financial assistance to the destitute old people, poor families who have lost primary breadwinners and poor expectant mothers. The three components of the programme are National Old Age Pension Scheme, National Family Benefit Scheme and National Maternity Benefit Scheme.

The Accelerated Rural Water Supply Programme (ARWSP) under the Rajiv Gandhi National Drinking Water Mission strives to assist the states and union territories providing safe drinking water, free from chemical and bacteriological contamination at 40 litres per capita per day (70 litres in desert areas) to under covered villages and habitations identified through surveys, within 1.6 kilometres in plains and 100 metres elevation difference in hills.

Under the scheme, submissions and programmes to control fluorosis, remove excess iron and brackishness, remove arsenic, conserve water and recharge of aquifers are taken up. They also promote human resource development research, information, education and communication health education and awareness generation.

The centrally Sponsored Rural Sanitation Programme (SRSP) strives to provide sanitation facilities to the rural population, generate awareness about hygiene at eradicate manual scavenging by converting all existing dry latrines into low cost sanitary latrines.

The activities under this scheme include construction of individual sanitary latrines with eight per cent subsidy to below the poverty line, stress on school sanitation, encourage other household to have facilities on their own, launch intensive awareness campaigns, establish sanitary complexes exclusively for women and promote total sanitation of village. Implementation through the State Government departments/Boards, Panchayati Raj Institutions through active involvement of the NGO's and through campaign approach.

The Drought Prone Areas Programme (DPAP) aims at the adverse effects of drought on the production of crops and livestock and productivity of land, water and human resources. It also strives to encourage restoration of ecological balance and seeks to improve the economic and social conditions of the poor and the disadvantaged section of the rural community. Village community including self-help development by planning and implementation of project on watershed basis is through watershed committees constituted from among themselves.

The government supplements their creating social awareness, imparting training and providing technical support through project implementation agencies.

The Desert Development Programme (DDP) aims at combating drought and desertification. It encourages, restoration of ecological balance by harnessing, conserving and developing natural resources—land, water, vegetative cover and raising land productivity.

It is a people's programme with government assistance and special arrangement for maintenance of assets. Area development is on watershed basis. A watershed is a unit of about 500 ha. for implementation. There is direct participation of local people in planning, development and maintenance.

The Integrated Wasteland Development Programme strives to develop non-forest wasteland on village and micro-watershed basis. The scheme also helps generate employment in rural areas besides, enhancing people's participation in wasteland development leading to equitable sharing of benefits and sustainable development.

Major activities taken up under this scheme and soil and moisture conservation, afforestation and pasture development, promotion of horticulture/agro-forestry, encouraging natural regeneration, wood substitution and fuel wood: conservation measures and dissemination of technology as decided by the user group living in or around the project area.

There are many other programmes in the area of health, mother and child care. caring for the girl child, nutrition, literacy entrepreneurship which are women oriented and the focus is more on rural and tribal women especially in the district of Deoghar, Dumka, Godda, Pakur, Jamtara and Sahibganj of Santhal Pargana.

11

National Commission for Women: An Appraisal

A nation or society goes ahead only through the contribution of all its members. Push the women into the backyards, and the society itself will be dragged behind. During the struggle for independence, Mahatma Gandhi realizing this, took special efforts to include women in political as well as economic and social struggles. Even before him, stalwarts like Raja Rammohun Roy, Swami Vivekananda and Mahatma Phule had laid great emphasis on women's participation in their revival programmes.

After independence, however, the progress of women and of the society seems to have retarded. Even after forty years, examples galore where on the one hand the sensitivity over women's issues are lacking and on the other hand atrocities against woman are rising.

The Committee on Status of Women in India (CSWI) recommended as early as in 1975, the setting up of a National Commission for Women. Many women activists and organizations also pressed for the demand and finally Parliament passed the Act in 1990 for setting up a Women's Commission. Actual formation and functioning of National Commission for Women started in 1992.

Women related issues have many dimensions but they can be summarized as violence, denial and deprivation. Violence can be in parental or matrimonial house, or at work place or elsewhere in the society. Denial comes as denial of the right to be born, or denial of nutrition, education, health, home, property etc. Deprivation results from debarring them from several opportunities of empowerment—political, economic or careerwise. Also important are the questions of women in jail (pre-trial or post conviction), women in mental asylums, single women and so on.

These are the problems. But what about the systems designed to solve these problems? How effective are they? For example, a review of legal system shows that right from the judicial system to police investigation to medico-legal recordings to the system of evidence have been twisted in the hands of advocates; everywhere we find systemic insensitivity. Similarly, take the social systems, economic or political, we find insensitivity to the women's aspirations for realizing their potential. Ultimately the buck will stop at the door steps of the society which itself has become too insensitive. But the buck has to be brought there through studies, debates, seminars, action plans etc.

All this provides the working ideology for National Commission for Women. The NCW Act, 1990 has some very strong and all encompassing provisions. The most important and operative part *i.e.,* Section 10 of the Act lists fourteen important areas in which the Commission has to function; they include investigation of all matters relating to safeguards of women, suggest amendments to various laws look into complaints relating to deprivation of women's rights, take up matters of non-implementation of Acts meant for achieving equality and development of women and non-compliance of policy decisions etc. The Commission can undertake investigations, call for special studies and find litigations involving women's issues of larger dimensions. The Commission can also inspect jails and investigate the conditions of women therein.

On the empowerment side Section 10 enjoins NCW to suggest ways for ensuring due representation of women in all spheres, to participate and advice on the planning process of socio-economic development of women and to evaluate such development.

As a tool of NCW's investigations, power of civil court for summoning a person summoning the record or taking statements on oath have also been given to the NCW. Upon investigation and findings. Commission may require different agencies of government to implement the recommendations made by it.

NCW can make reports on its findings and recommendations to government and can require that such a report be placed before Parliament or the State Assembly as case may be. This is one very powerful methodology in the hands of NCW. Thus Commission combines the powers of investigations coming to a judicious conclusion, make recommendations and get them implemented through the government machinery.

The Commission works mainly through its members and a team of officers. However, Commission can set up expert committee on specific issues. Similarly experts can be co-opted even as a part of investigating team. Thus NCW needs to maintain a strong network with academicians and NGOs working all over the country and can tap the best available brains and activists for the purpose of situation analysis and recommendations.

The best too to assess the work of the Commission is its annual reports. The annual reports from 1992–93 onwards tell us about the work done so far, the work methodology and the future direction. These reports have a set pattern. Every report has chapters on "Status of Violence against Women" and "Custodial Justice" to deal with the menace of violence which is naturally the first concern of NCW. There is a complaints and counseling cell which looks into complaints received and gives guidance to the visitors who come to seek help, legal advice or otherwise. Some of these complaints are not a serious nature where investigation by the Commission is warranted and undertaken. Details of these investigations can be seen in the annual reports.

The complaints cell is an interface between suffering women and National Commission for Women. It gives first hand information about the Women's problems and the non-functioning of the departments that are primarily responsible to redress the grievances. It gives insight about various social, administrative and legal maladies. To redress the complaint of the individual sufferer is no doubt the first objective of the complaints cell. But the Commission cannot just stop there. It must be able to use this knowledge as a feedback to the government and should be able to recommended systemic changes needed in various government sectors to ensure that women do not have to suffer in future. The complaint cell allows the Commission to understand larger issues involving policy decision, methods of implementation and method of monitory in various government departments and particularly their non-functioning. NCW needs a strong ability to analyze the data available from the Cell and to suggest systemic changes to other government departments. To the extent that the NCW can do this, the complaint cell will provide an interface between the suffering women and the concern administrative departments also.

Annual report also has chapters on "Review of Laws" done by Commission and recommendations given to government on various new bills or amendments to existing laws. Participation of eminent lawyers, judges, academicians and activists is enlished before these recommendations are made.

The Commission has some programmes for funding to voluntary organizations, academicians and other bodies. The programme of legal literacy camps is designed to organize a three-day legal awareness for a group of nearly 50 women by any organization. The Parivarik Mahila Lok Adalat (PMLA) is designed to give funding to voluntary agencies who can work along with District Family Courts or the District Legal Aid Service Authority to provide counseling to the disputing parties and bring about a speedy reconciliation. The third programme is the programme of public hearing under which hearing is given to a group of 30 or more women who are affected by a typical situation at one or more places. Funding is also given for holding seminars/workshops on topic relevant and important for women's questions. Fifthly, funding is also given to academicians to carry out surveys and other studies. The observations and recommendations received from these activities are compiled. The public wing of NCW has in past, brought out substantive publications on various issues.

The annual report gives the progress of what is happening on the side of empowerment by examining the scenario on political and economic front and in media. Political participation women, right from the village panchayat upto Parliament, avenues for economic independence to women at all levels and the portrayal of women in media are the matters of continuous advocacy in NCW. The reports also contain a chapter on our planning process and how specific planning can be helpful in removing gender disparities in various geographical and social arenas.

Special studies are undertaken and sponsored by Commission. Another tool is organization of national workshop and seminars. The subjects range from child rape to tribal women to food security to agricultural labour, to health related matters to credit policy for women and so on. More than three hundred recommendations have been made so far and nearly 100 publications have been brought out.

There are some ways to measure the success of NCW's work. It can be asked whether there was any perceptible change in the society because of any work done by NCW. One such example can be quoted. A project called Mangalam started by NCW in Pondicherry in 1994 which received further support from the successive Lt. Governors has worked very well in a cluster of about 50 villages resulting in high degree of awareness and empowerment of women even though they are not well educated. The idea behind his project was the women's group be formed and trained to support the cause of women by having a justice delivery system for women by the women. This empowerment of women is sought to be achieved by developing their expertise in elementary skill for delivering judgments. They are also put peer pressure on families or a better status of women within family in areas such as violence against women by the male members, malnutrition of girls, child-marriage, dowry harassment, better educational access to girl children etc.

Other ways of measuring success of NCW is through systemic improvements brought about in government offices, gender sensitization achieved perception of the government and the public about the role of NCW, new process or implementation started in any organization due to NCW's efforts, the degree of confidence among the public regarding how effectively NCW can tackle the problems and the feedback received from people about how they are benefited by the work of NCW.

The NCW has been designed as a watchdog on how the various government sectors perform *vis-à-vis* gender justice. In coming years NCW will have to focus on various government efforts to ensure that they have a proper strategy, proper execution plan and proper monitoring system rather than just having excellent recommendations.

The real index of empowerment of women will be that situation when the Commission does not have to exist anymore for them. But in our vision of the NCW, do we see that day possible sometime in future? Are our eyes on that day? Or is it a vision of perpetual existence of the Commission? Perhaps it is a little too early, but this question must remain in our mind as an index of NCW's success.

12

Promoting Child Development and Governmental Programmes: An Assessment

Child development as generally means all-around development of the child, physical, mental and social can only be enhanced, when the defined age group is provided with the basic services of both preventive and curative in nature in accordance with the needs and age of the child. The basic aspects which are to be looked after in order to stimulate early childhood development include:

1. Immunization;
2. Nutrition;
3. Health;
4. Early childhood education;
5. Parental education.

Apart from specifically designed child care programmes, most of all rural development programmes have one or more such components of early childhood development. Fig. 12.1

The major problems that do not bring expected results of these programmes may be the rapid growth of population, lack of proper education and status of women in the present day situation in India and the study region as well.

Children constitute about 43 per cent of the country's population, a major proportion which has remained almost constant through the past 79 years. This age distribution of the population is the combined effect of high fertility and steady decline in mortality. A crucial factor contributing to high fertility in India is the young age at which girls are married. In the absence of a foolproof system for marriage registration, data analysis reveals a small rise in age at marriage of girls from 13 years in 1901 to 15.3 years in 1951, 17 years in 1971 and 18.6 years in 1981.

The correlation between female illiteracy and infant mortality is equally clear. It is found that infant mortality was highest in the case of illiterate mothers both in urban and rural areas, but much higher in lager. As education levels increased, the mortality rate declined. The lack of education of women limits their awareness of

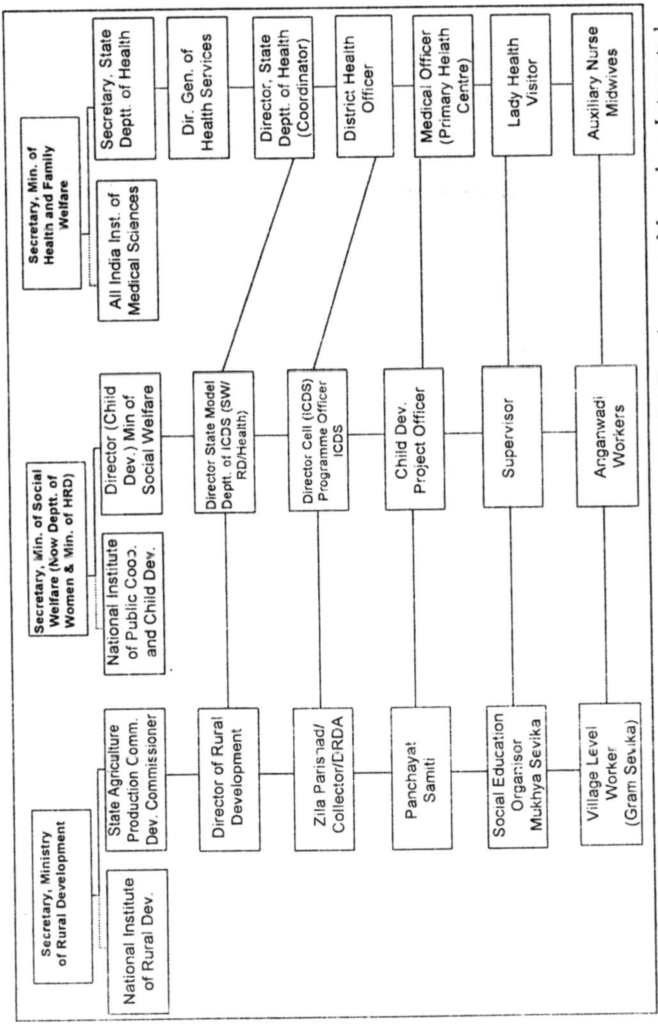

Source: National Institute of Public Corporation and Child Development. Manual on Integrated Child Development Services, New Delhi. 2003.

Fig. 12.1: ICDS Projects Administrative Chart

the benefits of learning for their children. Unless the women are educated, the efforts to open up learning opportunities to boys and girls from poor family is unlikely to succeed decisively. In fact, the most potent tool to create a social demand for early childhood development is the exposure to education of adults, particularly women.

Child cannot develop in vacuum. It needs support of the family and the community as a whole since the parents are the primary care takers of the child. The development of the child depends totally on the development of parents. A step to enhance child development through various rural development programmes is the inclusion of child development and parental education aspects as discussed earlier in the programme, frame. The next step is to build up a sound community participation base for the successful implementation of the programmes. The following measures are to be taken care of to make Rural Development Programme more child oriented:

- Parental awareness regarding the programme: objectives, services, beneficiaries etc.
- Timely services.
- Adult education by incentive schemes, involving the literate beneficiaries.
- Steps to equality of women.
- Population education.
- Parental education to stimulate the development of the child in home situation.
- Use of media, innovative technology in educating parents.
- Involving beneficiaries in need identification, prioritization of services, review and periodic assessment of the programme.
- Grass-roots level organization development and its involvement in the programme.
- Inter-personal relationship between beneficiaries and programme functionaries.

The very purpose, promoting child development through rural development programmes explains the idea that child development should be considered in the context of family and community, where the child lives. There is a need to include more child development aspects in rural development programmes and the parents, basically mothers should be equipped with required skill to stimulate the development of the child so that both work simultaneously to create a healthy intelligent and socially viable child to make our country prosperous.

The Scheme of ICD (Integrated Child Development Scheme)

An ICDS scheme was launched in 1975 for providing opportunities of physical and psycho-social development to children in age-group zero to six years through an integrated package of early childhood services. These services include supplementary nutrition, immunization, health check-up, referral service and treatment for manor illness for these children and expectant and nursing mothers, pre-school education for children in the age group of three to six years, and nutrition and health education for all women in the age group 15–45 years. The services are provided through the ICDS projects located mostly at the Block level. With its expansion in successive Five Year Plans, ICDS, is today a major programme of child development at the national level with the following main objectives:

- to improve the nutritional and health status of children in the age-group 0–6 years;
- to lay the foundation for proper psychological, physical and social development of the child;
- to reduce the incidence of mortality, malnutrition and school dropout;
- to achieve effective co-ordinations of policy and implementation amongst the various departments to promote child development; and
- to enhance the capability of the mother to look after the normal health and nutritional needs of the child through proper nutrition the health education.

The objectives are sought to be achieved by delivery on integrated package of early childhood services comprising supplementary nutrition, immunization, health check-up and referral services for children (0–6) and for expectant and nursing mothers by providing health and nutrition education to mothers and by imparting non-formal pre-school education to the children in the age group three to six years.

The objectives of the scheme are implemented through the projects located at the block level. Launched initially with 33 ICDS projects on 2 October 1975 on experimental basis in 22 States and the Union Territory of Delhi, the scheme covered 164 projects by the end of March 1978.

Objectives

The objectives of the study were following:

- To examine the organizational patterns for the implementation of ICDS projects and study their relation to the effective delivery of services;
- To analyse the process of management obtaining under different organizational patterns and compare their effectiveness in the delivery of services; and
- To suggest a more effective organizational system for better implementation of the projects.

Scope

The study was confined to rural ICDS project to make it feasible. It was undertaken Sahibganj, Dumka and Deoghar district, Jharkhand, where the Department of Social Welfare and Health and Family Welfare respectively were the nodel departments for the implementation of the ICDS scheme, with the objective of comparing the effectiveness of delivery of services under two different organizational and administrative systems.

Sample for the study

The major consideration underlying the selection of the villages was the location (distance from Project/PHC/Block) and their representative character. The first group represented the villages, which were near the Project/PHC/Block while another group represented those which were far from the project headquarters. A third group was found with villages, which were neither very near nor very far from the project office. Two other groups were also formed. However, the criterion for forming these five groups were as follows:

Sl. No.	*Group Criteria*	*Distance Criteria*	*No of Villages Selected*
1.	Near from the Project	0–10 Kms	2
2.	Far from the Project	40 Kms. and above	2
3.	Medium distance range	10–20 Kms.	2
4.	Near the Sub-centre/Dispensary	0–10 Kms.	2
5.	Remote village (No facilities)	40 Kms. and more	2
		Total	10

The villages were grouped according to the norms specified above. Having listed the names of the villages in each group, the final selection of villages was made in consultation with the CDPO, on the basis of the population/number of households. The sample for the study included 13 per cent (two from each group) of the Anganwadi villages. It was also ensured that the selected Anganwadi villages were geographically well distributed in the project area and the sample-included center located in the interior. The respondents comprised Anganwadi Workers (AWWs) beneficiaries and community leaders from the selected centers/villages. From each center/village two beneficiaries and two community leaders were selected following purposive sampling technique. Besides the respondents all the other ICDS functionaries, *viz.* CDPO, Medical Officer and BDO.

The number of different types of respondents interviewed in the field during the course of the survey in project under study may be seen below:

Sl. No.	*Types of Respondents*		*No. of Interviewed*
1.	Project Level Functionaries		
	CDS-CDPO		1
	Anganwadi worker		10
	Medical Officer		2
	Do		1
2.	Local Community		20
	Representative of Panchayat, village leaders, teachers etc.		
	Beneficiaries		20
		Total	**54**
3.	Number of Anganwadi Centres covered		10

In addition to this efforts were also made to collect and discuss the concern officer posted at district level *viz.* Welfare Officer, DSO etc.

Limitation of the Study

A study was confined to only one rural ICDS project of Santhal Pargana in Jharkhand State observations cannot be generalized in the case of other rural projects. However, the findings may at the most indicate trend in the case of other rural projects in the State and to that extent some of the suggestions given in respect of the project may be relevance of them.

The organizational set-up of ICDS in Santhal Pargana is given in Fig. 12.2. The ICDS project at Dumka, Deoghar and Godda covered 85 Anaganwadi Centers (AWCs) and five sectors but at the time of the study one sector supervisor was transferred. There were therefore, four supervisors and 95 workers in position and each worker was assisted by a helper. The project was headed by a Child Development and rroject Officer (CDPO). The CDPO was responsible for supervising and guiding the work of project team including Supervisors and Anganwadi Workers. He was to maintain close functional laison with the BDO and PHC Incharge and other functionaries at *i.e.* block level to avail the already existing infrastructure and resources for development for the effective implementation of the ICDS project. The CDPO was functioning as the drawing and disbursing officer for the project.

However, the staff position as on 6 February 2004 at the ICDS Project in Dumka is as follows:

Category	*Sanctioned*	*In Position*	*Trained*	*Under Training*
CDPO	1	1	1	—
Add./Asstt. CDPO	—	—	—	—
Supervisor	5	4	4	—
Anganwadi Worker	95	95	91	4
Medical Officer	5	5	—	—
LHVs	2	2	2	—
ANMs	25	20	20	—

Source: ICDS Project, Dumka

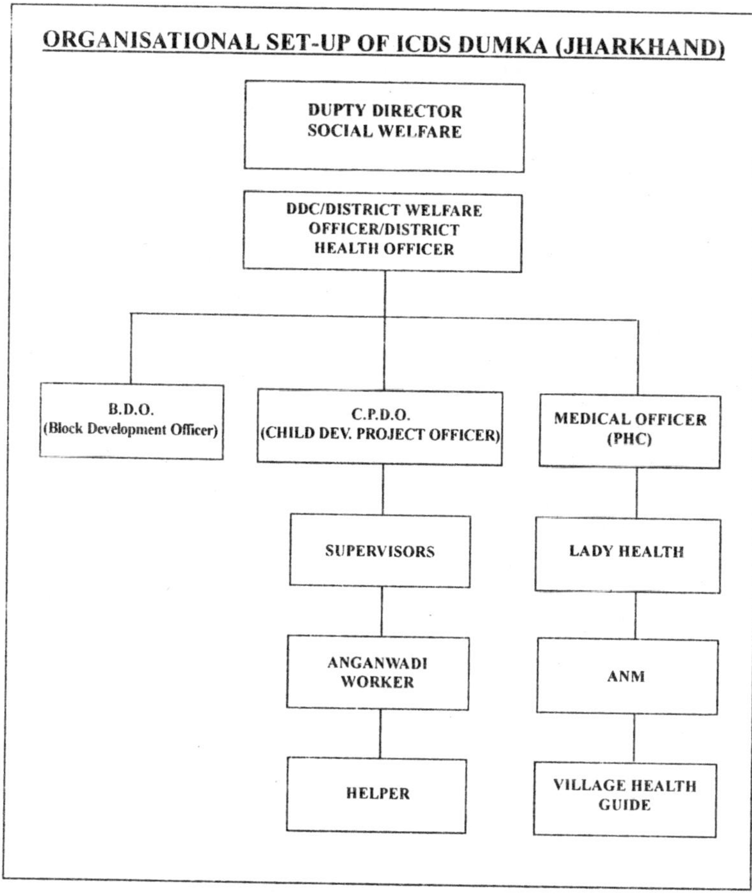

Fig. 12.2: Organisation set-up of ICDS Dumka (Jharkhand)

As mentioned about out of Anganwadi Workers only 91 are trained and four workers has been for training to Ranchi Training Centre, Ranchi, but the training programme was postponed.

The informations regarding infrastructural facilities available at the CDPOs Office and Anganwadi Centres are also collected and presented below:

Item	*Availability*
(a) At the CDPO's Office	
Jeep	One
Trailor	Nil
Typewriter	Nil-but required
Duplicator	Yes (One)
Slide Projector	Yes (One)
Slides/Film strips	Yes
Office furniture	Yes—but inadequate
(b) At the Selected Centres	
Weighing scales	Adequate
Coloured strips for UMAC	do
Registers	Inadequate
Health Cards	Inadequate
MPR Forms	Adequate
Guide book for AWW	do
First aid kit	Inadequate
Materials for pre-school activities	do

It was observed during field visit and also suggested by the CDPO that there should be one operator for slide projector and first aid kit and materials for pre-school activities were fairly inadequate in all the selected Anganwadi Centres.

The Anganwadi Workers

Among the 95 Anganwadi Workers of the project area, a little more than one-fifth or 22.10 per cent belonged to the scheduled castes community. Populationwise five out of the 10 selected villages under sample were predominantly inhabited by the scheduled caste. However, this did not coincide with the fact that five of the 10 Anganwadi Workers who belonged to the scheduled castes were coming from the same village were the scheduled caste population was high. Notwithstanding, in two villages where the SC population was predominant, the Anganwadi Workers did not belong to the SC community.

A brief profile a Anganwadi workers is presented in Table exhibit that more than one-third or 36.86 per cent workers belonged OBC (Other Backward Caste) category followed by SC (22.10 per cent) and Hindu low caste. Hindu high castes and Muslim community had the equal share, *i.e.*, 10.52 per cent, as far as caste-wise representation of Anganwadi Workers is concerned.

Profile of Anganwadi Workers

Variation	*No. of AWWs*	*Percentage*
Age: 15–20 Years	0	0.00
21–25 Years	45	47.38
26–30 Years	25	36.48
30 and Above	15	15.78
Total	**85**	**100.00**
Caste: S.C.	21	22.30
S.T.	0	0.00
Sub-Total	**21**	**22.30**
Other Backward Caste	35	36.86
Hindu High Caste	10	10.52
Hindu Low Caste	19	20.00
Muslim	10	10.52
Others	10	10.52
Total	**84**	**100.00**
Education: Upto Middle	59	62.12
Below High School	24	35.78
High School and Above	2	2.10
Illiterate	—	—
Total	**85**	**100.00**
Work Experience: Less than 1 year	4	4.21
1–3 Years	24	25.26
3–5 Years	32	33.68
5 Years Plus	35	36.85
Total	**95**	**100.0**
Training: Trained	95	95.78
Untrained	4	4.21
Total	**99**	**100.00**

Source: ICDS Project, Dumka

Age structure of Anganwaid workers was biased towards young. Majority of the Anganwadi Workers (45 or 47 per cent) were in age group 21–25 years followed by 26–30 years (35 or 36.84 per cent). About 16 per cent workers were in the age group 31 and above and none of the workers were from the age group 15–20.

As far as educational structure of the Anganwadi Workers is concerned, a little less than two-third or 62.12 per cent were educated upto middle only. About 36 per cent were below high school standard and only 2.10 per cent had crossed this bar. However, none of them were illiterate. A total of 91 underwent job training for the Anganwadi Workers and four were untrained. Their experience as Anganwadi Workers varied from less than one year to more than five years. Majority of them (35 or 36.58 per cent) were having more five than years experience.

Eight out of 10 Anganwadi Workers were local (staying in the same villages where their respective Anganwadi Centres were located) and rest two were coming from the neighbouring villages situated at a distance of one to five kilometres. The details regarding this are as follows:

	Number
Local	8
Non-Local (coming from a distance of 1–2 kms.)	1
Non-Local (coming from a distance of 3–5 kms.)	1
Total	**10**

Functioning of Anganwadi Centre

Time devoted by the Anganwadi Workers on different activities and informations regarding functioning of the centers were also collected. The services provided under the project included supplementary nursing for children in the age group 0–6 years and pregnant and nursing mothers, health check-up immunization and referral services for them, health and nutrition education for mothers and non-formal pre-school education for children in the age group three to six years. The Anganwadis, the focal points for the delivery of services under ICDS, were functioning from 10.00 A.M. to 2.00 P.M. With the following schedule of activities:

Time Devoted by AWCs	*Activity*
10.00 a.m. to 11.00 a.m.	Bringing of children to AWC by helper.
11.00 a.m. to 1.30 p.m.	Pre-school activity.
1.00 p.m. to 1.30 p.m.	Washing of hands and face of children.
1.30 p.m. to 2 p.m.	Distribution of supplementary food.

However, it was observed during field visit that in almost all the selected Anganwadi centers, the above mentioned programme schedule was followed except washing of hands and face of children. The programme schedule given above was broad and flexible in the sense that the Anganwadi Worker could adjust it keeping in view the local situation and take initiative in conducting the activities in a more interesting and effective manner. On the whole, it was observed that the Anganwadi Workers were not giving proper attention in washing of hand and face of children.

The Beneficiaries

The beneficiaries under the ICDS Scheme are categorized under expectant mother, nursing mothers, children (six months to three years) and children (three years to six years). However, under these categories number selected for supplementary nutrition and number of children registered for pre-school education in the complete ICDS project area were also selected and given in the table below:

Number of Beneficiaries Under the ICDS Project

Category of Beneficiaries	*No. Selected for SNP*	*Percentage*	*Children Registered for PSE*
Expectant mother	570	1,225 (6.03)	—
Nursing mother	570	1,225 (6.03)	—
Children (six months to three years)	4,507	(47.70)	—
Children (3–6)	3,800	(40.22)	3,800
Total	**9,447**	**9.92**	**3,800**

Source: ICDS Project, Dumka (S.P)

Above table shows that only 9,447 or 9.22 per cent of the total population were the ICDS beneficiaries for SNP in the block. As far as expectant and nursing mothers are concerned they were having equal share, *i.e.* 1.25 per cent. Among the total beneficiaries, children below three years (six months to three years) were having good share, 47.70 per cent. The corresponding figure for 3800 children in the ICDS project area were registered for pre-school education.

It is observed during the field visit to the selected Anganwadi centers that the attendance of children was very low. Only 10–20 children were present in majority of the Anganwadi Centres (six out of ten) for both the programmes. The number was less than 10 in one Anganwadi centre. However, detail information regarding this is presented in table below:

Attendance of Children at the Anganwadi Centres

No. of Children	*No. of AWCs showing Attendance of Children*	
	As Per Register	*During Visit*
31–40	3	0
21–30	5	3
10–20	2	6
Less than 10	0	1
Total	**10**	**10**

The number of children was more in three of the Anganwadi Centres, where the pre-school activity in an innovation way, was going on. In none of the Centres more than 30 children were seen though the number of children enrolled at various centers varied from 15 to 60 and 20 to 50 for children in the age groups six month to three years and three to six years respectively.

Having notice the poor attendance of children at the Anganwadi Centres, the reasons thereof were also identified, from both parents as well as Anganwadi Workers, which are as follows:

- At the time of field visit, supplementary nutrition was suspended due to interruption in food supplies (State Food Corporation). At some places children were not interested in having 'khichudi' only. And throughout the year they were given 'khichudi' and supplementary nutrition.
- The community were not properly educated about the ICDS programme. Because in PSE activities they were expecting something else and so not found it worthwhile to send their children to Anganwadi Centre.
- In the villages predominant by higher castes, parents preferred to send their children to school than Anganwadi Centre (even three years of children).
- In the Scheduled caste families, older children had to stay back at home to look after their younger siblings while both the parents went out for work.

- It was also complained by the villagers that Center used to remain close for longer period (10–15 days) in a month so they found it not worthwhile to send their children.
- This problem was discussed by the ICDS functionaries. As per their statement children will only come to the Centre when supplementary nutrition will be provided to them. Interruption in food supply leads to the poor attendance of children at the Aganwadi Centres.

Supplementary Nutrition

Under the programme, supplementary nutrition food was used to serve (not regularly) to the children and the pregnant and lactating mothers. Mostly they were given "khichudi" of rice and dal, which were locally available. However, the Anganwadi Workers were expected to see that the children wash their hands before the food under SNP was served to them. Though this was the practice at most of the Anganwadi Centres, the children observed were by and large untidy. The Anganwadi workers found fault with the parents for not keeping their children neat and clean. It was, however observed that no effort was made by the Anganwadi Workers to keep the children clean. The children were sent back home as they were at the end of the Anganwadi Programmes. If the Anganwadi Workers send them neat and tidy, it would give the parents a feeling that children are developing good habits while attending the Anganwadi Centres.

Most of the parents reported that they were sending their children regularly to the Anganwadi Centres, but it was observed that many of them were not doing so particularly when supplementary food could not be served due to delay in supplies. This was more so with the parents of the SCs community for whom the main attraction at the Anganwadi Centres was the food that was distributed. At one of the Centres it was observed that not even a single beneficiary was present.

The timing of food distribution was found not suitable, it being afternoon by that time, the presents were expecting a full meal for their children and therefore, they had a feeling that the quantity of the food, given was not sufficient.

As far as pregnant and nursing mothers are concerned, very few of them were going to the Anganwadi Centres for taking their share of supplementary nutrition food. Some of them felt it below their dignity to go to Anganwadi Centre just to have a little share of food while others did not find time to go there as they were busy in their fields or household work. It was also observed that not many women were aware that supplementary nutritions food was provided about the services available at the Anganwadi Centre.

By the large, the Anganwadi workers were not getting any help from the beneficiary mothers in running the centre. They were only coming sometimes to leave their children at the Centre and take them back at the end of the Anganwadi activities, as they used to keep themselves busy in own household/agricultural work. They were of the view that the Anganwadi worker does not require their help as she was provided with a helper to assist her. They, however, expressed their willingness to help the Anganwadi worker, if at all they required any help from them. These observations suggest that the mothers were not clear on how they could participate in the Anganwadi Activities. It could be that the Anganwadi Workers were not clear that how they could involve mothers in conducting programmes of they did not like to involve them.

Food supplies under SNP to the Centre were generally irregular (as per the response of both the workers and local people) and their quality unsatisfactory. It was also reported that warm-infested food material was supplied on one or two occasions. As reported by the ICDS functionaries, the community people were not at all in a position to contribute anything being very poor and affected by natural calamities like drought etc. in the case of Anganwadi Centre. Not approachable by road, the village people were not helping the Anganwadi Worker by picking up the supplies from the roadside and delivering them to the centre.

However, supplies of food material for SNP and medicines to the Anganwadi Centres were not regular as reported by the Anganwadi Workers. Four out of 10 Anganwadi Centres studies has inadequate facilities for storage of supplies. The article in these Centres were kept at a neighbouring house to avoid theft. All the Anganwadi Centres were provided at the beginning with very few utensils/ equipments for running the programmes, one-third of the Anganwadi Workers felt that certain items like bucket rope, plates and spoons should also be provided at the centre.

Pre-school Education

The next important activity of the programme is the pre-school education (PSE) with having the following main objectives:

- developing adequate muscular coordination and basic motor skills in the children;
- developing creativity and aesthetic appreciation and elementary hygienic sense;
- providing opportunity for interacting with other children of the same age-group;
- developing in the child the ability express his thoughts and feeling influent, correct and clear speech; and
- developing the habits of attending the AWC regularly.

The programme content of pre-school activity is, therefore centred on play activities as "play is the main activity by which child learns and develops". These play activities should be based on indigenous material and culture.

However, in the project under the pre-school activity was being conducted generally from 11.00 a.m. to 1.00 p.m.. The activity, starting with a payer, included recitation of nursery rhymes, teaching of numbers and narration of stories. It was observed that Anganwadi workers were not having sufficient kit materials to perform this activity. Many of the Anganwadi Workers were of the view that the play material became unusable and required replacement.

In most of the centers, the children were asked to recite the same old prayers, poems, and tell the same old stories narrates to them when the project started functioning. However, the workers were making efforts to involve children in outdoor games. They were trying to develop the concept of number, shape, colour, size etc. But it was observed that in almost all the centers those activities were repetitive. Thus, the pre-school activity, although conducted regularly, were repetitive and monotonous and not attractive enough for the majority of the Anganwadi Centres. It was also unattractive for them as the same old charts and play material provided when the project started functioning were used for these activities.

Health and Nutrition Education

Health and Nutrition Education to the target groups were mainly given by the Female Health Worker (FHW)/ANM, Multipurpose Health Worker, Anganwadi Worker and LHV as mentioned by the beneficiaries. Under this component ANMs were suppose to motivate the people for adoption of family planning practices and were suppose to educate them on the need to get their children immunized and keeping their surroundings clean.

It was however, observed that very few were imparting health and nutrition education to the people. Very few of the Health Functionaries make the visit of their allotted area/villages as reported by the villagers.

It was however, observed that very few were imparting health and nutrition education to the people. Very few of the Health Functionaries make the visit of their allotted area/villages as reported by the villagers.

Health Check-up, Immunization and Referral Services

As in the case of health and nutrition education, these three activities are also the main responsibility of the Primary Health Centre (PHC) and its dispensaries and sub-centres. In the project there was no regular health check-up at the Anganwadi Centre. The Medical Officer (MO) was conducting an over-all health check of children to identify infectious diseases, etc., when, immunization services were provided through mass campaigns.

Although weighing scales were available at each Anganwadi Centres but the weights of children were not taken as per the schedule. Growth charts and Health Cards were distributed to AWCs long back when the project started. It was also observed during the field visit that the mothers were usually not present when the weights of their children were taken at the Anganwadi Centre except in the case of those who were in the age-group of six months to two years. However, the mothers should be required to be present when the weights of their children were taken irrespective of their age-group as they could help in Anganwadi Worker in taking the weights. Their presence would also help in creating health awareness among them.

As regards immunization, services were being provided for mothers and children through the sub-centres. The children of Anganwadi Centres were usually immunized twice in a year against different diseases. The targets and achievements of the complete area of the PHC is given in the table.

It is evident from table that for none of the items achievements are more than 50 per cent. This problem was discussed with staff at PHC level. As per their statement the poor achievement is because of lack of manpower at both the level as well as PHC/dispensaries. However, supply of vaccines and medicines for each items are adequate.

Targets and Achievements Under Different Items of PHC Dumka (S.P.), 2003

Item	*Target*	*Achievements*	*Percentage*
(1)	(2)	(3)	(4)
DPT	3,950	1,820	4.07
D.T.	3,900	1,630	41.79
B.C.G.	4,077	985	21.95
Polio	4,077	1,685	41.32
T.T.	5,233	1,925	36.78
Vitamin "A"	—	75 Bottles	—
Iron Tabs (Children)	—	88,000	—
Iron and Folic Acid Tablets for (Women)	—	78,000	—
Simple Drug	—	Adequate	—

Source: PHC, Dumka

So far as the referral services are concerned, services were not provided in a regular and systematic manner. The FHWs/MPWs on their visits to villages, advised the present so far children suffering from typhoid, dehydration etc. requiring special attention to go to the nearest dispensing center of PHC or district hospital as the case may be. But there was no regular follow-up of such an advice as there was no formal referral service system at the project through a referral card or slip. There was no services or regular follow-up even in the case of malnourished children.

The opinion of parents varied in regard to the benefits received from the services rendered through the AWC. Most of them (60%) felt that their children benefited from the SNP. Next in order were the immunization and pre-school services (65%). Only about one-third of them mentioned that their children benefited from the service of health check-up. None of them was aware of the referral services provided through the AWC.

Services	*Benefited*	*Not benefited*	*Don't know*	*Total*
S.N.P.	12 (60%)	4 (20%)	4 (20%)	20 (100)
P.S.E.	13 (65%)	7 (35%)	—	20 (100)
Health Check-up	7 (35%)	—	13 (65%)	20 (100)
Referral Services	—	—	20 (100)	20 (100)

Most of the parents particularly those belonging to the scheduled caste community, could not, however, spell out how the services benefited their children. Only a few of them specified the benefits received as follows:

- They learnt good manners;
- Developed school going habit;
- Learnt the correct usage of words, etc.

Visits of Functionaries to the Anganwadi Centres

For proper functioning of the center, the Anganwadi Workers required the guidance and supervisors. It is, therefore, the information regarding visits of different functionaries (their frequency) to the AWCs were also collected and presented in the table.

Visits of Functionaries to AWCs During 2003

Frequency	*Functionaries Visited No. of AWCs*				
	CDPO	*MO*	*Supervisor*	*ANM*	*LHV*
2–5 times	6	8	3	7	9
6–9 times	2	1	3	3	1
10–14 times	2	—	2	—	—
Total	**10**	**9**	**8**	**10**	**10**

The above table reveals that the supervisor (ICDS) most frequently make visit of the Anganwadi Centres. Five out of 10 studies centers have reported that ICDS supervisor had made visit to their centers more than six times. High frequency of visit was followed by the CDPO. The Anganwadi Workers said that their supervisors helped them in solving some of the problems. They persuaded the parent to send their children regularly to the Anganwadi Centre. They explained different columns in the registers/reports and guided the workers in filling the required information, etc.

Co-ordination at Different Levels

As the ICDS scheme adopts an inter-sectoral approach involving more than one department or agency of the government, panchayats and voluntary agencies, there is all the more need for coordination of their efforts in delivering the package of services for children and mothers. Co-ordination will help maximum utilization of the available resources. The scheme provides for formal mechanisms through the constitution of co-ordination committees at the state, district and project levels.

On the whole, it was observed that at the block level BDO, CDPO and MO were having good co-ordination between each other but at the grass-root level co-ordination between the health functionaries and AWWs were not so.

Community Participations

The community participation in the effective implementation of the programme is a very important aspect which cannot be ignored. For the purpose of present study, representatives of panchayat, village leaders and influential persons of the village were considered. The primary school teacher who is usually a source of information and an agent for creating community awareness was also included under the category of leaders.

A total of 20 community leaders were interviewed. However, their observations may only indicate the general trend. Most of them said that they were visiting the Anganwadi Centre twice a month and some of them started almost every alternate day. They sought the advice of the leaders on various matters like improving the attendance of children at the AWCs, creating community awareness about the programme.

However, by and large it was observed that the community participation was poor in programme implementation. The conditions of all the visited centers were very poor. The AWWs used to keep the articles in nearby houses. During field visit "Mukhia" of the village panchayat was also consulted in this regard and few of them were agreed up on it and giving assurance that under the Jawahar Rozgar Yojana they are going to construct the building for Anganwadi Centre.

Suggestions and Recommendations

(a) About Proper Functioning

- The primary school teacher or one of the fellow villagers or elders or local persons should supervise/guide the helper in the distribution of supplementary nutrition food when the Anganwadi Workers are on leave or even in normal course also.
- The local people should help the Anganwadi worker in procuring the articles for Anganwadi Centre.
- For running the Anganwadi Centres more affectively in regard to programmes and activities, role of functionaries, supplies and equipments, support and participation of the beneficiaries and the village panchyats should also be enhanced.
- The community should be made more aware of the activities and programmes of the Anganwadi Centres.
- The priority should be given to the local girls for recruitment of Anganwadi Workers so that she can put more efforts in running the Centres.
- The Supervisors and the CDPO should make frequent visits to the Anganwadi Centres and provide necessary guidance to the Anganwadi Workers; and
- The Anganwadi Centre should be provided with adequate number of utencils and containers for storage of food material.

(b) About Supplementary Nutrition

- Food supplies under SNP by the State Food Corporation were very irregular and their quality was unsatisfactory. It was reported that worm infested food material was also supplied on one or two occasions. Hence, it is suggested that the food supplies should be regular and of a better quality.
- It is observed that since last one year only "khichudi" distribution of rice and dal was going on in all the Anganwadi Centres. There should be variety in the supplementary food given to mothers and children.
- When there is delay in food supply community should contribute the locally available food for the Anganwadi Centres.
- It was suggested by the parents that children may also be given sweets and biscuits sometimes in place of "khichudi".

(c) About Pre-school Education

- It was observed that pre-school activity, although conducted regularly, were repetitive and monotonous and not attractive enough for the children. It was also unattractive for them as the same old charts and play material provided when the project started functioning. Hence, it is suggested that some more teaching materials through the help of UNICEF should be supplied.
- Parents were in the opinion that Anganwadi Worker should give more emphasis on teaching numbers and alphabet to children. Thus, in this regard parents need to be educated by the functionaries on the concept of pre-school education.
- Toys may be provided or should be prepared by the AWWs/ Community through waste materials for children at the Anganwadi center to attract and educate them simultaneously.

(d) About Health and Nutrition Education

- Under this, the ANMs/FHWs were motivating the people only for adoption of family planning practices to achieve their targets. They should also give emphasis on the need to get their children immunized and keeping their surroundings clean.

- Very few of the Anganwadi Workers were imparting health and nutrition education during their home visit. But they should use puppets and posters to educate the community on the evils of alcholism, drug addiction, etc, through group meetings of the beneficiaries.

(e) About Health Check-up, Immunization and Referral Services

- The mother should be required to be present when the weights of their children were taken irrespective of their age-group as they could help the Anganwadi Worker in taking the weights. Their presence would also help in creating health awareness among them.
- The health functionaries working at the grass-root level (like, ANM/FHW, and MPW) should make regular visit at least twice in a month for health check-up and once in six months for immunization.
- Local people had a feeling that the Anganwadi Centre is only to look after children; so at least the ANM should be provided the required medicines during home visits.
- Long back when the project was started a medicine kit box was supplied to the Anganwadi Workers through UNICEF after that any medicine nor tool kits were given to the workers. It is therefore, suggested that atleast first-aid medicine should be supplied at the centre.
- Referral services were not provided in a regular and systematic manner. The beneficiaries by the large, were unaware of the referral services due to the fact that these not effectively provide. However, grass-root level health functionaries should given special attention and advised the parents to go to the nearest dispensing center or PHC or district hospital as the case may be.

13

Summary and Conclusion

Any study of the tribal society or can not ignore the four major characteristics of tribal life: (a) widespread poverty, (b) very high of illiteracy, (c) primitive nature of their culture characterized by the absence of modern outlook and (d) centuries old norms controlling social behaviour of the people. The present study is basically an analysis of gender role differential as exists among the Santhals, the most advanced and numerically biggest among all the tribes found in the State of Jharkhand. The specific area of study is home-management and the intention behind selecting the particular is that home is the sphere where the role of female is most intensive.

Various studies have been done in different societies regarding the role performance of the female in home-management. This forms an interesting subject of study because with the changes taking place in the socio-cultural spheres the pattern of home-management. For instance as a result of the changing status of women in developed and developing nations of the world the relationship between the spouses is also being replaced by the feeling of comradeship between the two instead of the relationship of dominance subordination existing during the past decades. In these societies drudgery of domestic works is no longer an exclusive business of the women. The men have come forward to assist the women in various aspects of home management. This has become more necessary because the women have opted in increasing number for gainful employment outside their homes. The small family norm, all over, have brought changes in the family structure, especially among the middle class and this has caused changes in the conception of home or family management. The children need more intensive care which is more a concern for the mothers than the male guardians of the family. With the increasing freedom of the women they also have been made to accept new role. At the first instance we can mention that women have started assuming the role of economic patterns of their husbands. They have also been entrusted with other tasks, which were done exclusively of the children, etc. Therefore, it is not absolutely correct to say that women in advanced or advancing countries have been able to shake off the domestic responsibilities to a great extent. Rather the correct version would be to say that they have been entrusted with many other responsibilities than merely home management as found in less advanced societies found in rural or tribal areas. Of course, it cannot be denied that many function like laundering etc. have been taken over by the specialized outside agencies and the appearance of many types of family budgets in the market—automatic power driven, semi-automatic and manually operated—gave much relief, both in terms of labour and time, the housewives in urban areas. The women in the backward societies, in rural and tribal areas, are deprived of it.

As per the new concept of home management it is considered not only significant but at the same time a complicated affair having several dimensions including budgeting, planning, execution of plan etc. In simpler societies, however, the pattern of home-management, however, largely depends on the cultural tradition. Home, in any society, is the most significant institution. It is the above of the family consisting of men, his wife or wives and children. The continuity of society is dependent of family because the procreation and upbringing of the children who take the place of the present generation. In our cotemporary world the practice of sexual promiscuity no longer exists and in each society, whatever may be its level of development, some sort of social sanction is needed for sexual relationship between man and woman. All over the world one of the most prevailing form of social sanction is marriage. After marriage man and woman, normally, hire in a home and form a family. Out of the many facets of family one is the management.

Since the dawn of human civilization woman has remained a working partner of man either having equal or subordinate status. But the gender role differentiation however existed all through the ages because of the physical constituents of the female. Tasks such as hunting, lumbering and mining are predominantly male roles.

Cooking, gathering vegetables products, carrying water and making as well as repairing clothes are largely female roles. Men undertake the more strenuous tasks such a lumbering, mining, quarrying, land clearance and house building because of his superior physical strength. Unlike the women he is free from the physical burdens of pregnancy and nursing. Therefore, man can range further allied to hunt, to fish, to hard or the trade. Woman, however, has no disadvantage in the lighter tasks *e.g.* gathering the vegetable products, fetching of water, preparation of food and the manufacture of utensils and clothing, which can be performed in a near home. Women are tied to the home because of her biological function of child bearing and nursing. This is also limited to less strenuous task because of her physique.

The above account is based on the concept of "sexual division of labour" and found working in almost all the societies of the contemporary world. The universality of the division of labour by sex can be explained on the basis of the advantages inherent in it. There is another concept of the division of labour between men and women based on their psychological characteristics. According to this concept the role of women in the family can be characteristics. According to this concept the role of women in the family can be characterised as "expressive" which means the provides warmth, security and emotional support. For effective socialization of the young this is considered essential. The expressive qualities of women are not exclusively meant their children but also applicable to their husbands. For the isolated nuclear family of the modern period this is very essential. This is also essential for stabilisation of adult personalities. Men are often exposed to stress and anxiety because of their instrumental role as the bread-winner of the family which requires them to spend his working days competing in an achievement oriented society. By providing understanding, love and consideration the expressive women relieve the weary bread winners from the tension. There must be a clear-cut division of labour between men and women in family in the absence of which it cannot operate as a social system efficiently. Like a button and a button hole the instrumental and expressive role complement each other. In order to promote family welfare and solidarity they lock together.

According to a third concept the division of labour between man and women is determined by culture and also largely directed by it. This concept has been evolved by sociologists. According to this concept the norms, values and roles are determined by culture and socially transmitted. The learned recipes for behaviour are shared by members of a society. From this point of view gender rates, roles and products of culture rather then biology. The respective male and female roles are learned by the individuals. The gender role differences are justified and supported as normal, right and proper by a belief and value system.

All the concepts of sexual division of labour discussed above have, however, been vehemently opposed particularly by the female sociologists and supporters of Women's Liberation Movement. On the basis of evidences collected from different culture all over the world they claim that sexual division is not universal and more over, there is no reason for its being universal. Diverse and endlessly variable human cultures were created by human inventiveness and not because of invincible biological forces. The sexual division of labour is neither universal nor it is correct to argue that certain roles are always performed by men and other by women. In most cases this view is biased because of the limited vision of the researcher who views if through his own cultured perspective and also through the eyes of male. The sexual division is more apparent in western world and it will be an error to judge all other cultures through this perspective.

The hollowness of the assumption that sexual division of labour is largely determined by biology can be established by mentioning the practices in different societies of the world. In many societies, for example, lumbering is done either exclusively by women or shared by both sexes. The task of land clearance is many cultures is the sole responsibility of the women. Cooking is also shared activity at many places. In India women constitute more than ten per cent of labourers on building sites. More than a quarter of the labour force in Asian and Latin American countries, working in mines is female. The biological characteristics do not act as a barrier to the female for performing any particular job. In fact, there is no work meant exclusively for the women.

Our discussion so far leads us to the following generalizations: Culture rather than biology determine the gender role; no task (apart from child bearing) is exclusively carried out exclusively by females;

and women are not debarred from particular occupations because of their biological characteristics.

On the basis of above discussion we can therefore, very well say that the domestic role of women in a cultural construction and the significant among the various roles is the role of household management. Management is the natural outgrowth of human association in the home environment. As soon as the family is established and persons begin to work together for common purpose needs arise from the development of a plan for action, for the delegation of responsibility and for organising and controlling the use of available human and non-human resources.

Many peoples look upon management as a way of life. They are home made up of human beings living together in an environment of love and affection and predominantly concerned with the quality of human association. In the concept management becomes a means of using resources for the attainment of family goals. Efficiency is measured in terms of sound standards and the use of resources that affect individual development and family living.

In general terms the concept management may be said to be planned activity directed towards accomplishing desired ends. It involves the weighing of values and the making of decisions. Everyone learns to manage in some manner, the resources at his disposal some people learn to manage well others not so well, but all manage in some degree of competence.

Early men managed but as life gradually grew more and more complex and the method he used become more refined. In earlier societies where resources were limited the situation were relatively fixed and the facilities to satisfy one's needs were simple, man's efforts to manage—that is to control his environment—were simple and direct. In our modern technique and technological environment Where situations are complex and highly flexible where many choices are possible and where values changes more rapidly, we must depend on reasoned ways of accomplishing results. Fixed rules or set ways of behaviour are not possible and traditional ways of doing things are less applicable. Under these circumstances mass is forced to make a choice of the means and the methods he will use to obtain what he wants to reach his ends.

Home management is a practical science. It cannot do away with a concept of degree or measurement. As in other practical sciences such as medicines, measurement of normal or abnormal health shows a state of being in terms of degree. In home management managing shows some degree of competence. Thus a home in which goals (ends) are being attained with some degree of satisfaction may be considered a well managed home.

Home management is the administrative side of family living. It is the force the mental work and power that puts the machinery of home making into action and keeps it going. It is dynamic. It involves decision-making that leads to action. It is a means of accomplishment. For a person or family management is planned activity directed towards the nurturing the values and satisfying of wants. It makes the use of the findings of sciences and of knowledge concerning all aspects of family life—economic, social, psychological, physical, spiritual and technological. It applies this knowledge in using the family's resources to meet living situations to solve problems and to help resolve conflict.

Simply, stated home management is planning, organising, controlling and evaluating the use of resources available to the family for the purpose of attaining family goals. Goals are in the realm of material and psychological, processes are in the realm of psychological and technological. The use made of the family's resources and the extent to which family goals are realised depend in large measurement on the managerial ability, interests and leadership to the home makers and their ability to motivate all members of the group.

The resources that individuals and families have at their disposal consist of the tools, capabilities and the ways and means they processes. These resources used are countless ways to achieve what is important to each person and to the family as a group. Assuming that decisions have been made concerning what is important to work for the question of how to use avoidable resources must be considered.

But first we will examine in more detail what the resources especially are. Two main groups are evident—the human and the non-human. Human resources are often over looked or their potential may not be attributed or made available as evident from their examination. Human resources include:

1. Abilities and skills of family members both native and acquired.
2. Attitudes, the opinions or feelings that activate or retard action. These can be very powerful activators in helping of hindering attainment of goals.
3. Knowledge possessed by each person both factual and in terms of relationship.
4. Energy or the power of members to carry on both physical and mental activities.

This group of resources is very important to the family, for not only are they the means of accomplishing desired and but in using them well the group ends and acts together in such a way that common goal seems more real and attainable and the quality of interpersonal relations can be lifted. One can easily underestimate or not be aware of these significant resources.

The non-human resources used in family living are tangible, more easily recognized and some are ardently sought after. Time, made up of shorter or longer period of duration in which activities are carried on. Time has the unique characteristics of being the one resource constant in amount for all. Its limited supply, felt by some, systems from the wide variation from person to person and from family to family in activity patterns carried on in a given period. Money and certain collateral fringe benefits now widely granted to wage earner and people on salary. In a predominantly exchange economy money is a pivotal resource because it is exchanged for commodities, services and mechanical power have added on impressive resource to family living, for they conserve money that otherwise might have to be used for certain family needs, such as costs of illness, hospitalisation or savings for retirement.

Goods, durable and perishable properly and other investments owned by the family make a large part of the non-human resources.

Community facilities for which the family does not pay directly but to which it has free access, such as parks, roads, schools, certain kinds to transportation, libraries and many other services, such as police protection, markets, medical facilities, free concerts and other entertainment, are all provided by the social group.

Conclusions

The present study was an in-depth study of the role of Santhal women in development and in home management. The significant of the study less on the fact that the study aimed at an analysis of general role in the tribal society. The overall findings of the study suggested that the roles of women were in the management of household were determined by the culture of the people. In the household sphere several aspects like household economy, decision-making, leisure time activities and the management of food and energy were taken into consideration, the analysis of the data collected revealed that the Santhals are very tradition ridden people and inspite of the absence of strict segregation of sexes the roles of the men and women were well demarcated by their traditional culture. In the household economy the males are supposed to play the major role as bread winner. But in a large number of cases the women were found working in order to add to the total income of the family. In other words, it can be said that among the Santhals the women are frequently found as the working partner of the male-folk. In view of that it can be said that the women shared quiet a significant role of the responsibility of running the family. She is supposed to manage the kitchen, looked after the children doing the domestic works like washing, cleaning and above all to work for supplementing the family income.

The leisure time was mostly spent in feminine activities like gossiping, washing, cleaning, knitting, basket making, tending the kitchen garden etc. Singing and dancing were very common and popular pastime for the Santhal women. However, in recent years there has been a shift from the traditional pattern of leisure time activities to the more sophisticated pattern found in the urban areas. The most important amount them was the film shows and film songs. Many respondents suggested that their traditional songs were also being effected by the film songs. But their traditional mode of entertainment like singing, dancing, visiting fairs or meals, jatras (rural theatre) etc. still draw large crowds.

Finally, the management of energy and food was also a part of women's role in the family. Traditionally the members of Santhals defended on the woods from the forest as the main source of energy. Like coal and kerosene were becoming popular. The women in Santhal villages very often go to the forest for picking dry woods and leaves and at times they also use the cow dung cakes as the fuel. The women were also entrusted with the tank of loading the domesticated animals and birds like chicken and ducks and they often sell the products of these animals and birds to earn money.

The milk is a source of food supply for the families, which keep domesticated animals. The Santhals is in recent years has become more inclined to keep piggeries in their houses. The pork was found a delicay among these people. But most of the respondents in this study reported that the supply of food or availability of food was insufficient. They attributed it to the factors like the absence of irrigation facilities, small size of land holdings and mortgage of tribal land to the non-tribals. Alcoholism which was very widespread among these people were mentioned as the cause of their poverty. With the clearance of the forests and absence of water reservoir the people seldom went for hunting and fishing. Lastly, the respondents suggested that certain measures which they thought could remove the economic hardship of the Santhals. These suggestion were included modernization of agriculture, creation of alternative source of income, avoidance of alcoholism and return of land mortgage to Santhals by dikus (non-tribals).

Recommendations

Women are part of the society and their problems should be treated as society's problems. Women's emancipation would lead to family emancipation, and ultimately emancipation of the country. Thus, it is in the men's interest that efforts should be made to improve women's social, economic, and political empowerment. Women, men, society, NGOs, state, and centre are stake-holders in this exercise. Hence, stake-holderwise responsibilities are suggested below:

For Women to Act

Women's empowerment is in their hands. They sold not misplace this opportunity. Once they get going, world will have to change. In order to make it a reality, women have to discharge certain responsibilities. In seeking to empower women, let us not forget that it is mothers who are essentially bringing up children. Education is a crucial input in this direction. Women should change their attitude towards girl child and accordingly provide necessary education, health care and affection on par with boys. Girl children should not be ill-treated and mothers should ensure sending them to school. They should follow small family norms. Further, child marriages, polygamy, and bride prices should be discouraged. Women should organize themselves into self-help groups and take an active part in village institutions like Anganwadi Center, health care center, co-operative, etc. Educated women voluntarily should come forward to conduct adult education classes, and awareness programme on health care, sanitation, family planning, superstition, etc. for women only happen through education. Women should also convince their menfolk about the advantages of educating girl child, monogamy, etc. Unless women become a political force, they cannot make an impact in this age of globalization. Transfer of power might lead to disruption of social system but we cannot expect men to change overnight.

For Men to Act

Men should realize the contribution of women to the household. They should also appreciate the special qualities of women. Men should encourage their spouses and children to take active part in decision-making not only in house but also outside homestead. Women should be given equal treatment and that should start from the home. Men should try to modify according to the changing environment, and practices like polyandry, polygamy, child marriage, bride price, conception of excess rice beer, etc. should be avoided.

For NGOs to Act

There are few genuine NGOs operating for emancipation of women in the state. Gyanodaya, Vivekananda Kendra, Our Welfare Association and a number of other NGOs are among them. They should collectively prepare an action plan for overall development of women. Exclusive school and boarding hostels for girls, women, old age homes, organizing self-help groups conducting health camps and adult education to women, taking up issues like child marriages, polygamy, polyandry, and bringing awareness among women about their position in society and expected roles should form agenda of these NGOs. Education and economic upliftment should form the first step in their overall objective of women's empowerment. Support from the state and central government, and international agencies can be sought for this noble cause.

For State to Act

The state government has a number of schemes for women. Of late, it has enacted the state women's progress in this regard is less than satisfactory. The state should apportion atleast 30 per cent of its total development expenses towards emancipation of women. Efforts should also be made to ensure that the allotted amount reaches the target group. Further, police, district administration, and judiciary should help women's cause, and a speedy redressed mechanism should be worked out. Women's commission should be given adequate powers and recourse to carry out its cherished goals. Appointments to the commission should be made non political and chairperson be given the rank of a cabinet minister. State also may follow the precedence of Government of Haryana which announced an incentive of Rs. 500 per month for opting family planning with two girl children. However, this amount may be deposited in the name of children in a national saving scheme which can be enchased after attaining majority. The state should give preference to girl in education, employment, and legislature. Thus, the state should not only create conducive environment for emancipation of women but also provide necessary financial support in achieving overall objective.

For Centre to Act

Centre should take the role of a friend philosopher, and guide. As it aware, Jharkhand is a sensitive area with numerous handicaps. Added to it, Jharkhandis are yet to form part to national mainstream. Further, women of Jharkhand need the special attention of Government of India. ICDS is being implemented in the state with central assistance. There is a need to strengthen Anganwadi Centres with play materials, adequate timely, and quality medicines SNP items, and necessary infrastructure. The rules followed in the rest of the country with regard to ICDS may not be applicable here. Jharkhand state is considered as a highly expensive area and such honorarium to worker and helper needs immediate hike. Further, it would be difficult for the locals to contribute towards construction of Anganwadi Centre. Government of India should consider providing 50 per cent grants towards their construction in the state. There is neither office accommodation nor quarters for the staff of ICDS. In an undulated region like this, it is a difficult task for the staff to get quarters. Government should make necessary provision for providing quarters and office accommodation to ICDS staff. Efforts also should be made to extend scheme to hitherto uncovered villages, and population.

A vast majority of the women in the state are interested in organizing Self-Help Groups. Women have opted for schemes like fish ponds, vegetable cultivation, horticulture, garment shop, petty trade, weaving, and breeding mithuns to be taken up through SHGs. Financial assistance from the government is required to implement these schemes on an experimental basis. This would go a long way in improving socio-economic status of these women. Government should also make available adequate grants for education of girl children, health care of girls, and pregnant, nursing, and old women. Such a liberal attitude from the Government of India would go a long way in not only improving emancipation of women but also building their loyalty towards India.

There is lot of differences between women, in Jharkhand state as described by Verrier Elwin and the present day women. They are marching towards progress, and are no longer passive spectators. There are women ministers, administrators, doctors, engineers, lawyers, nurses, typists, clerks, contractors, social workers, and they are in all fields. Selection of life partners is no longer restricted to rule of endogamy, many inter-tribal marriages have been taking place, and some of them got married to people from plains (rest of India). Young and educated women are crusading against polygamy. A good number of girl students are also studying outside the state. Due to rising unemployment and lack of alternative sources of income, there is unrest among educated youth. Many women have set up small businesses, and brought into focus irregularities practiced at fair price shops. They have also started literacy programmes for women and children. You will be surprised to know that there are eight beauty parlours and a training centre to train beauticians at Dumka/Deoghar conversations are in Hindi, English, and of course in their dialect. Age-old practices and traditions are coming on their way hindering progress. Thus, it is necessary to create congenial, social, political, and economic environment to enable women to participate in decision-making process. Whatever these women take up, they do it whole-heartedly and this attitude pays dividends.

There has been a drastic reduction in periodicity of Jhum cycle. As a result, Jhum plots became private property. Now it is the productivity of the Jhum lands and not number of Jhum plots which is significant. Some of them are now using improved variety of seeds, and fertilizers, and even going for off-seasonal vegetables, and horticultural crops. Keeping in view of the topography and crops grown, agricultural tools may be developed. Women have to learn by doing, by using technology, and not merely by being told. The method and approach of teaching and convincing them of utilizing information must be enhanced. It is necessary to train women facilitators on improved tools and equipment. There is a need to develop and encourage time saving technologies that can help women find time to participate in social, economic, and political activities. There is a need to strengthen support services and provide necessary inputs at subsidized rates to make them self-sufficient.

Reservation for women in education, employment, and legislature is necessary to bring about equality. Present 33 per cent reservation for women in State and Central Government employment is an affirmative section. There is a need to build women's capacities through education, organizing self-help groups, arranging economic activities, and providing agricultural extension activities. The aim should be to build women's capacities, give information, and construct a positive perspective of society. Eradication of illiteracy through education, and health care of pregnant, and lactating mothers along with newly born babies will have to be clubbed together to successfully impart family planning programmes. Efforts should be made to reduce/widening economic and social disparities among various tribes.

Limitations of the Study and Future Research

Like most study in social sciences the present research has also been conducted with certain limitations:

1. The prime objective of the present study was to investigate certain social, economic and psychological correlates of status and development of tribal and rural women of Santhal Parganas. Of the very many personal, economic, social and psychological factors only a few like three personal, three personality and four value orientation dimensions have been studied in relation to women's concern for status and development of child in the present research. The analysis of data, however, does suggest that there are many other relevant factors, which deserve studying in relation to women's concern for status and development of children. To mention a few among the background factors are rural-urban residence, education of women, job status of working women, parental attitude, and family as well as marital adjustment etc.
2. That, as detailed in Chapter IV, not getting sufficient and comparable number of cases on criteria of marital status, monthly family income and educational level in the groups of the literate and illiterate children's the 'working women' and the 'non-working women' in the districts of Santhal Pargana are an admitted limitation of the study. The researcher may like to plan some studies in future to examine their effects in a more planned manner, and if needed, in bigger cities.
3. That, the researcher has developed and standardized scale to measure women's concern for status and development of children. It has worked satisfactorily in the present research. However, the test needs further refinement, validation and preparation of norms before it is used in varied researches.

Appendices

APPENDIX-1

A Situational Analysis of Women and Children in Santhal Parganas, (Jharkhand) (SAWC Rating Questionnaire)

1. Age:
2. Religion: Illiterate/Literate/Less than Matriculate/Matriculates and above.
3. Are you a barning member: Yes/No
4. If yes, nature of job: Service/Business/Manual Labour.
5. If employed, please mention the monthly income? Rs. ....
6. Marital Status: Married/Widow/Deserted.
7. Husband's Education:
8. Number of Children: Son Daughter No Issue.
9. Does the male head of your family work outside the village. Yes/No
10. Who according to you bears the major burden of running the family in your society? Male/Female/Both.
11. Please, mention your religion: Hindu/Bongaism/Christian.
12. Are in favour of women being head of the family? Yes/No/Don't Know.
13. Do you like interference of your mother-in-law in your family affairs? Yes/No/Don't Know.
14. Which clan do you belong?
15. Please mention total income of your family per month Rs. ....
16. Do you think that women are determined against men while working outside? Yes/No/Don't Know.
17. Please mention the main source of your family? Service/Business/Agriculture/Manual Labour.
18. Number of earning members in your family? One/Two/Three/More.

19. Number of dependent members? One/Two/Three/More.
20. Does any of your married daughter live with you? Yes/No.
21. Do you think that the status of women in Santhal society has changed in recent years? Yes/No/Don't Know
22. Do you think that women share major responsibility in household economy? Yes/No/Don't Know
23. Do you think that the male members can run the family affair as efficiently as the female members? Yes/No/Don't Know
24. Do you prefer the idea of sharing the household works equally between male and female? Yes/No/Don't Know
25. Do you think that women contribute to the household economy through their services equally with the men? Yes/No/Don't Know
26. What according to you is the most difficult problem facing the tribal families? (a) Alcoholism, (b) Discord between husband and wife, (c) Low income, (d) Any other.
27. Do you feel that you can run the household smoothly out of the total income of your family? Yes/No
28. Do you make any effort to supplement the resources of your family? Yes/No
29. Do you maintain any kitchen garden in area adjacent to your house? Yes/No
30. Do you keep domesticated cattle? Yes/No
31. If yes, please mention the types? Cow/Buffalo/Pigs/Goat.
32. Do you keep any poultry? Yes/No
33. Do you practice weaving? Yes/No
34. Are you trained in basket making? Yes/No
35. Do you go to local hatia for marketing any commodity produced by you or your family? Yes/No
36. Do you engage yourself in food gathering like: tubers, roots, fruits, mahua etc.? Yes/No/Occasionally.
37. Are you aware of any scheme started by the government in your area which can augment your family resources? Yes/No
38. Do you agree with the view that god created women for the kitchen and man for the field? Yes/No/Don't Know
39. Is it correct to say that inspite of their hard labour and contribution to the household economy they are neglected by the men? Yes/No/Don't Know

40. Given an opportunity would you like to give up your domestic responsibilities? Yes/No/Don't Know
41. Do you agree with the view that women are born with an instinct for household works? Yes/No/Don't Know
42. Do you think that male members are better decision-makers than the women? Yes/No/Don't Know
43. Are you entirely free to take decision regarding matters relating to your personal life? Yes/No
44. Are you free to move about as you like? (a) Absolutely free, (b) to a great extent, (c) Restricted.
45. Who takes major decision in your family? Father-in-law/ Mother-in-law/Husband/Myself/Altogether.
46. Do you think that your opinion is sought while a decision is taken in your family? Yes/No/At times.
47. Do you think that the opinion of female members should be given equal consideration with the male members while the family decision is taken? Yes/No/Undecided.
48. Do you agree with the view that the opinion of working women is given more consideration while making a decision that of the non-working women in the family? Yes/No/Don't Know.
49. Do you agree with the view that the opinion in most cases of the women prevail in decision-making because the males act according to the advice of their female counterparts? Yes/ No/Don't Know.
50. Do you think that a women should be given full freedom to take decision on matters relating to her personal life? Yes/ No/Don't Know.
51. Is it correct to say that in most cases the female members in the household are reluctant to take part in decision-making? Yes/No/Don't Know.
52. Even today many males are of the opinion that female are incapable of taking any serious decision. How far do you agree with it? Agree/Disagree/Undecided.
53. Do you agree with the view that acceptance of decision taken by the male members of the family has become a matter of habit for the women members? Agree/Disagree/ Undecided.

54. Do you accept the view that in modern household women are increasingly participating in decision-making compared to the traditional homes? Yes/No/Undecided.
55. Do you think that the claim for equal participation in decision-making compared to the process leads to discontent in family life? Yes/No/Don't Know.
56. Do you participate in making decision about the family budget? Yes/No/Not always.
57. Do you participate in making decisions regarding family property? Yes/No/At times.
58. Do you think that the majority of your households the mothers have a greater sign in the matter related to their children? Yes/No/Don't Know.
59. Who takes decision about the marriage of the children? Father/Mother/Elderly members/altogether.
60. In matters related to religious aspects of the family who plays the major role in decision-making? Male/Female/Both.
61. Do you take an independent decision about your right at the time of election? Yes/No
62. In case you have a daughter-in-law will you like her to participate equally with other members in decision-making your family? Yes/No/Undecided.
63. Which of the following according to you is a possible barrier to the participation of women in decision-making process? (a) Traditional norm of the male dominance, (b) Reluctance of women for fear of being criticised, (c) Incapability of taking serious decisions, (d) Avoidance of responsibility.
64. Do you think that women enjoy same amount of leisure time as that of the men? Yes/No
65. Do you find time to take part in community activities outside your family? Yes/No/Seldom.
66. Do you take part in dancing with other women of the village? Sometimes.
67. Do you join the women ot your neighbourhood during the leisure time for gossip? Frequently/Infrequently/Rarely.
68. Do you visit place outside your village for a change? Quite often/Occasionally/Rarely.

69. Do your relatives or acquaintance visit your place frequently? Frequently/Infrequently/Rarely.
70. Do you visit the melas or hatias for the sake of recreation? Yes/No/Sometimes.
71. Do you tell stories to your children or grand children or your boys or girls of your family during your leisure time? Yes/No/Sometimes.
72. Do you have any taste for knitting during your leisure time? Yes/No
73. Is there any adult education centre in your locality? Yes/No/Don't Know
74. If yes, do the women of your village go their from learning something? Yes/No/Don't Know
75. Do you think that the educated women enjoy more leisure in their lives than the uneducated or illiterate women? Yes/No/Don't Know
76. What do you do during your leisure time? (a) work in the kitchen garden. (b) Gossiping with other women. (c) Engaged in cleaning and washing. (d) Take part in singing and dancing.
77. It is often said that if the women are allowed to more leisure they indulge more in quarrelling with other women. Do you agree? Agree/Disagree/Undecided.
78. Do you find any change in the leisure time activities of the women in recent times? Yes/No/Don't Know
79. If yes, mention the factor responsible for change? (a) Growing education. (b) Female employment. (c) Urban mode of recreation, like cinema. (d) Mass media like Radio/T.V.
80. Do you have any Radio/Transistor in your family? Yes/No
81. Which you prefer most as source of recreation? Jatra/Dance/Cinema.
82. Do you feel that the composition of folk-songs in your society has been effected by the film songs? Yes/No/Don't Know
83. Do you visit Cinema shows? Frequently/Sometimes/Rarely.
84. Do you agree with the view that people have developed preference for the Hindi film songs than your traditional folk-songs? Yes/No/Don't Know

85. Do you agree with the view that people belonging to the younger generations and drifting away from the traditional pattern of recreation which is closely linked with the traditional culture? Agree/Disagree/Undecided.
86. Do you have sufficient supply of fuel to run the kitchen? Yes/No
87. If no, who takes the major share in fuel management generally? Men/Women/Children.
88. Which is the major source of availability of fuel energy you are using? Forest/Mines/Market.
89. Do you get sufficient supply of kerosene oil? Yes/No
90. What is the main type of fuel you used? Coal/Wood/Cowdung Cakes/Dry leaf.
91. Do you go to forest for picking woods frequently? Regularly/Sometimes/Seldom.
92. Do you agree with the view that the use of wood as fuel causes the disappearance of forest? Yes/No/Can't Say.
93. Has there been any change in your society regarding the use of fuel for domestic purpose? Yes/No/Don't Know
94. Do you find it difficult at times to prepare meals for want of fuel? Yes/No
95. Is it because of shortage of fuel that Santhals are used to take stale food? Yes/No/Don't Know
96. Do you think that the average Santhal family can meet the daily requirement of foodstuff? Yes/No/Don't Know
97. What according to you is the main reason for the shortage of food supply? (a) Poor Agriculture, (b) Small holdings, (c) Exploitation of tribal by diku mahajans, (d) Any other.
98. Can you provide food to your children with the existing source of food supply? Yes/No
99. Do you agree with the view that the intoxication like mahua or handia are taken in most cases as alternatives to food? Yes/No/Don't Know
100. Do the women of your village are able to gather sufficient food at least for few days for the family? Yes/No/Don't Know
101. Do you have any source of green vegetables or fruits from the jungle as supplement for food supply? Yes/No

102. Is there any Governmental or Semi-Governmental agencies distributing food and nutritious among the Santhals? Yes/No/Don't Know
103. Do you get any food supply from the church or Christian mission? Yes/No.
104. Do you get any food supply from the church? Do you supplement the milk of the domesticated cattle as food for the family members? Yes/No.
105. Do the male members of your family go to fishing with a view to supplement food resources? Yes/No.
106. Do the male members of your family go for hunting? Yes/No/Rarely.
107. Which measure you suggest to remove the economic hardship of the Santhals? (a) Modernisation of Agriculture, (b) Creation of alternative source of income, (c) Avoidance of alcoholism.

English Version (Questionnaire)
ATDWC Rating
(Objective Question Only)

---

1. (a) Name : ______________________
   (b) Age : ______________________
   (c) Religion : ______________________
   (d) Caste : ______________
   (e) Profession or Occupation : ______________
   (f) Address :
   Local : ______________________
   ____
   ____
   ____
   Home : ______________________
   ____
   ____
   ____
   (g) Sex : ______________________
   (h) Educational Qualification : ______________

Please check your answer by putting (√) (×) in the places marked.

Yes/No

2. Do you think your family is :

(a) Conservative?	☐	☐
(b) Of liberal view?	☐	☐
(c) Modern?	☐	☐

3. Are you Married? Yes ☐ No ☐
4. Date of Marriage : ______________________

5. How many children you have:

Male		Female	
Alive	Dead	Alive	Dead
☐☐☐☐	☐☐☐☐	☐☐☐☐	☐☐☐☐

6. Please fill in the following interval period (in months) 1st birth (from the 2nd birth, 3rd birth, 4th birth, 5th birth date of marriage in)
7. What spacing do you like to have among your children?
   1st 2nd 3rd 4th 5th
8. What is your average monthly income? ____________
9. What is your average monthly expenditure? ____________
10. (a) Net savings before the birth of your children?
    (b) Increase or decrease in savings after the birth of your children ☐ ____________ ☐ ☐
    Increase Decrease Deficit
11. (a) Number of your sons reading in School:
    (b) Number of your sons reading in College:
    (c) Number of your daughters reading in School:
    (d) Number of your daughters reading in College:
12. Total Annual expenditure on the education of your children:
13. How many children do you want to have?

	Boys	Girls
One	☐	☐
Two	☐	☐
Three	☐	☐
Four	☐	☐
More than four	☐	☐

14. What is your opinion on the following:
    (a) Godwill necessarily provide food for all of your children.
    Yes ☐ No ☐
    (b) The Children will be a source of your spiritual salvation.
    Yes ☐ No ☐
    (c) The Children will add to your financial burden.
    Yes ☐ No ☐
    (d) The Children will add to the wealth of your family.
    Yes ☐ No ☐

(e) A large number of children will impoverish the family.
Yes [ ] No [ ]

15. Would you like to practise some kind of control that would limit the birth of children in your family?
Yes [ ] No [ ]

16. Are you in favour of birth control?
Yes [ ] No [ ]

17. Which of the following method would you prefer:
(a) Use of mechanical contraceptives. [ ]
(b) Observation of Safe Periods. [ ]
(c) Oral medicines. [ ]
(d) Surgical Operations. [ ]
(e) Celibacy [ ]
For (i) Male (ii) Female

18. Do you practise any measure for birth Control?
Yes [ ] No [ ]
(a) Use of mechanical contraceptive.
(b) Oral medicines.
(c) Surgical Operations.
(i) For Male : __________
(d) Observation of Safe periods.
(ii) Female : __________
(e) Celibacy.

19. Do you think that :
(a) The use of drugs and implements to prevent birth of children will lead to an increase in dandestine sexual affairs?
Yes [ ] No [ ]
(b) Such methods will lead to the beak-up of family?
Yes [ ] No [ ]
(c) Such methods of birth control will lead to depopulation?
Yes [ ] No [ ]

20. Do you think that the rapid increase in the population of the country is one of the causes of the poverty of the masses?

    Yes ☐ No ☐

21. Are you in favour of Sterilization of defective and criminals?
    (a) Defective: Yes ☐ No ☐
    (b) Criminals: Yes ☐ No ☐

22. If you are in favour of family planning *i.e.,* birth control, you have any hesitation in propagating.

    Yes ☐ No ☐

    If your answer is in the affirmative, please state what stands in the way of family planning?
    (a) Conservative nature of people. ☐
    (b) Natural gearing for children. ☐
    (c) Need of a son for Mukit. ☐
    (d) The greater the number of sons the greater the income of the family. ☐
    (e) Fear of dandestive affairs. ☐
    (f) Issueless persons looked down upon by society. ☐
    (g) Taking a wife necessarily required family to have a daughter to give as Kanyadan. ☐
    (h) Birth control is considered irreligious. ☐
    (i) Lack of scientific information of family planning and birth control. ☐
    (j) Involves regular expenditure and botheration. ☐
    (k) Any other reason. ☐

24. Could a natural method of population control be favoured without using any birth method and only by rising the age of marriage, *e.g.* strict observance of Sarda Act?

English Version (Questionnaire) Awareness Test Towards Family Welfare Programme

---

1. (a) Name : ____________________
   (b) Age : ____________________
   (c) Religion : ____________________
   (d) Caste : ____________
   (e) Occupation/Profession : ____________
   (f) Sex : ____________________
   (g) Address : ____________________
   Local : ____________________
   ____
   ____
   ____
   Home : ____________________
   ____
   ____
   ____
   (h) Educational Qualification : ____________

Please check your answer by putting (Yes/No) in the places marked:

2. Do you know about Family Planning?
   Yes ☐ No ☐
   (a) If yes, what do you understand by Family Planning?
   (b) When did you first hear of Family Planning?
   (c) From Whom did you first hear about Family Planning?
   (d) What do you think, is Family Planning advantageous.
   Yes ☐ No ☐
   (e) What do you think is Family Planning advantageous to you. If yes, give reasons for it.
   (f) Is Family Planning advantageous to your wife?
   Yes ☐ No ☐

(g) Is Family Planning advantageous to your Children.
Yes [ ] No [ ]

(h) Is Family Planning advantageous to your country?
Yes [ ] No [ ]

3. (a) Do you know about the different Family Planning Programme of Government.
Yes [ ] No [ ]

(b) Has Government Opened any Family Planning Centre in your areas.
Yes [ ] No [ ]

(c) Have you ever visited a Family Planning Clinic?
Yes [ ] No [ ]

4. (a) Does the Government give any economic aid for sterilization.
Yes [ ] No [ ]

(b) Do you know any such Family Planning Centre, Which distributes free contraceptives?
Yes [ ] No [ ]

5. Please State Favourable reasons for Family Planning? (in 3 sentences)

6. Please State Reasons for Non-adoption of Family Planning? (in 3 sentences)

7. Please State view Regarding Copulatory Sterilisation. (in 3 sentences)

8. Are you in favour of Taxation on Large Families?
Yes [ ] No [ ]

9. Are you in favour of compulsory Sex Education.
Yes [ ] No [ ]

10. Please give your suggestion regarding publicity and propaganda. (in 3 sentences)

APPENDIX-4

Important Statistics of the Region

Table 1: Tribes

SANTHAL
Total Population
426897

1. Soren
2. Marandi
3. Murmu
4. Hembrem
5. Kisku
6. Hansda
7. Tudu
8. Besra
9. Baski
10. Choure
11. Pauria
12. Sauria

PAHARIA
Total Population
101094

1. Mal Paharia
2. Kumar Bhang
3. Sauwaria

KOHL **MOHLI** **KAMAR**
Total Population
10536

POPULATION STRUCTURE OF S.P.

Table 2: Surveyed Subraces of Paharia Tribal Population (S.P.)

Block	*Village Surveyed*	*Subraces*			
		Sauria	*Kumarbhag*	*Mal*	*Total*
Sundarpahari	58	3755	1020	953	5728
Boarijor	45	3504	—	—	3504
Porayahat	06	—	—	142	142
Godda	08	252	—	206	458
Grand Total	**117**	**7511**	**1020**	**1301**	**9832**

Table 3: Total Paharia Population Surveyed Under Tribal Blocks of Santhal Pargana of Paharia Villages

Race	*Sauria*			*Kumarbhag*			*Mal*			*Total*		
Age	*M*	*F*	*T*	*M*	*F*	*T*	*M*	*F*	*T*	*M*	*F*	*T*
Infants (0—3)	479	796	1275	69	119	188	110	147	257	658	106	1720
Children (4—12)	775	652	1427	99	102	201	147	102	249	1021	856	1877
Teenagers (13—19)	490	757	1247	62	88	150	66	54	120	618	899	1517
Youngs (20—35)	1169	901	2070	130	138	268	152	151	303	1451	1190	2641
Elders (36—40)	540	472	1012	84	67	151	111	104	215	735	643	1378
Olders (51—65)	218	191	409	34	25	59	74	72	146	326	28	614
Oldest (Above 65)	25	33	58	02	01	03	04	07	11	31	41	72
Total	3696	3815	7511	480	540	1020	664	637	1301	4840	4992	9832

Notations: M = Male, F = Female, T = Total

Table 4: Paharia Population Structure in Relation to Age, Sex and Race Under Sundarpahari Tribal Block

Subrace	*Sauria*			*Kumarbhag*			*Mal*			*Total*		
Age Groups	*M*	*F*	*T*	*M*	*F*	*T*	*M*	*F*	*T*	*M*	*F*	*T*
Infants (0—3)	230	418	648	69	119	188	87	116	203	386	653	1039
Children (4—12)	406	356	762	99	102	201	107	75	182	612	533	1145
Teenagers (13—19)	212	394	606	62	88	150	45	43	88	319	525	844
Youngs (20—35)	585	465	1050	130	138	268	100	103	203	815	706	1521
Elders (36—40)	281	214	495	84	67	151	86	83	171	453	364	817
Olders (51—65)	94	81	125	34	25	59	63	46	99	181	152	333
Oldest (Above 65)	09	10	19	02	01	03	02	05	07	13	16	29
Total	1817	1938	3755	480	540	1020	482	471	953	2779	2949	5728

Notations: M = Male, F = Female, T = Total

Table 5: Paharia Population Structure in Relation to Age/Sex and Race Under Boarijor, Porayahat and Godda Blocks

Subrace	*Sauria*			*Mal*			*Sauria*			*Mal*			*Total*		
Age Group	*M*	*F*	*T*	*M*	*F*	*T*	*M*	*F*	*T*	*M*	*F*	*T*	*M*	*F*	*T*
Infants (0—3)	236	349	585	06	11	17	13	29	42	17	20	37	30	49	79
Children (4—12)	332	269	601	15	12	27	37	27	64	25	15	40	62	42	104
Teenagers(13—19)	260	353	613	14	09	23	18	10	28	07	02	09	25	22	37
Youngs (20—35)	573	415	988	25	16	41	11	21	32	27	32	59	38	53	91
Elders (36—40)	228	235	463	07	07	14	31	23	54	16	14	30	47	37	84
Olders (51—65)	111	92	203	07	11	18	13	18	31	14	15	29	27	33	60
Oldest (Above 65)	15	23	38	00	02	02	01	00	01	02	00	02	03	00	03
Total	1755	1736	3391	74	68	142	124	128	252	108	98	206	232	226	450

Notations: M = Male, F = Female, T = Total

Table 6: Literacy and Education Among Paharias (S.P.)

Block	*Population (Above 4 Years)*			*Literacy (Number)*			*Frequency of Literacy (%)*		
	M	*F*	*T*	*M*	*F*	*T*	*M*	*F*	*T*
Sundarpahari	1588	1547	3135	268	70	338	16.9	04.5	10.8
Boaruor	1519	1411	2930	244	97	341	16.1	06.9	08.3
Porayahat	68	57	125	26	08	34	38.2	14.0	27.2
Godda	201	177	378	06	01	07	03.0	00.6	02.1
Total	3376	3192	6568	544	176	720	74.2	26.0	48.4

Notations: M = Male, F = Female, T = Total

Table 7: Literacy and Education in Paharia Under Four Tribal Blocks of Santhal Pargana

Blocks	*Sub Races*	*Population Group above 4 Years*	*Illiterate*	*Literate*				*Primary Education*				*Secondary Education*				*Intermediate Education*				*University Education*			
				M	*F*	*T*	*%*	*M*	*F*	*T*	*%*	*M*	*F*	*T*	*%*	*M*	*F*	*T*	*%*	*M*	*F*	*T*	*%*
	S	1553	1330	171	52	223	14.4	128	50	178	79.8	39	02	41	18.4	—	—	—	—	04	—	04	1.8
Sundar	K	832	763	58	11	69	8.3	52	11	63	91.3	06	—	06	8.7	—	—	—	—	—	—	—	—
Pahari	M	750	704	39	07	46	6.1	29	04	33	71.7	08	02	10	21.7	02	01	03	6.5	—	—	—	—
	T	3135	2797	268	70	338	10.8	209	65	274	81.1	53	04	56	16.9	02	01	03	0.9	04	—	04	1.2
Boarijor	S	2930	2589	244	97	341	11.6	138	74	212	62.2	93	23	116	34.0	01	—	01	0.2	12	—	12	3.5
Porayahat	M	125	91	26	08	34	27.2	15	05	20	58.6	08	03	11	32.4	03	—	03	8.8				
Godda	S	209	206	02	01	03	1.5	02	01	03	100												
	M	169	185	04	—	04	2.4	04	—	04	100												
	T	378	371	06	01	07	1.9	06	01	07	100												

Notations: M = Male, F = Female, T = Total, % = Frequency, S = Sauria, K = Kumarbhag, M = Mal

Table 8: Average Annual Income of Paharia Family Under S.P. (Rs./Family)

Resources	*Deoghar*	*Dumka*	*Godda*	*Sahibganj*
Agricultural Products	17,463	30,394	4,457	4,052
Forest Production	6,817	2,642	1,889	1,312
Livestock	162	64	102	79
Other Products	594	864	3,400	3,600
Government and Other Jobs	304	264	600	750
Total	25,340	34,228	10,448	9,793

Relevant Maps of the Region

	Population		*Male*		*Female*	
	Total	%	Total	%	Total	%
1. Dumka	621484	41.55	314616	50.62	306868	49.38
2. Godda	216047	25.09	109314	50.60	106733	49.40
3. Deoghar	119085	12.76	60945	50.18	58140	48.28
4. Sahibganj	347321	23.72	257135	50.68	250186	49.33
5. Santhal Pargana	1463937	31.89	742010	50.69	721927	49.31

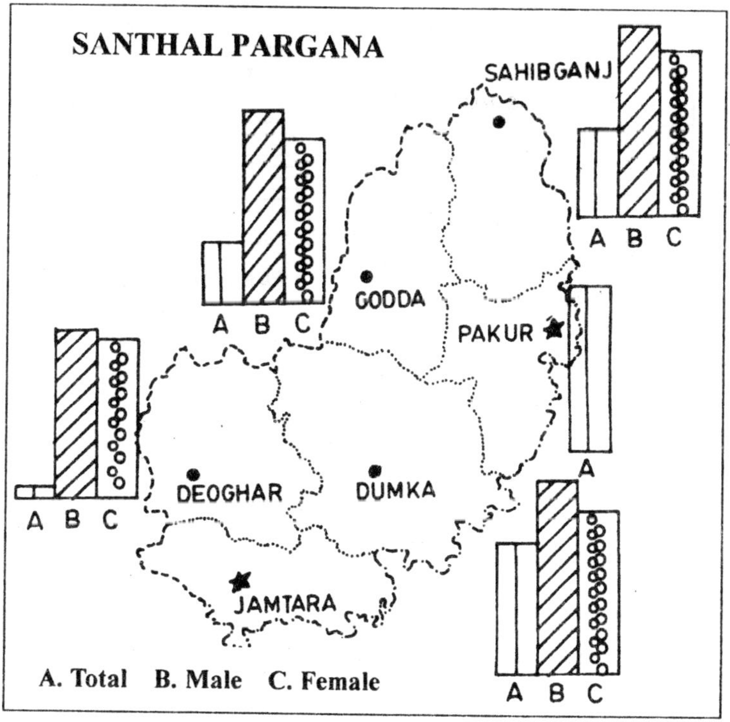

Fig. 1: Scheduled Tribe Population (Male and Female)

	Population		*Male*		*Female*	
	Total	%	Total	%	Total	%
1. Dumka	1404794	93.92	715993	50.97	688801	49.03
2. Godda	837545	97.26	435224	51.96	402321	48.04
3. Deoghar	807954	86.59	419914	51.97	388040	48.03
4. Sahibganj	1206087	92.70	620894	51.48	585193	48.52
5. Santhal Pargana	4256380	92.71	2192025	51.50	2064355	48.50

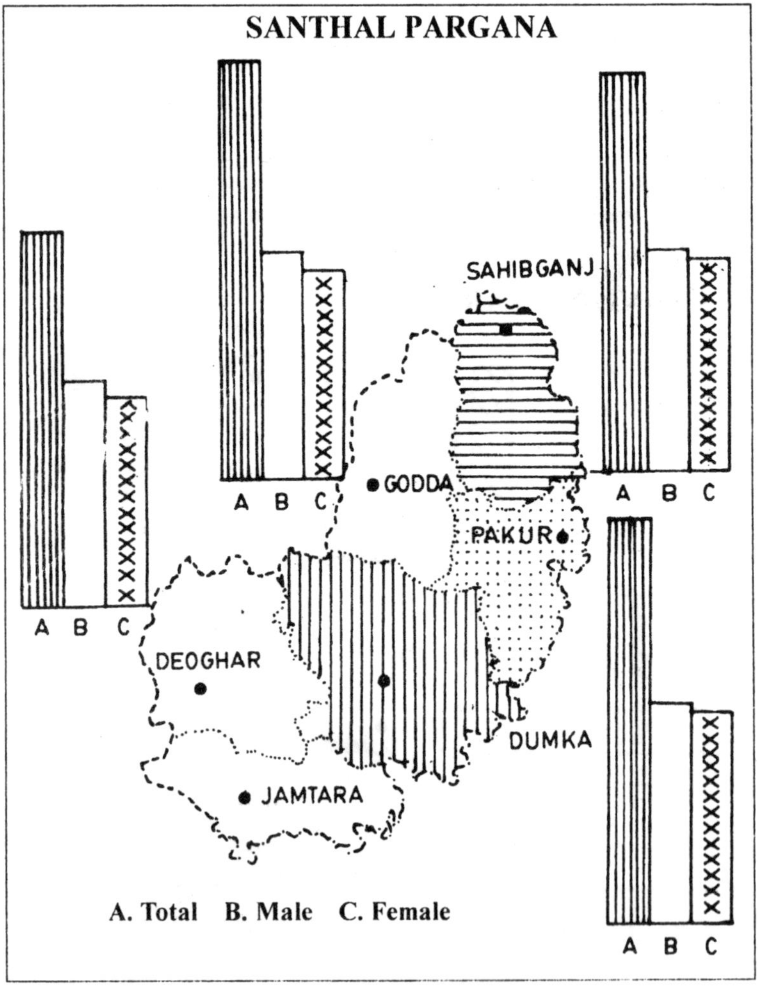

Fig. 2: Rural Population

	Urban Population		Male		Female	
	Total	%	Total	%	Total	%
1. Dumka	90915	6.08	49009	53.91	41906	46.09
2. Godda	23637	2.74	12848	54.36	10789	44.64
3. Deoghar	125159	13.41	68315	54.58	546844	45.42
4. Sahibganj	95001	7.30	50837	53.51	44164	56.49
5. Santhal Pargana	334712	7.29	181009	54.08	153703	45.92

1. Dumka, 2. Godda, 3. Deoghar, 4. Sahibganj, 5. S. Pargana

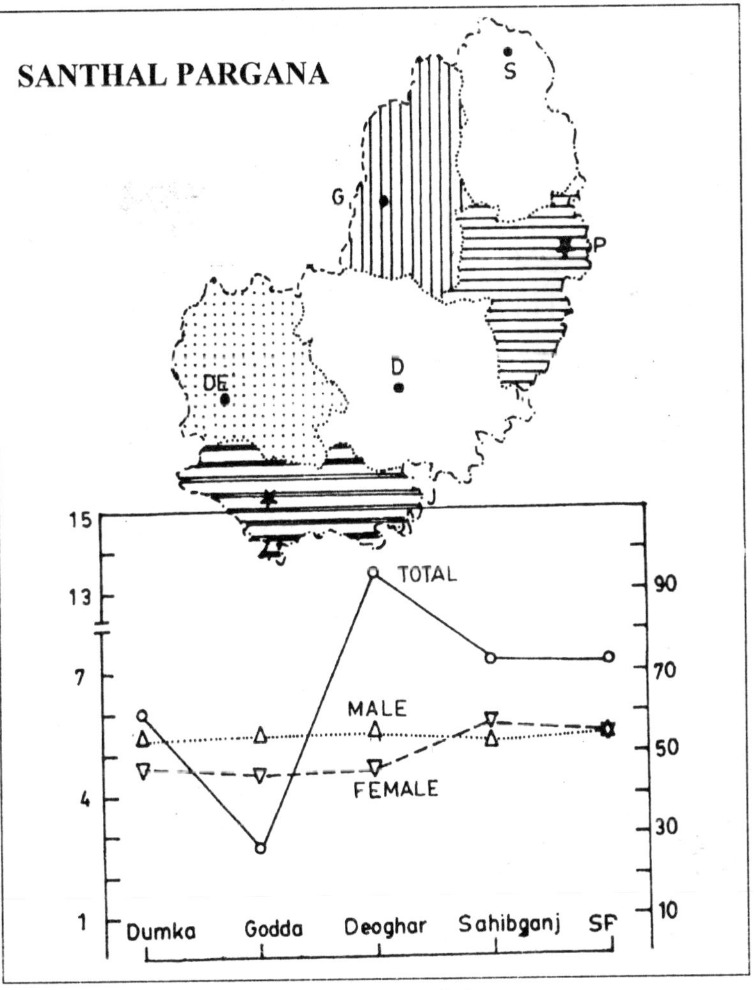

Fig. 3: Urban Population

	Rural		*Urban*	
	Total	%	Total	%
1. Dumka	616449	43.88	5035	5.54
2. Godda	214936	25.66	1111	4.70
3. Deoghar	116368	14.40	2717	2.17
4. Sahibganj	504119	41.80	3202	3.37
5. Santhal Pargana	1451872	34.21	12065	3.60

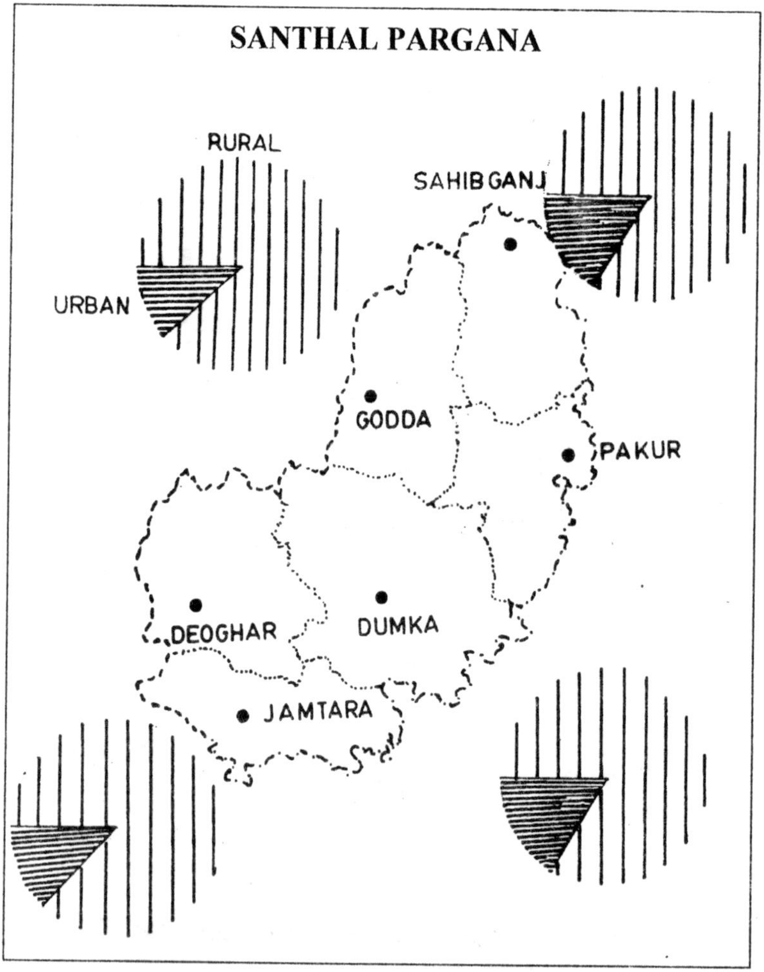

Fig. 4: Population of ST (Rural and Urban)

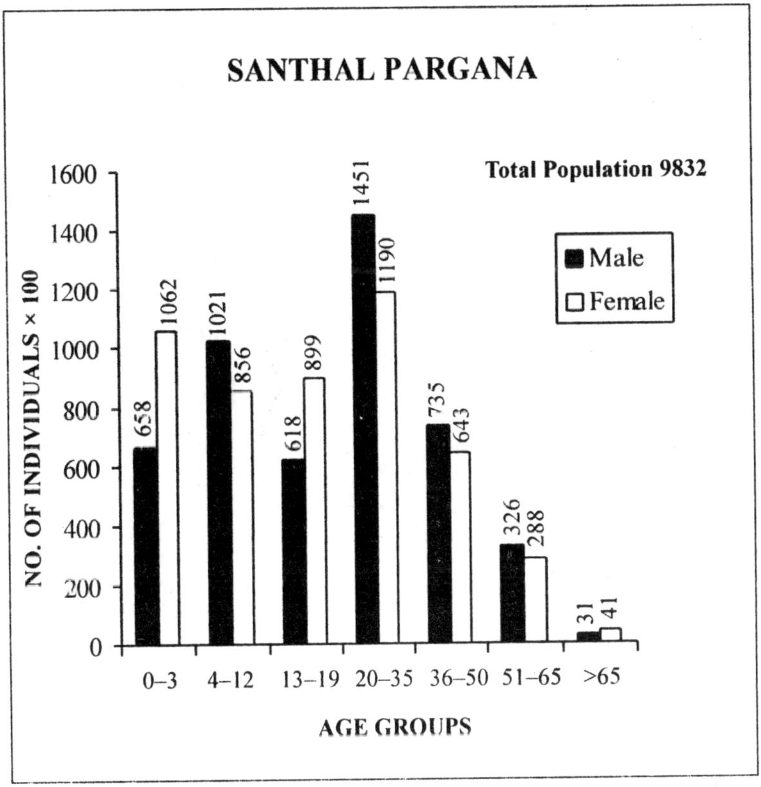

Fig. 5: Analysis (Age and Sex) of Paharia Population Structure

	Main		*Male*		*Female*	
	Total	%	Total	%	Total	%
1. Dumka	537933	35.97	408834	76.00	129099	24.00
2. Godda	281044	32.63	227198	80.84	53846	19.16
3. Deoghar	274881	29.46	237269	86.32	37612	13.68
4. Sahibganj	443568	34.09	347780	78.41	95788	21.59
5. Santhal Pargana	1537426	33.49	1221081	49.42	316345	20.58

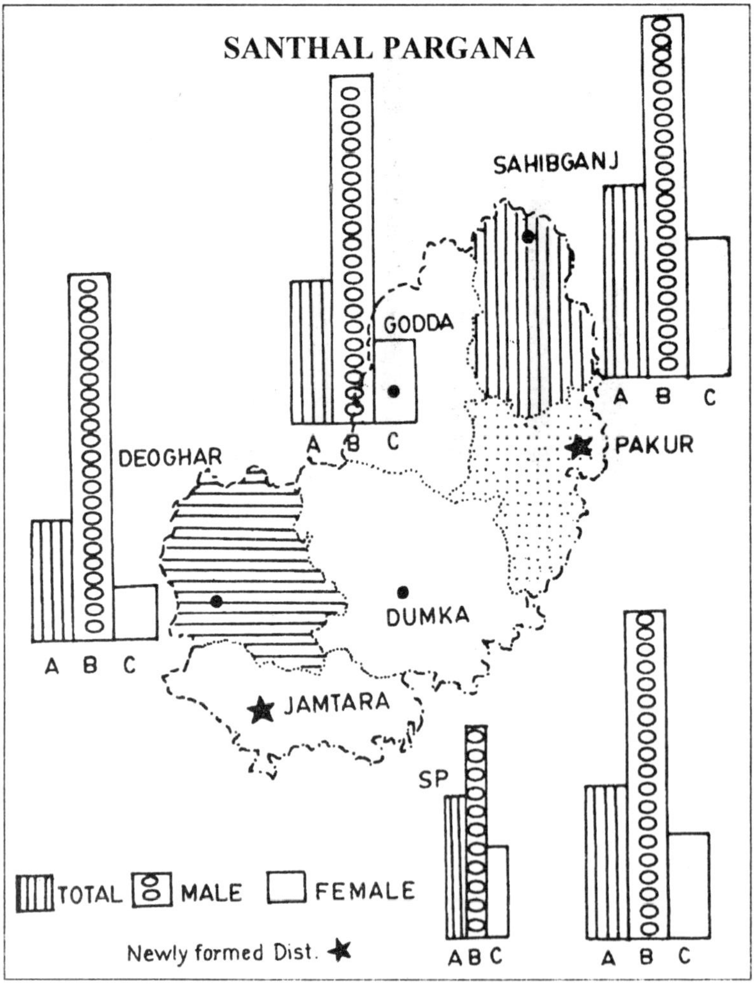

Fig. 6: Male and Female Workers

	Rural		*Male*		*Female*	
	Total	%	Total	%	Total	%
1. Dumka	514906	95.72	387668	75.29	127238	24.71
2. Godda	275323	97.76	221846	80.58	53477	19.42
3. Deoghar	244767	89.04	208815	86.31	35952	14.69
4. Sahibganj	421227	94.96	326683	77.56	94544	22.44
5. Santhal Pargana	1456223	94.72	1145012	78.63	311211	21.37

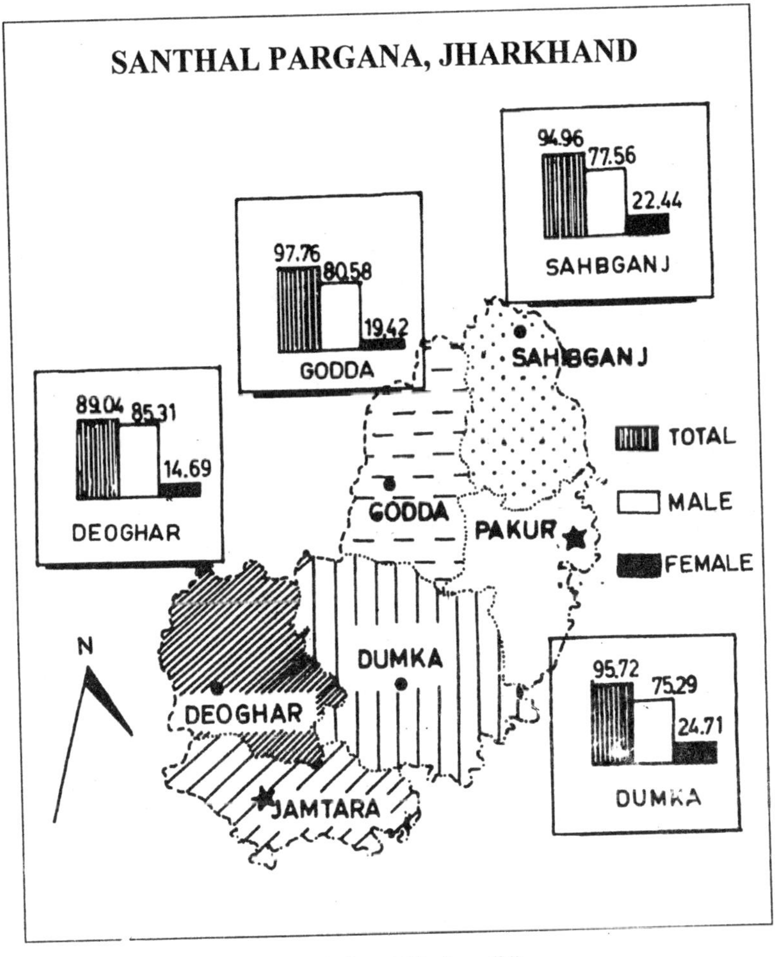

Fig. 7: Rural Workers (%)

	Urban		*Male*		*Female*	
	Total	%	Total	%	Total	%
1. Dumka	23027	4.28	21166	91.92	1861	8.08
2. Godda	5421	2.04	5352	93.55	369	6.45
3. Deoghar	30114	10.96	28454	94.49	1660	5.51
4. Sahibganj	22341	5.04	21097	94.43	1244	5.57
5. Santhal Pargana	81203	5.28	76069	93.68	5134	6.32

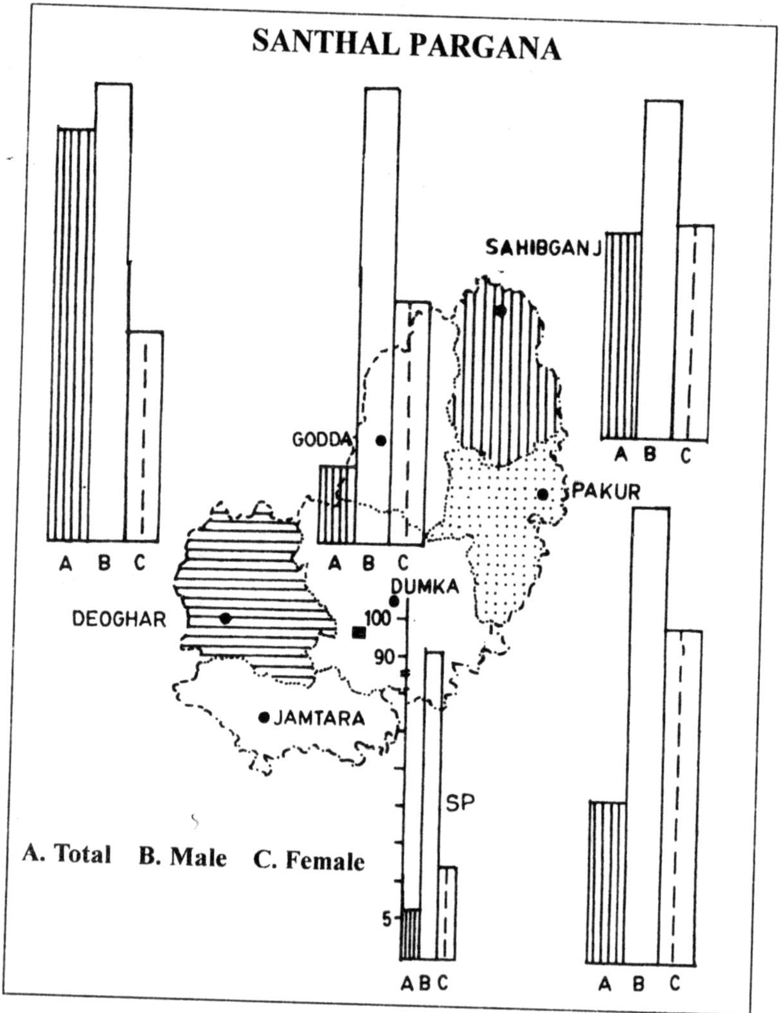

Fig. 8: Urban Workers (Male and Female)

	General		*Rural*	*Urban*
	Total	%		
1. Dumka	102203	19.00	101065	1138
2. Godda	84759	30.16	84152	607
3. Deoghar	47688	17.35	46429	1259
4. Sahibganj	129323	29.16	126496	2827
5. Santhal Pargana	363973	23.67	358142	5831

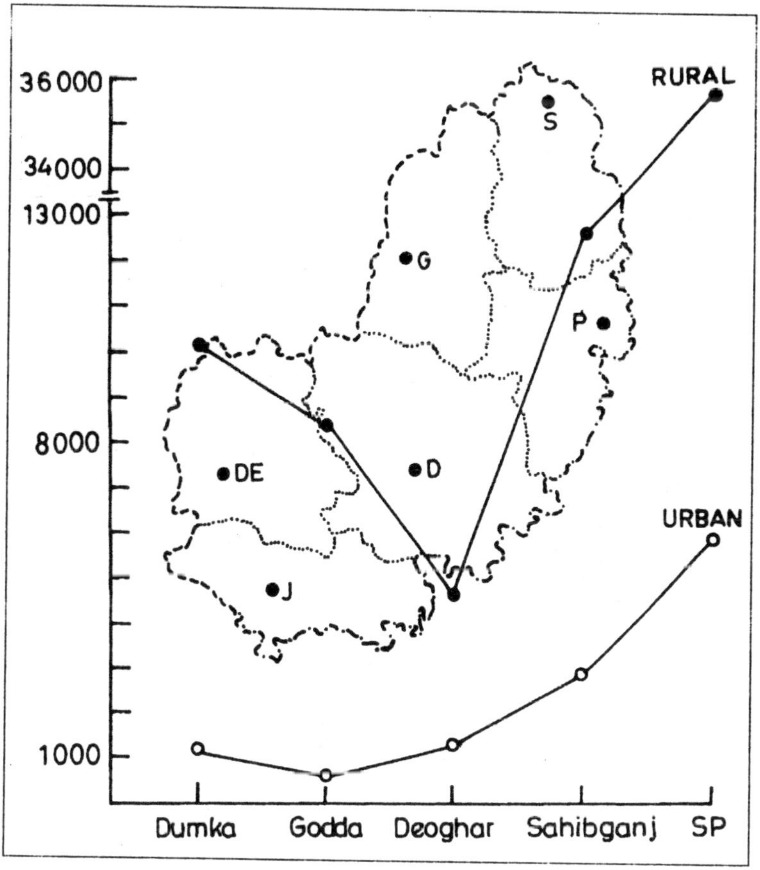

Fig. 9: Agricultural Workers (Rural and Urban)

	General		*Rural*	*Urban*
	Total	%		
1. Dumka	3356	0.62	2806	550
2. Godda	838	0.30	817	21
3. Deoghar	1761	0.64	11521	610
4. Sahibganj	2111	0.48	1741	370
5. Santhal Pargana	8066	0.52	6515	1551

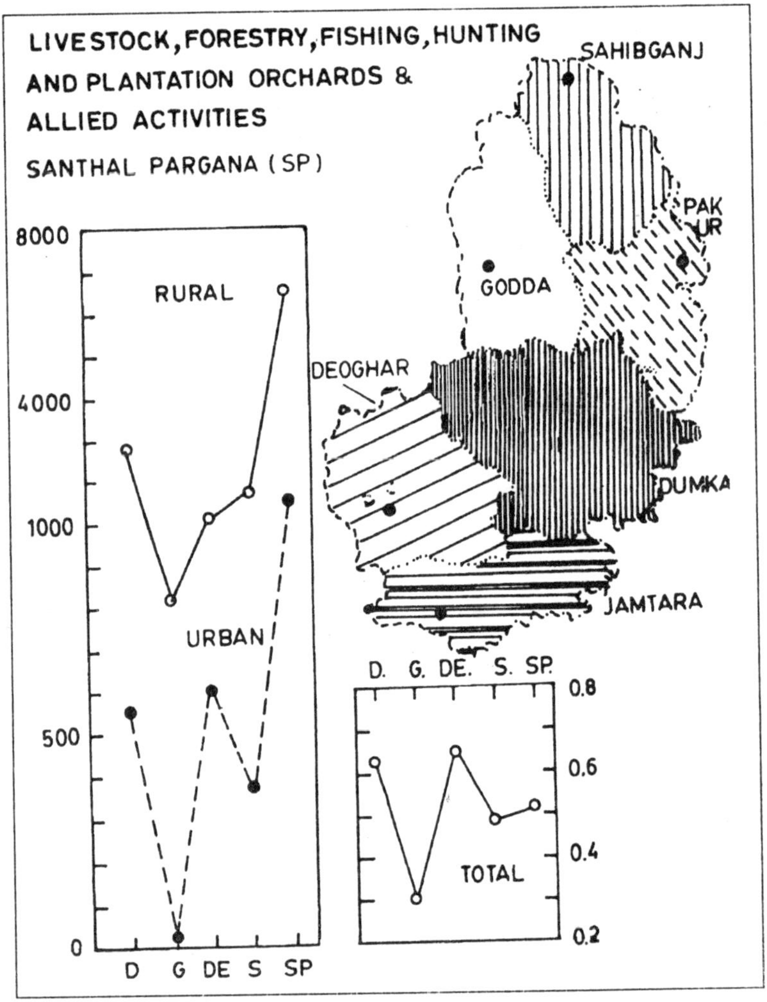

Fig. 10: Rural, Urban and General Workers

	General		*Rural*	*Urban*
	Total	%		
1. Dumka	2387	0.44	1776	611
2. Godda	805	0.29	652	153
3. Deoghar	3018	1.10	2035	983
4. Sahibganj	2514	0.57	2034	480
5. Santhal Pargana	8725	0.57	6497	2227

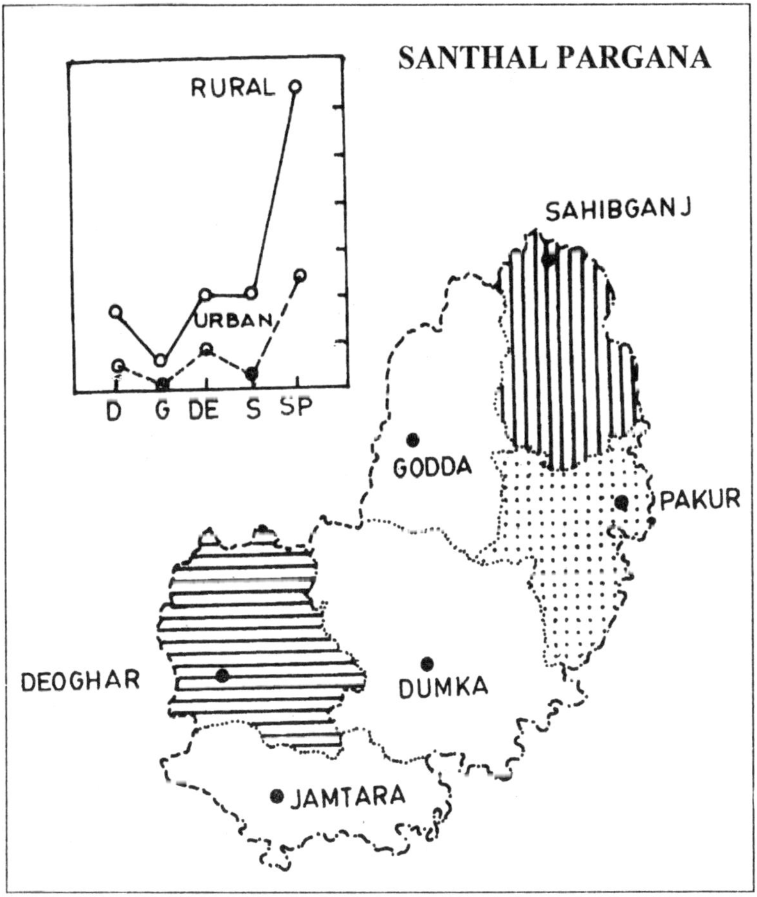

Fig. 11: Construction Workers

	General		*Rural*	*Urban*
	Total	%		
1. Dumka	16944	3.15	11474	5470
2. Godda	5332	1.90	4328	10
3. Deoghar	12405	4.51	4655	7750
4. Sahibganj	15922	3.59	12085	4837
5. Santhal Pargana	50603	3.29	31542	19061

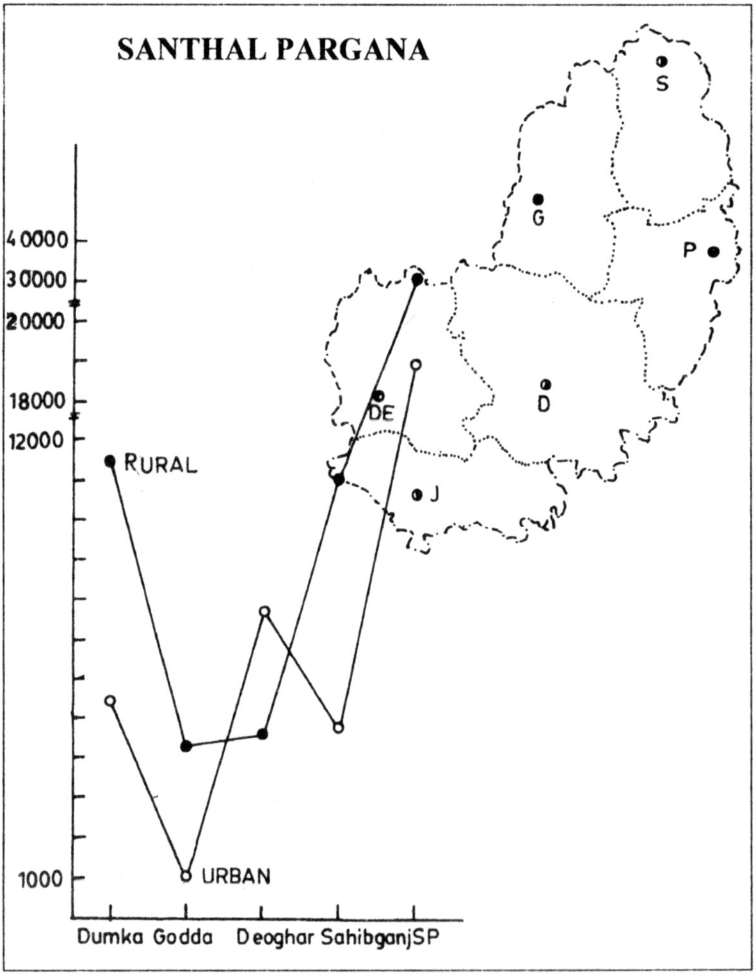

Fig. 12: Trade and Commerce Workers

	General		*Rural*	*Urban*
	Total	%		
1. Dumka	137617	25.58	136401	1216
2. Godda	59942	21.33	59184	758
3. Deoghar	50570	28.40	50056	514
4. Sahibganj	80242	18.09	79791	451
5. Santhal Pargana	659721	42.91	355432	2939

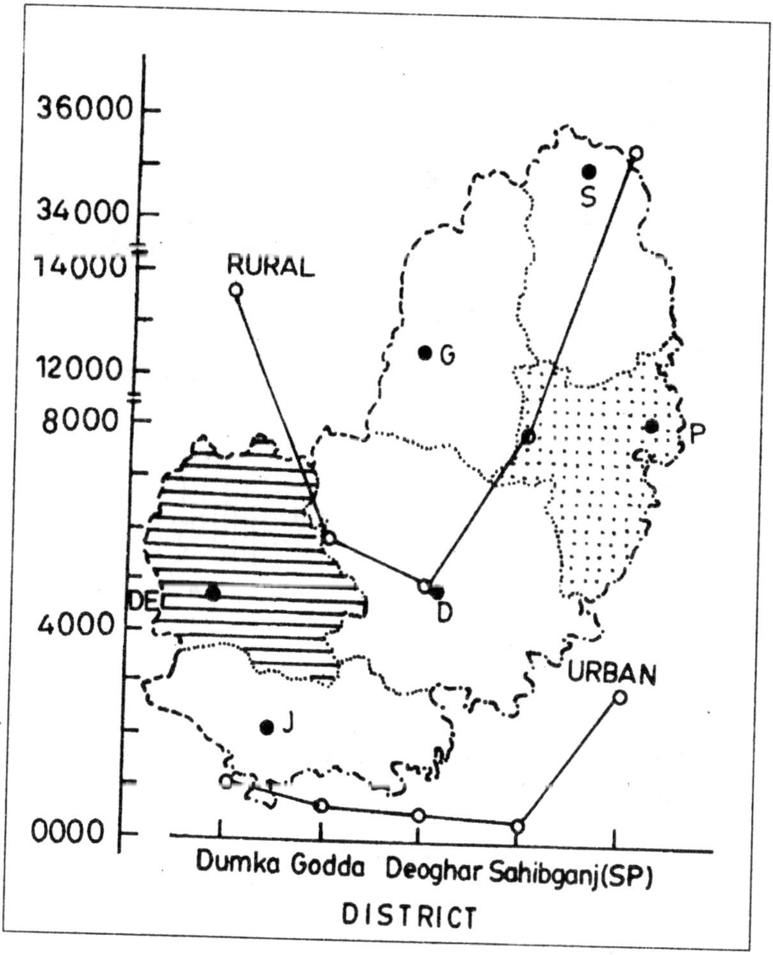

Fig. 13: Marginal Workers

	General		*Rural*	*Urban*
	Total	%		
1. Dumka	2240	0.42	2160	80
2. Godda	1115	0.40	1089	26
3. Deoghar	3680	1.34	3594	86
4. Sahibganj	1855	0.42	1776	76
5. Santhal Pargana	8890	0.58	8619	268

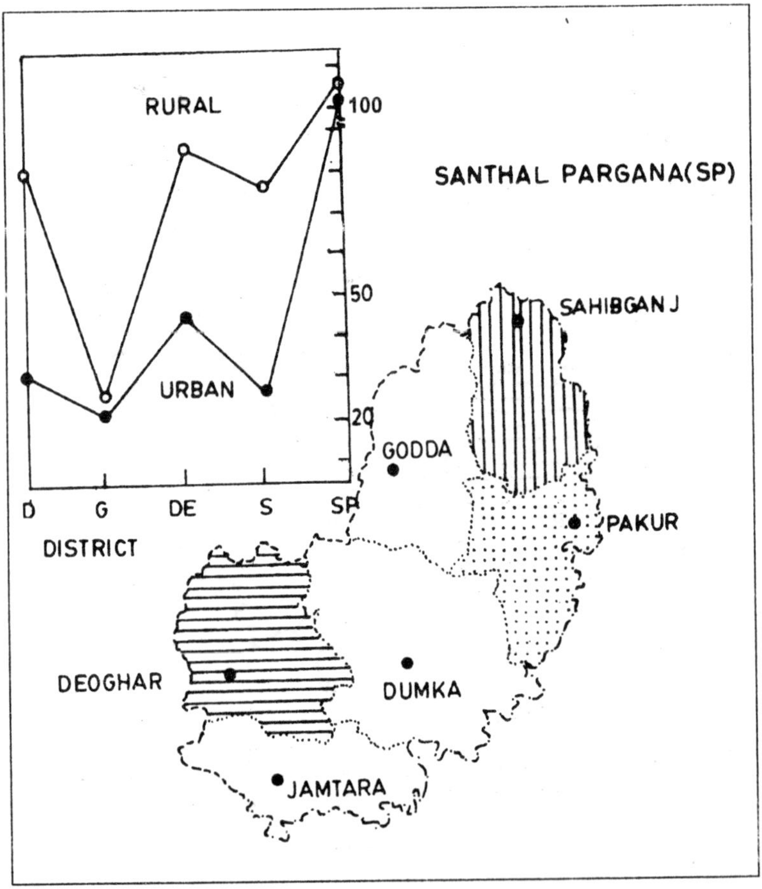

Fig. 14: Mining and Quarrying (Rural and Urban)

	General		*Male*		*Female*	
	Total	%	Total	%	Total	%
1. Dumka	354539	23.70	351966	99.27	2573	0.73
2. Godda	162856	18.91	161549	99.20	1307	0.80
3. Deoghar	159217	17.60	158037	99.26	1180	0.47
4. Sahibganj	233897	17.98	230910	98.72	2987	1.28
5. Santhal Pargana	910509	19.83	902462	99.12	8.47	0.88

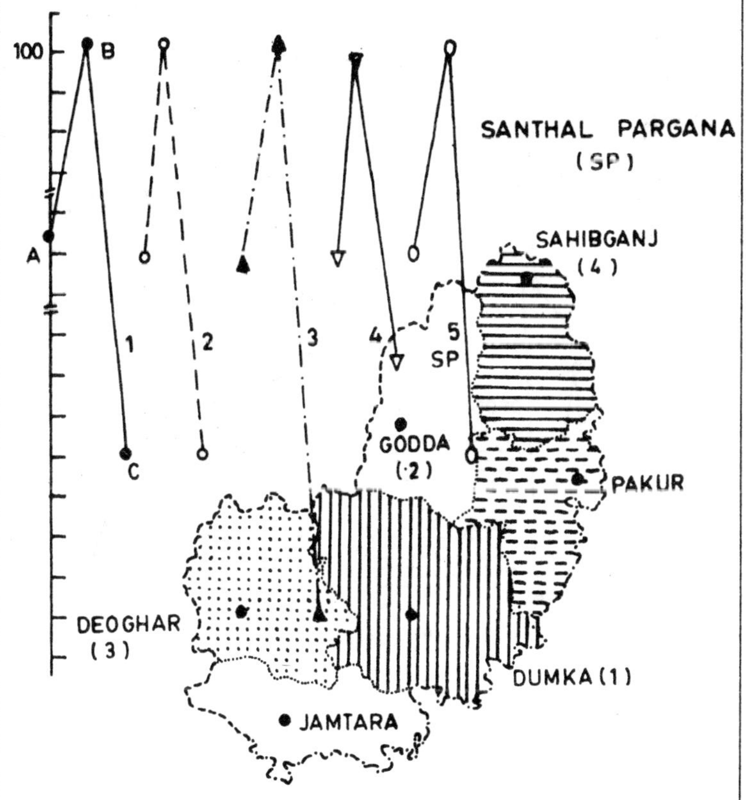

A. Total B. Rural C. Urban

Fig. 15: Cultivators Workers (Rural and Urban)

	General		*Rural*	*Urban*
	Total	%		
1. Dumka	25830	4.80	18837	6993
2. Godda	14706	5.23	12901	1805
3. Deoghar	25936	9.44	13491	12445
4. Sahibganj	20526	4.63	14601	5925
5. Santhal Pargana	86998	5.66	59830	27168

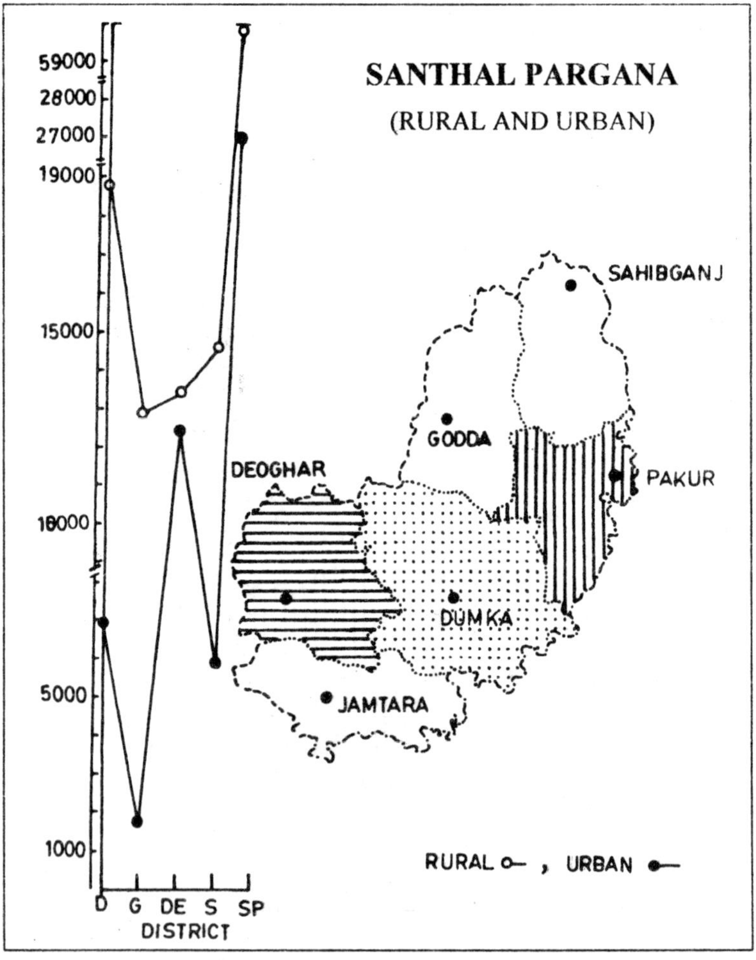

Fig. 16: Other Workers (Services)

	General		*Rural*	*Urban*
	Total	%		
1. Dumka	6484	1.21	4280	2204
2. Godda	1194	0.42	1008	186
3. Deoghar	4799	1.75	2609	2190
4. Sahibganj	6389	1.44	3862	2527
5. Santhal Pargana	18866	1.23	11759	7107

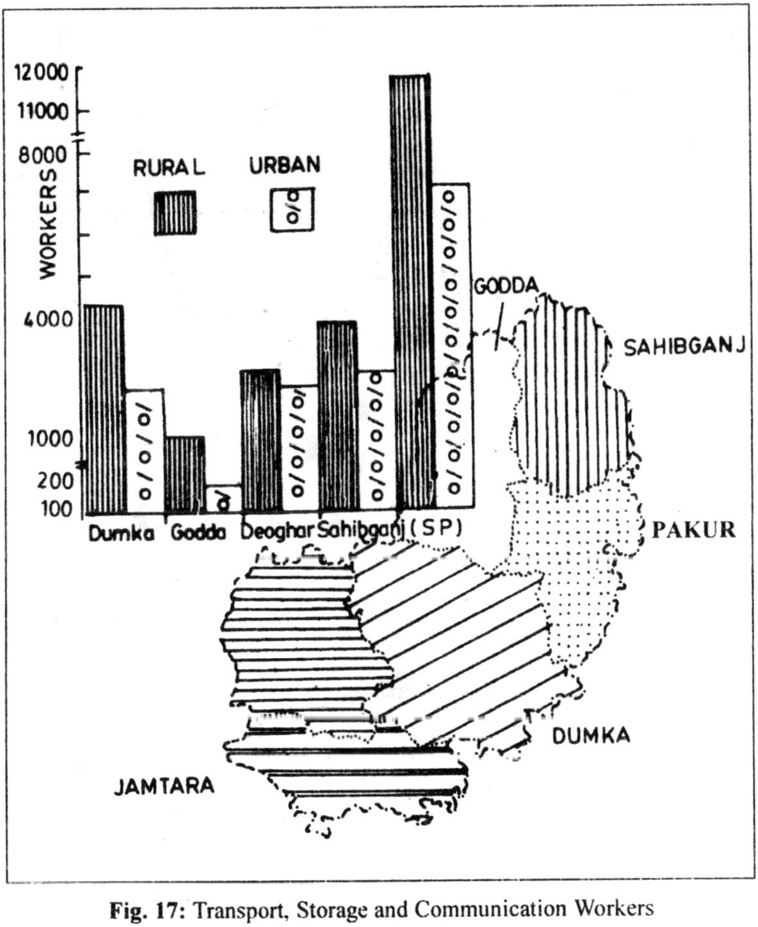

Fig. 17: Transport, Storage and Communication Workers

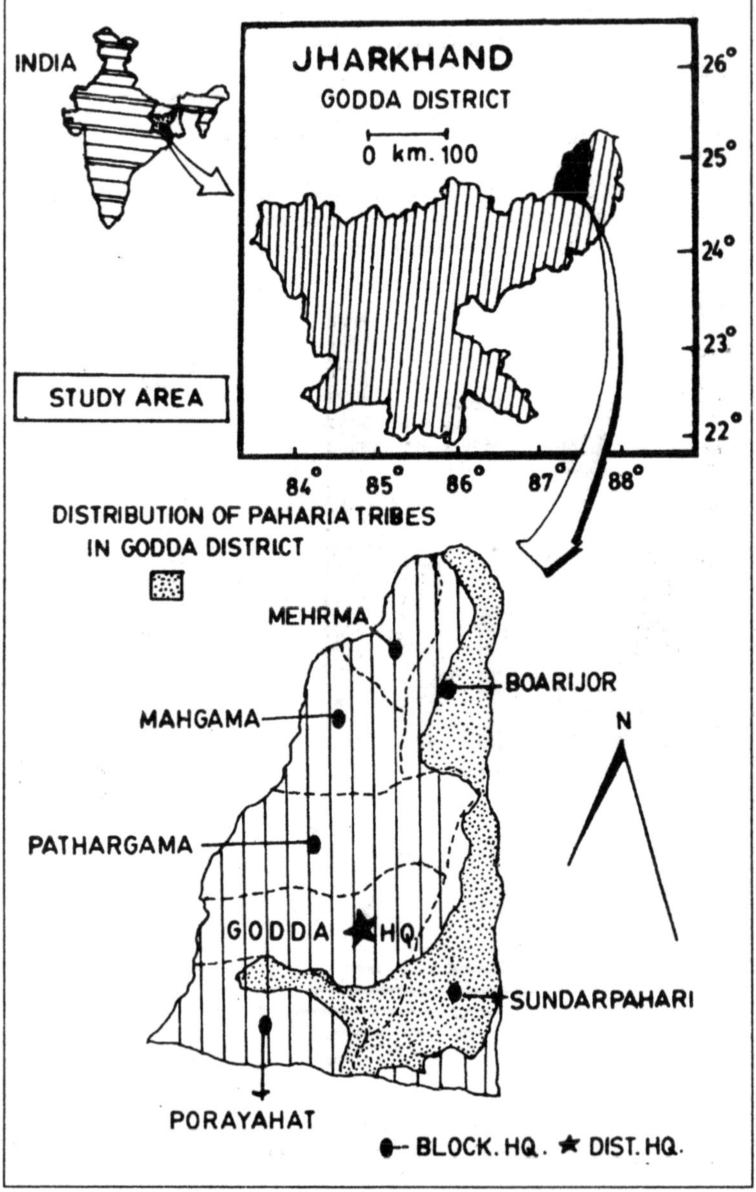

Fig. 18: Location Map of Godda District

Bibliography

Amartya Sen, Individual Freedom: "Basis for a Social Commitment", *The Times of India,* October 16, 1998, p. 12.

Archer, W.G.: *The Hill of Flutes,* George Allen and Unwin, London, 1966.

Bajpai, S.R.: *Samajik Anusandhan Tatha Sarbekshan,* Kitab Ghar, Kanpur, 1904.

Bajpai, S.R.: *Samajik Anusandhan Tatha Sarbekshan,* Kitab Ghar, Kanpur, 1984, p. 9.

Bakan, D. (1966). *The Duality of Human Experience.* Chicago: Rand McNally.

Balasaheb Dev Ras, *RSS—A Force for Social Change* (1981), pp. 11–22.

Barry, H., Bacon, M.K. and Child, I.L. (1957). A Cross Cultural Survey of Some Sex Differences in Socialization. *Journal of Abnormal and Social Psychology,* 55, 327–332.

Bell, Rber R. (1975). Significant Roles Among a Sample of Australian Women. Australian and New Zealand, *Journal of Sociology,* 11(1), 2–11.

Bem, S.L. (1977). On the Utility of Alternative Procedures for Assessing Psychological Androgyny. *Journal of Consulting and Clinical Psychology,* 45, 196–205.

Bennett, Barbara W. and Grasser, George, S. (1981). Movement Towards Aandrogyny in College Females Through Experimental Education. *Journal of Psychology,* 107 (2), 177–183.

Benson, Donna (1977). *Sexual Harassment: A Hidden Issue.* Published by Project on the Status of Women, Association of American College.

Betz, Ellen L. (1982). Need Fulfilment in the Career Development of Women. *Journal of Vocational Behaviour,* 20 (1), 53–66.

Bhattarjee, Pratima and Bhatt, Kusum K., (1983). Family Adjustment of Married Working and Non-working Women. *Indian Journal of Clinical Psychology,* 10(2), 497–501.

Biaggio, Mary K., Mohan, Philip J. and Baldarn, Cynthia (1985). Relationships Among Attitudes Towards Children, Women's Liberation and Personality Characteristics. *Sex Roles,* 12 (1–2), 47–62.

Bingham, William C., and Turner, Carol J. (1981). Modified Questionnaire on the Occupational Status of Women. *Educational and Psychological Measurement,* 41 (3), 909–915.

Biswas, D.K.: *Society, Polity and Economy Firma,* L. Mukhopadhyaya, Calcutta.

Bodding P.O.: *Santhal Folk Tales,* Vol. I, Oslo, Aschehoug and Co., 1929.

Bodding, P.O.: *Santhal Folktales,* Vol. I, Oslo.: A Santhal Dictionery, Vol. IV.

Bodding, P.O.: *How to Santhals Live,* p. 434.

Bodding, P.O.: *Santhal Dictionery,* Vol. I, Oslo, Aschehoug and Co., 1929.

Bodding, P.O.: *Taboo, Customs Amongst the Santhals,* J.A.S.B., Part III, 1898.

Bouchart, Godard A. (1978). One Kills the Mother: Liberation of Women and Paternal Space (Fren.) *Bulletin de Psychologie* 32 (3–7), 383–387.

Cella Van Sackle: *Consumer Use and Purchase of Furniture in Flint,* Michigan, 1951, p. 4.

Chakravarti, Satyabrata: *Santhal Women in Agriculture: Observations in a Burdwan Village.*

Choudhary, N.C.: *Women in Tribal India.*

Choudhary, P.C. Roy: *Bihar District Gazetteer, Santhal Parganas,* Secretriat Press, Bihar, 1965, pp. 946–947.

Choudhury, Neerja (1984). Cornered in the Dark. *The Stateman,* Delhi, October 29.

Cloud, K. (1994), "Women, Households and Development: A Policy Perspective", in Romy Borooah *et al.* (edu.) *Capturing Complexity,* Sage Publications, New Delhi, p. 81.

Cooper, Joseph, D.: *The Art of Decision Making,* Doubleday and Co. Inc., 1961.

Cooper, Joseph, O.: The Art of Decision Making, Doubleday and Co. Inc. 1961.

Davis, Richard A. (1981). Female Labourforce Participation, Status Integration and Suicide 1950–1969, *Suicide and Life Threatening Behaviour,* 11(2), 111–123.

Desai, Neera (1957). *Women in Modern India.* Bombay: Vohra and Co.

Deshi, S.L.: *Praramvik Samajik Manav Vigyan,* Vikas Publishing House Pvt. Ltd., Kanpur.

Dewer, John and Tuffs James, H.: *Ethic,* Macmillan, New York, 1938, p. 303.

Diesing, Paul: *Reason in Society, Five Types of Decision and Their Social Conditions,* Urbena, Illinois, 1962. p. 108.

Doshi, S.L.: *Praramvik Samajik Manav Vigyan,* Vikas Publishing House, Pvt. Ltd., Kanpur, pp. 140–150.

Dowey, John: *How You Think,* D.C. Health and Co., New York, 1910, p. 8.

Dr. Ashu Pasricha, *Department of Gandhian Studies,* Punjab University, Chandigarh, "The Women in Changing World".

East Lasing: *Conceptual Frameworks, Process in Home Management,* Home Management Conference, Washington, 1964.

Elizabeth H. Wolgest: Consumer De Husbands or Wives Make the Purchasing Decisions, *Journal of Marketing,* Vol. 23, No. 2, pp. 151–158.

Elizabeth, H.N.: Do Husbands or Wives Makes the Purchasing Decisions, *Journal of Marketing,* Vol. 25, No. 2.

Encyclopaedia of Social Science: Vol. XIII, Macmillan, London, 1924, p. 330.

Erdwins, Card. J.: Tyer, Zita E. and Mellinger Jeanne C. (1982): Achievement and Affliation Needs of Young Adult and Middle Age Women. *Journal of Genetic Psychology,* 141(2), 219–224.

Erickson, E. (1964). Inner and Outer Space: Reflections and Womenhood. *Daedalus,* 93, 582–606.

Fairchild, H.P.: *Dictionary of Sociology,* Little Field Adams and Co. Peterson, New Jersey, 1962.

Fairchild, M.P. *et al.*: *Dictionary of Sociology,* Little Field Adams and Co. Peterson, New Jersy, 1962.

Farley, Lin (1978). *Sexual Shakedown.* New York: McGraw Hill, 20–21.

Faver, Catherine A. (1982). Achievement Orientation Attainment Values and Women's Employment. *Journal of Vocational Behaviour,* 20 (1), 67–80.

Fenchel, Gerd (1979). Patternity and Changing Role of Women. *Issue in Ego Psychology,* 2(1), 5–11.

Ferree, Myra M. (1983). The Women's Movement in the Working Class. *Sex Roles,* 9(4), 493–505.

Fine-Davis, Maragret (1979). Social Psychological Predictors of Employment Status of Married Women in Ireland. *Journal of Married and the Family,* 41(1), 145–158.

Frankel, Judith; Monogul, Mary A. and Paludi Michelle (1982). The Employed Mother: A New Social Norms? *International Journal of Women's Studies.* 5(3), 274–281.

Fuchsle, Traude (1983). *Partnerschaft Bei Berufrataligen and Nicht Berufrtstigen jungeren and Alteren Frauen, Intimage.* Relationship of Younger and Older Working and Non-working Women (Germ). *Parterberatung,* 20 (2–3), 128–142.

Garofalo, James (1979), Victimisation and the Fear of Crime, *Journal of Research in Crime and Delinquency,* 16, 80–97.

Ghei, Amarnath and Ghie, P.: *Text Book of Food and Nutrition,* Sagar Publications, Ved Mansion, Janpath, New Delhi, 1973, p. 3.

Gocharane, W.W. and Carolyn, S. Bell: *The Economics of Consumption,* McGraw Hill, New York, 1956, pp. 33–35.

GOI (1974), Towards Equality, Report of the Committee on the Status of Women in India, Delhi.

Goode, W.J. and Hatt, P.K.: *Methods in Social Research,* Prentice Hall, New Jersy, 1975, p. 40.

Gray Janet, D. (1983). The Married Professional Women: An Examination of Her Role Conflicts and Coping Strategies. *Psychology of Women Quarterly.* 7 (3), 235–243.

Grazia, de, S.: *Of Time, Work and Leisure,* The 20th Century Fund, New York, 1963.

Green, A.N.: *Sociology: An Analysis of Life in Modern Society.* McGraw Hill Book Co., New York, 1964.

Gross, I.H. and E.W. Crandall: Management for Modern Families, New York, Appleton-Century-Crofts, 1963, p. 338.

Gupta, Sarita, Shah, M.A., Beg, M.A. (1982). Education and Socio-economic Status as Determinants of Indian Women's Attitudes

Towards Equality of Women. *Journal of Social Psychology,* 118 (1), 139–140.

Hafstorm, Jeanne I. and Dunshing, Marilyn M. (1978), Socio-economic and Social Psychological Influences on Reasons Wives Work. *Journal of Consumer Research,* 5 (3), 169–175.

Halas, Celia M. (1974) Sex-role Stereotypes, Perceived Childhood Socialization Experiences and the Attitudes and Behaviour of Adult Women. *Journal of Psychology,* 88 (2), 261–275.

Halgund, S.V. (1978). Relationship Among Adjustment Variables and Sex-role Orientation in College Women: A Construct Validation of Psychological Androgyny. *Dissertation Abstracts International,* 38, 3880-B.

Hambrum, P.C.: *Status of Women in Santhal Society.*

Harris, T.L. and Sejwan, R. (1979). Women's Liberation Extremity and Dogmatism. *International Behaviour Scientist,* 8 (4), 57–58.

Harry Sharp and Paul Mott: Consumer Decision in the Metropolitan Family, Journal of Marketing, Vol. 23, No. 2, pp. 149–156.

Hem Lata Swarup and Pam Rajput (ed.), *Women and Globalisation* (1994), p. 102.

Heralambos, M.: *Sociology, Themes and Perspectives,* Oxford University Press, Walton Street, Oxford, 2005, pp. 369–371.

Heralambos, M.: Sociology: Themes and Perspectives, Oxford Univ. Press, Delhi, 1980.

Herbert, A. Silon: *New Science of Management Decision.*

Herbert, A. Simon: *Administrative Behaviour,* New York, Macmillan 1961, p. 88.

Herbert, A. Simon: *New Science of Management Decision,* New York, Harper and Row, 1960, 2.

Hirway, I. (2001), "Economic Reforms and Gender Issues in India", *The Indian Journal of Labour Economics,* Vol. 39, No. 3 July–September, p. 582.

Holahan, Carolek and Gillbert, Lucia A. (1979). Inter-role Conflict for Working Women: Career *versus* Jobs. *Journal of Applied Psychology,* 64 (1), 86–90.

Holmquist, Carin and Sundin, Eli Sabcth: *Indian Economic Survey (1999–2000),* Government of India, New Delhi, March 2000.

Honey, R. *et al.*: *Decision Making in the Use of Family, Financial Resources* 1939, pp. 5–6.

Houseknecht, Sharon K. and Macke, Anne S. (1981). Combining Marriage and Career: The Marital Adjustment of Professional Women. *Journal of Married and the Family* 43 (3), 651–661.

Humphirės, J. (1977), "Class Struggle and the Persistence of the Working Class Family", *Cambridge Journal of Economics*, Vol. 1.

Huser, Willa R. and Grant, Claude W. (1978). A Study of Husbands and Wives from Dual Career and Traditional Career Families. *Psychology of Women Quarterly*, 3, 78–89.

Huth, Carol M. (1978). Married Women's Work Status; The Influence of Parents and Husbands. *Journal of Vocational Behaviour*, 13(3), 272–288.

ICSSR, *Critical Issues on the Status of Women, Suggested Priorities for Action*, New Delhi.

Jeans, W.J.: Science and Music, The University Press, Cambridge, 1961.

Jephcott, P. Seear, N. and Smith, J.H. (1962). *Married Women Working*. London: George Allen and Unwin Ltd.

Jordon, V., Fassberg. E.S. and Michael, V.T. (1976). Feminism, Androgyny and Anxiety. *Journal of Clinical and Consulting Psychology*, 44, 870–871.

Junge, Maxine and Maya, Vernetts (1985). Women in Their Forties: A Group Portrait and Implications of Phychotherapy. *Women and Therapy*, 4 (3), 3–19.

Jussawalle, J.M.: Natural Dialectics, A Handbook of Food, Nutrition and Health, Vikas Publishing House Pvt. Ltd., New Delhi, 1979, pp. 1–4

Kapplen, Max: *Leisure in America: A Social Inquiry*, New York, Willey, 1960.

Kapur, Promilla (1970). *Marriage and the Working Women in India*. New Delhi: Vikas Publication.

Kapur, Promilla (1974): Women's Liberation in America, Spain, 15 (I) 20–27.

Kenkel, W.F.: Influence of Differentiation in Family Decision Making, Sociology and Social Research, Vol. 42, No. 1, 1975.

Keown, Charles F., and Keown, Ada, L. (1982) Success Factors for Corporate Women Executives. Group and Organisaion Studies, 7 (3), 445–446.

Khoo, Seiwlan, Krishnamoorthy, Soorirajulu and Trlin, Andrew D. (1974). Attitudes Towards Roles, Women's Employment and Anticipated Family Size Among Young Unmarried Adults. *Australian Journal of Sex, Marriage and Family,* 5 (3), 147–157.

Knoll, M.: Economic Conditions to and from Individual Members of Families and Households, *Journal of Home Economics,* Vol. 42, No. 5, 1955.

Knoll, Marjorie: Economic Condition to and From Individual Members of Families and Households, *Journal of Home Economics,* Vol. 47, No. 5, May, 1955.

Krishna, K.P. (1982). Rape and its victim in India. *Journal of Social and Economic Studies.* 10(1 and 2), 89–100.

Krogh, Kathryn M. (1985) Women's Motives to Achieve and to Nature in Different Life Stages. *Sex Roles,* 12 (1–2), 75–90.

Lang, Katherine, A. (1978) Suggestions for Counselling Women Who Want to Enter a Non-traditional Occupation. *Journal of Employment Counselling.*

Lazer, William and Smallwood John, E. (1977). The Changing Demographics of Women. *Journal of Marketing,* 41 (3), 14–22.

Lebe Doryann, M. (1986) Female Ego Ideal Conflicts in Adulthood. *American Journal of Psychoanalysis,* 46(1), 22–32.

Lewin, T.H.: *The Wild Races of South-Eastern India Social Research,* 1942.

Liwen, T.H.: *The Wild Races of South-Eastern India,* 1867.

Locke, H.J. and Mackeprang, M. (1979). Material Adjustment and Employed Wife. *American Journal of Sociology,* 54(6), 329–330.

Loo, Robert and Logan, Pamela (1982). Personality Correlates of the Attitude Towards Woman Scale. *Personality and Industrial Differences,* 3 (3), 329–330.

Lovell-Tory, Lawrence, A. (1983). Anomia Among Employed Wives and Housewives: An Exploratory Analysis. *Journal of Marriage and the Family.* 45 (2), 301–310.

Lundberg, G.A.: *Social Research,* Longman Green and Co., New York, 1942, pp. 118–19.

M.G. Chitkara and Harbans Garg (Retd.) Director, Art, Culture and Language, H.P. Shimla.

Mackinnon, Catherine (1979). *Sexual Harassment of Working Women,* New Heaven: Yale University Press.

Mahajan, V.S. (ed). (1989), *Women's Contribution to India's Economics and Social Development* (quoted form), Deep and Deep Publications, New Delhi.

Man, E.G.: *Santhalia and the Santhals,* Londonm, 1966.

Marx, K.: *Kapital: A Critique of Political Economy,* Vol, I.

Mayes, Sharon S. (1979). Women in Positions of Authority: A Case Study of Changing Sex Roles. *Sighs,* 4 (3), 556–568.

Mazumdar, Datta, N.: *The Santhal: A Study in Cultural Change,* Govt. of India Press, Calcutta, 1956.

McCall, Suzanne, H. (1977). Meet the Work Wife: *Journal of Marketing.* 41 (3), 55–56.

McDermott, M.J. (1979). *Rape Victimization in 26 American Cities, Washington, D.C.*: U.C. Department of Justice.

Michael Zunich: Teenagers Influence on Personal and Family Purchases, *Journal of Home Management,* Vol. 58, No. 6, June, 1966, p. 483.

Mitra, A. (1979), *The Status of Women: Literacy and Employment,* New Delhi.

Miyahira, Sarah D. (1975). Marriage and the Employment of Women. In S.H. Osipow (ed.) *Emerging Women: Career Analysis and Outlooks.* Columbus, Ott: Charles E. Merill XIII, 95.

Molm, Linda, D. (1978). Sex Role Attitudes and the Employment of Married Women. *The Direction of Casually Sociological Quarterly,* 19(4), 522–533.

Moulton, Ruth (1977). Women with Double Lives. *Contemprorary Psycho-analysis,* 13 (1), 64–84.

Mr. Justice S. Mohan, "Social Justice in India", A.I.R. 1995, *Journal Section,* pp. 98.

Mukherjee, R.N.: *Samajik Manavshastra Ke Rooprekha,* Vivek Prakashan, Jawahar Nagar, New Delhi, 1983, p. 201.

Mukhopadhyay, Maitrayee, *Silver Shackles: Women and Development in India,* Oxford: Oxfam.

Murthy, C.S. (1997), "Human Development in a Dynamic Setting: The Indian Case" (Mimeo).

Nadelson, Carol C., and Notoman, Malkah, T. (1981). To Marry or Not to Marry: A Choice. *American Journal of Psychiatry,* 138 (10), 1352–1356.

Nadelsons, Theodore and Eisendberg, Leon (1977). The Successful Professional Women "On being married to one. *American Journal of Psychiatry",* 134 (10), 1071–1076.

Nair, Tara S., Enterpreneurship Training for Women in the Indian Rural Sector: A Review of Approaches and Strategies, *The Journal of Enterpreneurship,* Vol. 5, No. 1 (1996).

Nevill, Dorothy, D., and Damico, Sandra (1978). The Influence of Occupational Status on Role Conflict in Women, *Journal of Employment Counselling,* 15 (2), 55–61.

Newberry, Phyllis: Wiseman, Myrna M. and Myres, Jerome K. (1979). Working Wives and Housewives: Do They Differ in Mental Status and Social Adjustment? *American Journal of Orthopsychiatry,* 49 (2), 282–291.

Nickell, P. and Dorsey, J.M.: *Management in Family Living,* Willey Eastern Ltd. New Delhi, 1967, pp. 60–76.

Nye, I.F. (1959). *Employment Status of Mothers and Adjustment of Adolescent Children. Marriage and Family Living,* 21.

O'Malley, L.S.S.: *Bengal District Gazetteer, Santhal Praganas,* Logos Press, New Delhi, pp. 89–95, 102–104.

Oppenheimer, V. (1990), *The Female Labour Force in the United States,* University of California, Berkeley.

Orville, C. Brim: *Personality and Decision Processes,* Stanford University Press, California, 1962, pp. 10–11.

Oslo.: *Taboos, Customs Amongst the Santhals,* J.A.S.B. Part III, 1898.

Overstreet, H.A.: *The Mature Mind,* W.W. Norton and Co., New York, 1949.

Pandey, Rajendra (1986) Rape Crime and Victims of Rape in Free India. *The Indian Journal of Social Work,* 47 (2), 169–186.

Parkar, S.: Work and Leisure, in Butterworth and Weir, 1970. In the *Sociology of Leisure,* George Allen and Unwin, London, 1976.

Parsad, Onkar: *Santhal Music,* Inter-India Publications, New Delhi, 1985.

Parsons, T. and Bales, R.F. (1955). *Family Socialization and Interaction Process,* New York: Free Press.

Phillips, Susan D. and Johnston, Susan L. (1985). Attitudes Towards Work Roles for Women. *Journal of College Student Personnel,* 26 (4), 334–338.

Powell, Barbara (1977), The Empty Nest Employment and Psychiatric Symptoms in College-educated Women. *Psychology of women Quarterly,* 2 (1), 35–43.

Prager, Karne J. (1986): Identity Development Age and College Experience in Women. *Journal of Genetic Psychology,* 147 (1), 31–36.

Prasad, Pramil, and Bhushan L.I. (1984). Perceived Role Conflict Among School Teachers, *Research in Psychology,* 3, 41–48.

Prevey, E.E.: Developing Good Habits in the Use of Money, *Journal of Home Economics,* Vol. 38, Feb. 1946.

Ramaswamy, U. 1992, "Women and Development", in A.N. Sharma and Seema Singh (Eds.), *Women and Work: Changing Scenario in India,* B.R. Publication and Class, Harvard, Cambridge, Mass.

Rathore, B.S. and Dhameja, S.K. (Eds). *Entrepreneurship in the 21st Century,* Rawat Publications, Jaipur, 1999.

Reinke, Barbara J. (1985): Psychosocial Changes as a Function of Chronological Age. *Human Development,* 28 (5), 266–269.

Reuben Hill: Judgment and Consumership in the Management of Family. *Resources, Sociology, and Social Research,* Vol. 47, No. 4, (July, 1963) pp. 446–60.

Roemer, J. (1982), *General Theory of Exploitation and Class,* Harvard Cambridge, Mass.

Ruth, C. Freeman: Spending and Saving Patterns of Illinois Farm Families from 1933 to 1950, University of Illinois, Agriculture Experiment Station, Bulletin 592, Sept. 1955.

Sachidanand: *Profiles of Tribal Culture in Bihar,* Firma, K.L. Mukhopadhya, Calcutta, 1965.

Sahoo, F.M., and Dash, P. (1984). *Androgyny and Life Stress.* Unpublished Reprot, Utkal University, Bhubaneshwar.

Sahoo, F.M., Rout, Jayashree and Rout, A.K. (1985). Androgyny and Psychological Rigidity. *Psychological Studies,* 30–(2), 111–115.

Samir, Doman Sahu: *Santhal in Bihar K.C. Adivasi* by L.P. Vidyarthi College Center, Patna, 2005, pp. 53–54.

Sastry, Nalini (1990). Anxiety, Sex Role Orientation and Age Married Women in Urban India. *The Indian Journal of Social Work,* 51(4), 659–668.

Saxena, R.P.: *Tribal Economy in Central India,* Firma, K.L.M., Calcutta.

Saxena, Shobha: *Crimes Against Women and Protective Law,* Deep and Deep Publications, New Delhi, 2004.

Schlesinger, Benjamin: A Survey of Methods Uses to Study Decision Making in the Family, *The Family Life Coordinator,* Vol. 11, No. 1, Jan. 1962, pp. 8–14.

Sethi, Jyotsna: Women Enterpreneurship In India: A Brief Comment, *SEDME,* Vol. 21, No. 4, 1994.

Shah, M.A. and Varshney, K. Mukul (1982). A Comprehensive Study of the Attitude of Married and Unmarried Women Towards Religion, Equality of Women and Birth Control in Relation to Their Adjustment. *Asian Journal of Psychology and Education,* 9(1), 15–20.

Shaines, Netalie (1980). The Working Wife and Mother: A New Women? *American Journal of Psychotherapy,* 34 (3), 374–386.

Shanmugasundaram, Y. (1993), *Women Employment in India,* Allied Publishers, Madras.

Sharma, R.N.: *Bharat Me Gramin Samajsastra,* Rajhans Prakashan Mandir, Meerut.

Shenwik, W.S.W.S.: A Tour Thought, The Rajmahal Hills, *J.A.S.B* 1861.

Sherwill, W.S.: *A Tour Through the Rajmahal Hills,* Jan. 13, 1851.

Shorter, E. (1977). *On writing the History of Rape,* Sings 3, 2.

Siddiqui, M.I., *Child Labour: How to Investigate?* Deep and Deep Publications, New Delhi, 2003.

Singh, D.P. *Women Workers in Organized Sector,* Deep and Deep Publications Pvt. Ltd., New Delhi, 2005.

Singh, D.R. (1981). Current Trends and Forms of Crime Against Women. *The Indian Journal of Social Work,* 42 (1), 33–40.

Singh, S.N., and Sharma, Neelima (1975). Child Rearing Practices of Working and Non-working Educated Women. *Manas,* 22 (2), 113–119.

Smith, Elsie J. (1981). The Working Mother: A Critique of the Research. *Journal of Vocational Behaviour,* 19 (2), 191–211.

Smith, H.W.: *Strategies of Social Research,* Prentice Hall, New Jersy, 1975, p. 10.

Spence, J.T., Helmreich, R. and Stapp, J. (1975). Ratings of Peers on Sex Role Attributes and Their Relation to Self-esteem and Conceptions of Masculinity and Feminity. *Journal of Personality and Social Psychology,* 32, 29–39.

St. John-Parsons, Donald (1978). Continuous and Dual Career Families: A Case Study. *Psychology of Women Quarterly,* 3(1), 30–42.

Stafford, Inge P. Setan Hall U. (1984). Relation of Attitudes Towards Women's Roles and Occupational Behaviour of Women's Self-esteem. *Journal of Counselling Psychology,* 31(3), 332–338.

Stane, Steve and Morrow, Lisa (2005). Race Differences in Feminism and Guilt. *Journal of Economic Issues,* 61(1), 70–74.

Stein, Sandara L. and Weston, Louise C. (1982). College Women's Attitudes Towards Women and Identity Achievement. *Adolescence,* 17 (68), 895–899.

Stinnet, Nick; Knaub, Patrica K., O'Nal, Sunny and Waltors James (1983). Perceptions of Panamonian Women Concerning the Roles of Women. *Journal of Comparative Family Studies,* 14(2), 273–283.

Strober, Myra H., and Weinberg, Charles B. (1977). Working Wives and Major Expenditures. *Journal of Consumer Research,* 4 (3), 141–147.

Swarup, Hem Lata, "Ethnicity, Gender and Class" in *Ethnicity, Class and Gender,* (2005).

Symonds, Alexendra (1986). "The Dynamics of Depression in Functioning Women: Sexism in the Family." American Academic of Psycho-analysis Seminar on Women's Emerging Identity. Journal of Ameircan Academy of Psycho-analysis, 14 (3), 395–406.

Teleporas, Elizabeth (1977). Motivational Patterns in Attitudes Towards the Women's Liberation Movement. *Journal of Personality,* 45 (4), 481–500.

Theodere, B. Hohannis: Teenager Perception of Family Decision Making, *The Family Life Co-ordinator,* Vol. 4, pp. 59–60, 70–74.

Tomer, R.S.: *Social Research with Statistics,* Shriram Mehra and Co. Agra, 1959.

Travis, Cheryl B. (1976). Women's Liberation Among Two Samples of Young Women. *Psychology of Women Quarterly,* 1(2), 189.

Uma Devi, S. (1989), "Role of Women in Economic Development", in V.S. Mahajan (Ed.), *Women's Contribution to India's Social and Economic Development,* New Delhi.

Usher, Sarah and Fels, Mort (1985). The Chellenge of Feminism and Career for the Middle Aged Women. Special Issue: Feminist Psychology: Single Life and Married Life and Women's Sexuality. *International Journal of Women's Studies,* 8 (1), 47–57.

Veblen, T. (1934), *The Theory of the Leisure Class,* New York.

Verma, S.B.: *Status of Women in Modern India,* Deep and Deep Publications Pvt. Ltd., New Delhi, 2005.

Verma, Sudhir: Women's Development: Policy and Adminsitration, Aalekh, Jaipur, 1992.

Vinsaint, C.E.: Familia Spoumia: The Adaptive Function, *Journal of the Marriage and Family,* Vol. 28, No. 1, 1966.

Walker, Loraine and Friedman, S. Thomas (1977). Professional Women's Attitudes Toward the Dual Role of Women. *Psychology Report,* 41(1), 327–334.

Welch, Reenate (1979). Androgyny and Derived Identity in Married Women With Varying Degrees of Non-traditional Role Involvement. *Psychology of Women Quarterly,* 3 (3), 308–315.

Wojceichowski, Denise (1982). I am a Working Mother but Who am I? *Journal of Employment Counselling,* 19 (3) 106–112.

Women of Arunachal Pradesh Flay Customary Laws Bill, *Indian Express,* July 22, 1955.

Yin, R.P. (1980). Fear of Crime Among the Elderly, Some Issues and Suggestions. *Social Problems,* 27: 492–504.

Yogev, Sara (1982). Are Professional Women Over Worked? Objective *versus* Subjcctive Perceptlon of Role Leads. *Journal of Occupation and Psychology,* 55 (3), 165–169.

Zapalska, Alina M.A.: A Profile of Women Entrepreneurs and Enterprises in Poland, *Journal of Small Business Management,* Vol. 35, No. 4, October 1997.

Zhang, Yon Yun, A High Priced Slot in the World of Work, *World of Work,* 110, No. 12, May/June 1995.

Zimmermen, Gerepon: Kids and Money, *Look,* Nov. 2, 1965, p. 49.

Index

Aberration, 106
Accelerated Rural Water Supply
    Programme (ARWSP), 207
Achievements, 237
    motivation, 45
Adam and Eve, 151
Adult education, 216
Adult Education Centre, 166
Adult franchise, 146
Adulteration, 177-78
Age and Basket-making, 116
Age and education, 72
Age and husband's education, 78
Age and income, 164
Age and marital status, 78
Age and weaving, 115
Agreement, 142, 171-72
Agricultural development, 119-20
Agricultural economy, 113
Agricultural expension, 14
Agricultural extension programmes, 15
Agricultural household economy, 119
Agricultural and industrial occupation,
    7-8
Agricultural labourers, 72-73, 102
Agricultural operation, 97-98
    stages of, 103
Agriculture, 14-15
    modernisation of, 194, 245
Ajing, 32
Alcoholic drinks, 182, 190
Alcoholism, 110, 189, 245
Anganwadi training centres, 11
    attendance of children, 226-27
    beneficiaries, 225-26
    functionaries, 224-25, 232-33
Anganwari Workers (AWWs), beneficiaries of, 219-22
    profile of, 222-23
    programmes of, 227
Animal husbandry, 19
Animal sacrifice, 28, 33
Anti-poverty programmes, 10
Anti-social activities, 178
Anxiety, 44
Aphorism, 160
Appropriate methodology, 52
Artificial irrigation, 96
Atrocities, 201
Attitude Towards Women Scale
    and Eysenek Personality
    Questionnaire, 45
Awareness, 117, 213
Awareness Test Towards Family Welfare Programme, 262-63

Balance between income and expenditure, 111-12
Bales, Parsons, 43
Balwadi Nutrition Programme, 11
Bapla (marriage songs), 160
Basi Bhat, 188
Basket-making, 115-16, 244
Bell, R.R., 36
Bennett, Barbara, 37
Benson, Donna, 42
Betz, E.L., 46
Bhattacharjee, Pratima, 40
Biogrammar, 26
Blue money, 151
Bodding, P.O., 104
Bogardus, E.S., 56

Boldia Sanitation Project, Pakistan, 22
Bride-burning, 201
Bride-Price, 103, 246

Cash crops, 20
Centrally Sponsored Rural Sanitation Programme, 207
Chae-Champa areas, 31
Changing World's economy, role of women in, 18-19
Chaudhary, Neerja, 42
Child bearing, 28
Child development, 214
Child marriage, 244
Child rearing, 20-21, 98, 132
Childhood socialisation, 35
Chipko movement, 22
Chitkara, M.G., 34
Chotanagpur plateau, 56
Clan membership, 82
Committee on Status of Women in India (CSWI), 209
Committing suicide, 39
Communication, 152
 technology, 203-04
Community participation, 233-34
Communal tensions, 154
Complaints cell, 211
Complex problems, 129
Comradeship, 237
Constitutional obligation, 198
Consumership planning, 133
Coordination, 233-34
Correlation between female illiteracy and infant mortality, 215
Corruption, 178
Cottage industries, 115, 183
Creches, 13
Criminalisation, 24
Culture, bearers of, 155
Curt Sacha, 153
Custodial Justice, 211
Customs, 105, 175, 181

Dance and songs, 153-54
Dancing gossipings, 163
Data collection, tools of, 56-57
Davis, R.A., 39
Decision-making 127, 244
 concept of, 127
 management, 123-48
 participation of women in, 147
Deliberation, 126, 129
Democratization, 205
Deoghar district, 60-61
 women's average annual income of, 87
Deprivation, 209
Desai, Neera, 37, 47
Desert development programme, 207
Designs, types of, 55-56
Dewey, John, 123
Dhanki, 179
Differentiation, 131
Differences between male and female harmones, 27
Differences between tribal man and women, 102
Discrimination, 23, 83
Dogmatism, 45
Domestic cattles, 113
Domestic responsibilities, 238
Domesticated animals, 245
Doty, Ghaffaradili, 45
Dought Prone Area Programme (DPAP), 207
Dumka district, 60-62
 women's average annual income, 85
Dumka-Deoghar conversation, 247
DWCRA scheme, 10, 11
Dysphoria, 44

Early Childhood Care and Education (ECCE), 11-12
 strategy and implementation, 13
Economic activities, 133

Economic backwardness, 110
Economic status, 175
Economy, 140
Education, 20, 35-37, 42-43, 134-36, 141-44, 162, 246
Educational infrastructural facilities, 61
Eighth Five Year Plan, 198
Electronic media, 152
Elwin, Verrier, 248
Emotional Bond, 27
Employed married women, 40
Employment, 7, 8, 15, 37, 112, 136, 189, 237
Employment Assurance Scheme (EAS), 206
Energy, new sources of, 175, 185-86
Entertainment, mode of, 244-45
Environmental degradation, 19
Equal partnership between husband and wife, 143
Erdwin, Card J., 36, 47
Erickson, E., 43
Exchange economy, 91
Exchange labour, 148
Expenditure, patterns of, 92
Experimental design, 55
Exploitation, 1, 22, 110
Export, producing crops, 14

Family budgets, 143-44, 238
  women's contribution to, 13-14
Family decision-making, teenager perception of, 130
Family funds, mismanagement of, 93
Family income, 91, 111-14, 117, 166, 183
  sources of, 166-67, 192-93
Family life cycle, 132
Family management, role of women in, 17-32
Family planning methods, 247
  programmes, 249
Family's real income, 93-94
Family welfare programmes, 10
Female behaviour, 121
Female education, 108
Female employment, 169
Female literacy rate, 5-6
Female workers, employment categories of, 9-10
  percentage distribution of, 7-8
Feminine activities, 244-45
Femininity, 43-44
Fermentation, 182
Festivals, 115, 154-55
Five Year Plans, 9, 203, 217
Folk songs, 154-160
  characteristics of, 158
  cultural significance, 158
  types of, 155
Food and Agricultural Organisation (FAO), 204
Food, classes of, 104, 181
  crisis, 178
  crops, 20
  gathering, 100, 117, 191-92
  habits, 179
  production, 13-14
  shortage of, 178
Food management, 174-190
  problem solution, 194-96
Food supply, shortage of, 189-90
Forest plants, 97
Formal girls education enrolement, 64
Fox, Robin, 26, 27
Fraukel, Judith Monogul, 48
Freedom movement, 135, 154
Frenchise right of women, 146
Frustration, 111
Fuchsle, Traude, 48
Fuel collection, 20
Fuel management, 184
Funding, 212

Garofalo, James, 42
Gender issues, 23-24
Gender Justice, 197

Generalisation, 127, 240
Ghei, Amarnath, 196
Globalisation, 17
Gods and Goddesses, 157
Godda, W.J., 61
Gonong (bride-price), 32
Gossiping, 163, 167-68, 244
Green revolution, 14
Green vegetables, 113, 167
  availability, 192
Gross, I.H., 122
Gupta, Sarita, 37
Gurus, 105
Guy Mint, 24
Gyanodaya, 246

Hajla mela, 153
Halas, Celia, M., 35
Halgund, S.V., 44
Hambrum, P.C., 85
Harassments, 201
Harmonious sexual relationship, 40
Harris, T.L., 4
Hartley, E.L., 125
Harvesting, 100
Health check-up, 230-31, 236
Health and nutrition education, 235
Heckscher, August, 150
Heralambos, M., 151
Hijla Pahar, 163
Hirway, I., 16
Holahom, C., 41
Home-makers, 20-21
Home management, 132, 237, 240-42
  pattern of, 238
Horsey, John, 150
Horticulture crops, 249
Household duties, 41-42
  economy, 106, 111, 244-45
    management of, 91-120
  income, 187-88
Human Development Report, 2
Human Right for All, 202
Humphires, J., 34
Hunting, 26-28, 96, 153, 194
Huth, C.M., 41

Illegal falling of trees, 187
Illiterate women, 15
Illiteracy, 4-5, 17-18, 72-74, 80-82, 112-14, 117-18, 137-38, 162, 166-68, 187-88
  eradication of, 249-50
  international comparison of, 6
Immunization, 230-32, 236-37
Inadequate representation, 200-202
Income management, 92
Indian Administrative Service (IAS), 200
Indian Police Service (IPS), 200
Indira Awas Yojana (IAY), 206
Industrialised countries, 17-18
Industrialisation, 140, 183
Infant mortality rate, 79
Infactious diseases, 177
Infrastructural facilities, 60-61
Inorganic compounds, 174
Integrated Child Development Service (ICDS), 111, 217-18, 220, 233, 247-48
  beneficiaries 225
  objectives of, 217-18
Integrated Rural Development Programme (IRDP), 10
Integrated Wasteland Development Programme, 208
Intelligence activities, 124
Iowa State University, 132
Irrigation, water resources of, 183
Ishopanishad, 18

Jawahar Rojgar Yojana (JRY), 10, 234
Jephcott, P., 40
Jharkhand, 89, 202, 218, 237, 247, 248
Jhuggi markets, 24
Jhum lands, 249
Jhum plots, 148
Joint family system, 39

Jordon, V., 44
Junge, M., 36
Jungle-millets, 96
Justice delivery system, 213

Kajhi, 31
Kamin, 103
Kapur, Promilla, 35
Kenyan Green belts, 22
Keown, C.F., 38
Kerala, 5
Khet, 96
Khichudi, 226-28, 235
Kitchen garden, 122-13, 167
Knitting, 165, 244
Koening, E.J., 37
Krishna, K.P., 42
Krohy, K.M., 38, 45

Lazer, William, 38
Leisure activities, categories of, 150-51
  extention pattern of, 152
  forms of, 165
  neutrally pattern, 152
  opposition pattern, 152
Leisure Time Management, 150-170
Lewin, T.A., 159
Liberalization, 18
Life expectancy, international comparison of, 4
Life insurance, 130
Literacy , 72-74, 80-82, 112-13, 117, 137-38, 162-63, 166-68, 187-88
Locke, H.J., 40
Loo, Robert, 45
Lottery method, 70
Lovell-Troy, L.A., 40
Lucidity, 157
Lumbering, 28
Lundberg, G.A., 55

Mackinnon, C., 42
McCall, S.H., 38
McCarrison, Robert, 176
Mahatma Gandhi, 98, 154, 209
Mahila Mandal, 201
Majumdar, R.C., 24
Male idiosyncrasy, 141
Malnutrition, 127, 177-80
  problems of, 176
Man, E.C., 159
Management, quality of, 94
Managerial responsibilities, 25-26
Manual labourers, 71, 112, 166, 186, 189-90
Man, E.G., 172
Mantra, 18
Marillineal societies, 102
Marriage, 39, 100
  ceremonies, 144
Marital harmony, 40
Marital relationship, 38-39
Marital status, 78-79
Masculinity, 43-44
Matkin, T.A., 158
Melbourne metropolitan area, 36
Melody, 160
Menstruation, 99-100
Migration, 14, 29
Minnesota family, 133
Modernity, 44
Modernization, 29, 142
Modmandialies, 152
Molestation, 201
Monoculture, 14
Monthly income, 77, 82
Motherhood, 99-101
Moulton, Ruth, 41
Mukherjee, Charulal, 180
Murdock, George Peter, 27
Murthy, C.S., 16

Nadalson, Theodore, 39
National Commission for Women (NCW), 198, 209-12, 214
  investigation, 210
National Family Benefit Scheme, 206

National Maternity Benefit Scheme, 206
National Old Age Pension Scheme, 206
National Prospective Plan (NPP), 200
National Social Assistance Programme (NSAP), 206
Natural food, 175
Natural resources, 19, 60
Negotiations, 145
Nevill, Dorothy, 39
Newcomb, T.M., 125
Ninth Five Year Plan, 198, 205
Nodelson, T., 38
Non-agricultural employment, 102
Nutrition education, 230
Nutrition programme, 137
Naykers, 31

Occupation, 40, 80-82, 105, 114, 139-40, 144-46, 161-62
Occupational castes, 154
Occupational categories, 83, 154, 186, 190
Ojha's desciples, 161
Omission, 106
Oppengeimer, V., 16, 38
Organic compound, 174
Other Backward Castes, (OBC) 222
Our Welfare Association, 246
Oxidation, 174

Pachwai, 104
Paharia Tribal Belt, education status in, 76
  population, 264-68, 273
Pakistan, 17, 22
Panchayati Raj Institutions, 207
Pandey, Rajendra, 42
Parivarik Mahila Lok Adalat (PMLA), 212
Pensions, 93
Personality, 124
  development of, 152
  dimension of, 46
Phillips, S.D., 36
Pigcurry, 180
Pilchubuddhi, 29, 31
Ploughing, 96
Poisonous drug, 177
Policies and Programmes, 9
Political participation, 212
Pollution, 18, 127
Polygamy, 246
Population, 3-4
Poverty, 19, 24, 110, 248
  alleviation programmes, 10, 205
Prager, Karne J., 35
Pre-school education (PSE), 235-36
  objectives of, 229-30
Price control, 154
Primitive hunting, 100
Promoting child development, 214-230
Protective foods, 176
Psychic income, 93-96
Psychological factors, 43-44
Psychological phenomenon, 142
Purdah, 39, 116
Purposive Sampling method, 56

Quarrying, 28

Rajiv Gandhi National Drinking Water Mission, 207
Rajmahal, 63
Random Sampling, 56, 70-71
Rape, 201
Rashtriya Mahila Kosh (RMK), 10
Real income, 93-95
Recreation, sources of, 169-72
  policy, 151
Referel services, 230-31
Reinve, Barbara, J., 36
Relationship between Mother-in-law and daughter-in-law, 81
Reservation for Women, 249-50
Responsibilities, 25-26, 105-108, 129-30, 147-48
Rice beer, 180

Roemer, J., 1
Roy, Raja Rammohan, 22, 209
Rural development programme, 214-17
Rural-urban literacy, 74
Rural women, objectives of Media strategy for, 204-05

SAWC, 251-52
Sahibganj district, women's average annual income, 88
Sampling method, 56
Santhal community, 29-32
Santhal economic activities, 97
Santhal economy, 96
Santhal Parganas, 58-59
- agricultural workers, 277-78
- districtwise literacy, 75
- educational institutions, 60-62
- formal girls education enrolment, 64-65
- medical facilities, 67
- rainfall of, 60
- rural population, 270
- rural workers, 275
- sex ratios, 267-68
- urban population, 271
- urban workers, 276
- women's development and child care, 12
- women and children situation analysis of, 251-57

Santhal songs, 160
Santhal women, leisure time activities, 161
Scout, Flatcher, 158
Sastry, Nalini, 44
Satisavitri, 98
Satyagraha movement, 154
Save forest campaign, 184
Seasonal crops, 103
Seclusion, 116, 135
Self-actualization, 44
Self-employment, 2, 8
- programmes, 206

Self-Help Groups (SHGs), 248
Semi-governmental agencies, 192
Sen, Amartiya, 17
Sericulture, 22
Sex crime, 42
Sexual assault, 42
Sexual division of Labour, 26-28, 107, 121, 239-40
Sexual freedom, 144
Sexual harassment, 42
Sexual promiscuity, 238
Sexual relationship, 105, 238
Shainess, N., 45
Slesinger, D., 55
Smith, E.J., 40
Social development, 197-200
Social phenomenon, 53
Social problems, 154
Social-economic factors, 35-36
Solution problems, 123-24
Source of income, 82, 85, 188
Source of water, 115
Spinning, 22
Status of women, 89-90
Stephenson, Mzassy, 55
Stinnet, N., 37
Strober, M.H., 51
Structural Adjustment Policies (SAP), 23
Suicide, 39
Sundried rice, 180
Supplementary nutrition food, 227
Sustainable development, 118-19
Swami Vivekananda, 209
Swarna-Jayanti Gram Swarozgar Yojana (SGSY), 206
Symonds, A., 36

Teenager perception, 130-32
Telephoras, E., 45
Tiger, Lionel, 26, 27
Training and Employment Programme for Women (STEP), 10
Transplanting, 103
Travis, C.B., 39

Tribal areas, educational facilitaties, 72
Tribal communities, 99
Tribal population, concentration of, 71, 99-100
TRYSEM, 10

UN's Fourth International Conference in Women, Beijing, 197
UNICEF, 10, 235
Underemployed women, 40
Under nutrition, 176-78
Undifferentiated sex rate, 44
Unemployment, 8, 248, 250
  insurance, 93
Urban areas, primary sector activities, 7

Value judgement, 128
Values orientation, 46
Veblen, T., 2
Violence, 209
Vivekananda Kendra, 246
Vocational education, 39

Wage discrimination, victims of, 199
Walker, Loraine, 39
Weaving, 22
Welch, Reeneto, 51
Widowhood, 101
Wife beating, 201
Wild animals, 105
Wild plants, 97
Williams, Ralph, S., 157
Women, agents of change, 211-22
  agricultural sector in, 20
  basic problems of, 22-23
  economic backwardness, 110
  economic development, 2-3
  economic participation, 121-22
  economic status, 175
  education of, 35-36
  employment of, 6-7, 15
  liberation movement, 45, 109, 240
  personality characteristics of, 44
  representation, 198-99
  welfare, 197-202
Women empowerment, 9-10, 197, 201, 245-46
  national policy for, 198
  real index of, 213-14
Wojciechowski, Denise, 41
World Bank, 200
World Food production, 13

Yin, R.P., 42
Yogev, Sara, 41

Zimmerman, Gereon, 132
Zunich, 131